THE SUPPRESSION OF THE MONASTERIES
IN THE WEST COUNTRY

St Mary's Chapel, Glastonbury.
*The twelfth-century portal to this chapel which was dedicated in 1186, and is one of the few
substantial pieces of architecture surviving on the site of the greatest of all English abbeys.*

THE
SUPPRESSION OF THE MONASTERIES
IN THE WEST COUNTRY

J.H. BETTEY

ALAN SUTTON
1989

ALAN SUTTON PUBLISHING
BRUNSWICK ROAD · GLOUCESTER · UK

ALAN SUTTON PUBLISHING INC
WOLFEBORO · NEW HAMPSHIRE · USA

First published 1989

British Library Cataloguing in Publication Data

Bettey, J.H. (Joseph Harold), *1932*–
    The suppression of the monasteries in the West Country.
    1. South-west England. Monasteries. History
    I.Title
    271'.009423

ISBN 0-86299-594-9

Cover design by Martin Latham
Cover picture: Lacock Abbey, the cloister.

Typesetting and origination by
Alan Sutton Publishing Limited.
Printed in Great Britain.

Contents

ᑲ᙭ᔐ List of Maps and Illustrations ᑲ᙭ᔐ

Maps showing the major monastic houses and friaries of the west country

List of illustrations in the text

ᏽ Preface ᏽ

Throughout the Middle Ages the West Country was notable for the number, antiquity, wealth and splendour of its monastic houses, and even in the early decades of the sixteenth century it would have seemed incredible that they could be totally abolished, apparently so easily and over a period of no more than five years. It would have seemed equally incredible that most of their magnificent buildings, many of them only recently completed, and so much of their great accumulation of artistic treasures, should so quickly be demolished and destroyed.

The purpose of this book is to trace the remarkable story of the fall of these great monastic houses and of the friaries in Gloucestershire, Wiltshire, Somerset, Dorset and the neighbouring areas, to show how the destruction was accomplished and the effects which it had on all aspects of life throughout the region. Much of the book is based on record sources which are unpublished or not easily available, since the subject has not previously been studied in detail at a local level in this region, although there are numerous national studies including the indispensable work of the late Professor David Knowles, and the detailed researches of Professor Joyce Youings of Exeter University; their work, as well as the many other sources which have been used, will be found listed in the notes and bibliography. Because of the large number of monastic institutions which were to be found in the region, and the paucity of evidence concerning the fortunes of some of the smaller houses, this book will concentrate on the larger monasteries and nunneries and will not be concerned, except incidentally, with the numerous colleges, hospitals, almshouses, chantry foundations and other small religious establishments. A list of the major monastic houses in the region is given in Appendix I and the major friaries are listed in Appendix II. Above all, this book is concerned to show the dramatic nature of the Dissolution in the West Country: the great wealth, power and splendour of the major monasteries, their widespread estates, magnificent buildings and enormous influence; to tell the story of their fall; and to indicate the widespread effects of their suppression upon all aspects of life throughout the region.

For the sake of clarity, the spelling and punctuation of sixteenth-century documents have been modernised, and accounts originally written in Latin have been translated. As far as possible place names are given in their modern form.

∽✺∽ Acknowledgements ∽✺∽

I am grateful to various colleagues with whom I have discussed this subject or who have kindly read earlier drafts of the book, especially Michael Aston, James Bond, Dr John Chandler and Dr Robert Dunning. Michael Aston kindly prepared and drew the maps, and also supplied some of the photographs. Other photographs were supplied by Richard Bryant and Colin Miller. Gordon Kelsey provided help and advice on the illustrations, and Jim Hancock allowed me to use photographs from his collection of aerial views. I am grateful to Dr Celia Miller for her help throughout all stages of the production of this book.

J.H. Bettey
University of Bristol

Abbreviations

B.&G.A.S.	Bristol & Gloucestershire Archaeological Society
D.N.B.	*Dictionary of National Biography*
D.N.H.&.A.S.	Dorset Natural History & Archaeological Society
L.&P. Hen. VIII	*Letters & Papers of Henry VIII*
P.R.O.	Public Record Office
S.A.&N.H.S.	Somerset Archaeological & Natural History Society
V.C.H.	*Victoria County History*
W.A.M.	*Wiltshire Archaeological Society Magazine*

Chapter 1

The West-Country Monasteries before the Suppression

It is not easy to arrive at a balanced judgement on the state of the West Country monasteries in the decades before the Dissolution, and it is important to beware, on the one hand, of easy generalisations, of sweeping condemnation of undoubted scandals, abuses and failure to live up to high, difficult ideals and, on the other, of romantic regret for the passing of venerable institutions, the destruction of so much magnificent architecture, so many works of art and the ending of noble traditions. There are numerous examples of scandalous conduct, bad behaviour or failure to live up to monastic ideals in the monasteries of the region during the later Middle Ages, but it is important to remember that this evidence comes from episcopal and other visitations which were concerned only with reporting faults and which are generally silent about houses where all was well. Moreover, there were many monks and the criticisms often apply to only one or two in each monastery, while we hear little of the monks who quietly followed the daily routine of their Rule, carried out their duties and did nothing to attract the attention or condemnation of their superiors.[1]

The quality of religious life and spiritual endeavour leaves no record and cannot be measured by the historian; only the external and incidental features of the dedicated monastic life can be discerned, such as charitable works, hospitality, almsgiving or scholarship, and these things, although in themselves praiseworthy, were not the basic reason for monastic life. The central purpose was to provide a framework within which men and women could devote their whole lives, unceasingly and without distraction, to the service of God, but long years of selfless devotion to such a difficult ideal and strict adherence to a rigid, austere Rule, defy all the efforts of historical research. By its very nature, little evidence survives of the daily life within the monasteries, nor of the regular performance of their essential function – the maintenance for the benefit of the whole of society of a continuous service of prayer and praise, day and night, to the Almighty. Nor is it surprising that, with the passage of time, some monastic houses and some monks and nuns should slip from the harsher austerities of their original routine, especially those who were increasingly occupied in the administration of the monastic estates or in the ever more complex affairs of such wealthy institutions. None-theless many of the monastic houses continued to be respected as powerful centres of spiritual life. For example, when a Dorset gentleman, George Twynyho of Turnworth, made his will in 1524, he made numerous bequests to the nunnery at Shaftesbury where his aunt had been abbess (1496–1505) and his uncle a steward of the abbey lands. His bequests included

1

Provision for the priests of the abbey church to sing masses for his soul
for twenty-one years after his death.
A bequest of £40 'to my Lady Abbess of Shaftesbury'.
Bequests of 3s. 4d. to every nun who attended his funeral, and 4d. to
every nun to pray for him.
£5 to each of the abbey chaplains.

Clearly for George Twynyho, Shaftesbury Abbey was a respected
focus for spiritual life, the place in which to be buried, the place in
which to be prayed for.[2]
There is no doubt that there had been a great decline both in the
fervour and in the popularity of the monasteries. The foundation of
new monastic houses came almost entirely to an end after the Black
Death in the mid-fourteenth century, and likewise the stream of
bequests and gifts to the monasteries, which had been such a feature
of the twelfth and thirteenth centuries, dried up during the fifteenth
century; the typical late-medieval religious foundations were colleges,
chantries, almshouses and hospitals or gifts to parish churches. The
Lollards and other critics of the Church were particularly strong in
parts of the West Country, especially in Bristol and in the cloth-
working areas of Gloucestershire and Wiltshire, and there were many
who questioned the Church's teaching on purgatory, prayers for the
dead, images, pilgrimages and the whole basis and purpose of the
monastic life.[3]
Nonetheless, the ancient monastic houses continued to dominate
everywhere in the West Country with their spectacular buildings and
vast estates, while in the larger towns the four orders of friars played
an important part in urban life through their preaching and work with
the poorest classes of society. Nowhere in the region was more than a
few miles from a major monastery or nunnery, and their widespread
lands, farms, granges and other properties, as well as their appropriation of so many parish churches and parochial tithes, meant that
scarcely anyone could escape their influence. So much was destroyed
in the decades after the Dissolution that at many west-country sites it
requires a powerful effort of imagination to visualise the former extent
and splendour of the monastic buildings, but those that survive at
Tewkesbury, Gloucester, Malmesbury, Sherborne or Milton Abbas,
and the remaining fragments at sites such as Bristol, Lacock, Glastonbury, Cleeve or Forde, are a potent reminder of what was lost in the
revolutionary changes of the sixteenth century. Not only were the
monasteries impressive as landmarks, but the needs of the monks and
nuns encouraged the growth of towns and villages around them;
towns such as Lacock, Keynsham, Bruton, Glastonbury, Amesbury or
Cerne Abbas were almost completely dependent for their economic
survival on the great monastic house around which they had
developed. Monastic estates and economic influence were widespread
throughout the region. For example, the estates of Glastonbury

Map 1.
Major Monastic Houses of the West Country I: Cluniac, Benedictine, Cistercian and Carthusian.

stretched across the Somerset Levels and included lands on Mendip, in east Somerset and north-west Wiltshire, and manors in Dorset.[4]

St Augustine's Abbey in Bristol had numerous properties in Bristol itself and large landholdings in south Gloucestershire and north Somerset, as well as lands in Dorset and south Wales.[5] The estates of the Augustinian nunnery at Lacock included the town of Lacock and the surrounding area, several other manors in Wiltshire and lands in Hampshire and the Isle of Wight.[6] The dominant position of the Church in late-medieval Bristol was evident everywhere in the town; the religious houses and parish churches were the principal landmarks on the Bristol skyline and included the house of Augustinian canons, the priory of St James and the four orders of friars – the Black Friars or

Dominicans in Broadmead, the Grey Friars or Franciscans in Lewins Mead, the White Friars or Carmelites near the site of the present Colston Hall, and the Austin Friars near Temple Gate. As shown in Appendix II, there were also friaries in Gloucester, Salisbury, Bridgwater, Ilchester, Melcombe Regis, Dorchester and Marlborough. Throughout the later Middle Ages the monastic house had acquired a substantial proportion of the tithes of many parish churches by 'appropriation'. This was the process whereby the monastery became the rector of the parish and collected the 'great' tithes of corn and hay, while appointing a vicar to minister to the spiritual needs of the parishioners, and allowing him the less profitable and less easily collected 'lesser' tithes on other produce of the land.

Many monastic houses outside the region also had extensive lands in the West Country, including Westminster Abbey, the monks and nuns of Syon and Romsey, and the abbeys of Pershore and Evesham. The evidence of the impact of the monastic owners upon the landscape is still apparent. Great monastic granges and barns survive at Stanway, Farmcote, Frocester, Lacock, Bradford-on-Avon, Pilton, Doulting, Abbotsbury and elsewhere; the fifteenth-century barn at Tisbury is one of the largest medieval barns in England. Nearly 200 feet long with an enormous thatched roof 1,450 square yards in area, it was, like the barns at Kelston and Bradford-on-Avon, part of the estates of the nuns at Shaftesbury, the wealthiest nunnery in England. The original barn at Abbotsbury was 272 feet long, while at Great Coxwell the magnificent thirteenth-century barn, which belonged to Beaulieu Abbey, remains as impressive evidence of monastic wealth. The expensive building work engaged upon by the monastic houses meant that they exploited the resources of their estates as fully as possible. The surviving records of the Benedictines at Winchcombe and of the Cistercian abbey at Kingswood show the careful administration of their lands and farms and the detailed management of their great sheep flocks.[7] The canons of St Augustine's Abbey in Bristol were extending their lands at Almondsbury by draining the marshy banks of the Severn. Similarly, the records of Glastonbury show the monks managing their estates to best advantage, carefully planning the use of their arable lands, moving stock and produce between their various manors, while regular consignments of produce arrived at the great barn in Glastonbury for the use of the monastery.[8] Glastonbury was also involved in large-scale drainage work in the Somerset Levels and undertook land reclamation and sea-defences along the coast on its manors of Brent, Berrow and Lympsham. The early fourteenth-century Fish House at Meare is another reminder of the way in which the Glastonbury monks exploited the resources of their estates.[9]

In order to appreciate fully the number, wealth and widespread estates of the west-country monasteries during the later Middle Ages, it is useful to imagine a traveller taking a journey from the north Cotswolds to the Dorset coast in c. 1500. He would start his journey in

Great Coxwell barn near Faringdon.
This huge barn belonged to the Cistercian abbey of Beaulieu in Hampshire and was used to store the produce of their large estates in Berkshire. Its size and magnificence, larger than many parish churches, is an indication of the wealth of the monastery and of the abundance of its food production.

a region dominated by the estates of the ancient Benedictine abbeys of Evesham, Pershore, Winchcombe and Tewkesbury and by the Cistercian abbey of Hailes which had grown rich from the offerings of pilgrims coming to the shrine of the Holy Blood. As he travelled across the Cotswolds, everywhere he would see the great monastic sheep flocks, while to the west in the Severn Vale he would see the great tower of the rich Benedictine abbey of St Peter at Gloucester; at Cirencester he would encounter the lands of the Augustinian abbey, while before him would soon appear the huge church and two towers of Malmesbury Abbey, one of the towers surmounted by a steeple taller than the spire of Salisbury Cathedral. In the vale of Berkeley and the Cotswold edge he would cross the lands of the Cistercian abbey at Kingswood, while Glastonbury Abbey's manors were spread across the southern Cotswolds. Beyond the Forest of Chippenham lay Stanley and Lacock, while to the west were the lands of the abbeys of Bath, Keynsham and St Augustine's, Bristol. Along the Wiltshire–Somerset border our traveller would pass close to or through the lands of the Carthusians at Hinton Charterhouse and Witham, the Augustinians at Maiden Bradley and the Bonhommes at Edington, while away to the west lay the great Somerset Benedictine houses of Glastonbury, Muchelney and Athelney, and to the east the ancient nunneries of Amesbury and Wilton. A landmark leading travellers to the hill-top town of Shaftesbury was provided by the tower of the wealthy nunnery, visible for miles around, while to the west was the Benedictine abbey at Sherborne. Across the Dorset chalklands there were monastic lands on every side, belonging to the ancient and wealthy Benedictine abbeys of Dorset – Sherborne, Cerne, Milton and Abbotsbury – or to the house of Cistercian nuns in the isolated valley at Tarrant Crawford – one of the richest of all English nunneries.

One feature of all these religious houses which our imaginary traveller in *c*. 1500 could hardly have failed to notice was the extent and magnificence of recent building work; everywhere he would have seen masons and labourers employed in lavish and expensive enterprises, enlarging churches and building new cloisters, gatehouses, refectories, and separate, opulent apartments for abbots and abbesses. The modern visitor, viewing the fragments that remain, is impressed by the late medieval work in the cloisters at Hailes, Gloucester and Lacock, by the abbot's lodging at Muchelney and the abbot's kitchen at Glastonbury; by the refectory at Cleeve, the gatehouses at Montacute and Cerne; by Abbot William Middleton's fine hall at Milton and Abbot Thomas Chard's palatial lodging at Forde.

Finally, we have to ask what was the state of religious observance in these monasteries in the decades before the Dissolution? How far was the monastic Rule observed and what evidence exists for genuine piety, devotion and spiritual life on the one hand, or for laxity, abuses and indiscipline on the other? In considering this question, it must always be borne in mind that it is far more difficult to find evidence of

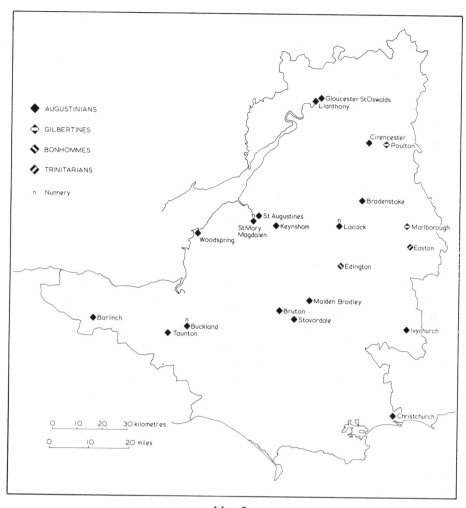

Map 2.
Major Monastic Houses of the West Country II: Augustinians, Gilbertines, Bonhommes and Trinitarians.

excellence than it is to uncover tales of scandal, licentiousness or failure to live up to a strict code of personal discipline. For a few monasteries in the region there is positive evidence of high standards and excellence. The house at Winchcombe, under the long rule of Richard Kidderminster (abbot 1488–1525), one of the most distinguished monks of his time, became a noted centre for the study of theology as well as of philosophy and literature, and its fame as an intellectual and academic institution spread widely.[10]

As will be shown later, the royal commissioners could find little to criticise at Glastonbury, Bruton or Lacock, while the Carthusians at Witham and Hinton Charterhouse continued to observe the austerities of their severe Rule, and no criticism was voiced of the life at either house. The prior of Hinton Charterhouse from 1523 to 1529 was John Bateman who wrote a book refuting some of Luther's ideas, while another scholar among the Carthusians at Hinton during the 1520s was Thomas Spicer who, amongst other writings, produced a commentary on St Paul's Epistle to the Galatians.[11] At Sherborne, the monastic life appears to have continued satisfactorily and, although there is no evidence of spiritual fervour, no criticism has been found of the moral and religious life of the monks, nor of their alms- giving, charity, and educational activity.[12] The spiritual and temporal affairs of the Augustinian house at Bradenstoke and of the Bonhommes at Edington seem to have been in a satisfactory condition.[13] A reasonably strict religious life continued to be observed at St Augustine's Bristol; the income of the house was carefully husbanded and, as far as can be observed in the surviving records, the spiritual duties were performed, the buildings were kept in repair, hospitality was maintained, alms were given to the poor, and bread, fish and other food as well as clothing were distributed at the abbey gates. A careful examination of the surviving account rolls of St Augustine's has revealed that the life of the twelve canons could not be described as particularly harsh or demanding, but equally it was not unduly luxurious:

> . . . about one-third of each year's income was spent on food, clothing and other domestic needs. The amounts of food and drink consumed are not in any way evidence of gluttony or drunkenness although they should have been fully adequate. Comfort, ease and sufficiency there certainly was but no excess.[14]

During the last few months of their existence, however, the Augustinians at Bristol had at least one canon who could hardly be considered as a model of the monastic life. This was John Rastle, who had been sent as a student to Oxford where perhaps he had acquired bad habits; when he returned to Bristol he was accused of being 'a public player of dice and other unlawful games'. He was eventually tried before the Court of Chancery for illegal gaming, although the monastery was dissolved before the case was heard. When it was heard in 1540 another ex-canon, Nicholas Corbet, who had become a secular priest at St Philip's in Bristol, declared that he knew John Rastle as a great dicer and carder and that he had heard that Rastle 'got at dice and cards of divers men in his chamber at the late monastery, £10, £5, and 5 marks' (£3 6s. 8d.), especially in the year before the dissolution of the monastery.[15] Details of Rastle's subsequent career are given in Chapter 7. In defence of the Augustinians it should be said that since their Rule required them to preach and to minister to the laity much more than other orders, they were far more subject to temptation and wordly corruption than were, for example, the enclosed, remote Carthusians.

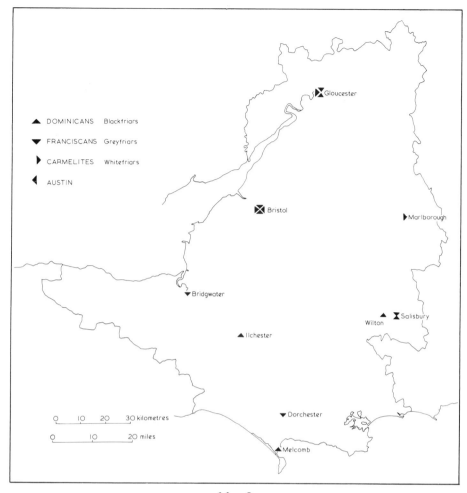

Map 3.
The West-Country Friaries at the Suppression.

Abbot Middleton of the Benedictine house at Milton has sometimes been criticised for his lavish expenditure on his own apartments, including the building of a magnificent hall which survives, but he also founded a free grammar school for the sons of townspeople in 1521. Several other west-country monasteries maintained fine libraries and others had schools in which local children as well as their own choristers and novices were taught. During the later Middle Ages, for example, there are references to schools at Gloucester, Cirencester, Llanthony, St Augustine's Bristol, Sherborne and elsewhere. A grammar school was founded in the Augustinian monastery at Bruton in 1520 and the foundation deed was signed by the abbots of Glastonbury, Witham and Bruton as well as by local gentry.[16] The record of the appointment of a schoolmaster in 1537 to teach grammar to the

The Ruins of St Oswald's Priory, Gloucester.
St Oswald's was a ninth-century minster founded by Aethelflaeda of Mercia, daughter of Alfred the Great. It was converted into an Augustinian Prior in the twelfth century and dissolved in 1536.

boys of the monastery survives from Forde, while at Glastonbury in 1534 the abbot appointed James Renyger to be organist in the Lady Chapel and to teach six boys pricksong and descant; at Ivychurch in 1536 a schoolmaster and five 'children for the church' were living in the monastery.[17]

For many of these schools few records survive, but one document gives a fascinating glimpse of a school at the small, remote Augustinian priory of Barlinch near Dulverton. This is a schoolboy's notebook written during the early sixteenth century; without it, the existence of the school would be unknown. The notebook reveals that it was a grammar school with a professional schoolmaster. The boy was probably a novice, expected to enter the monastic house, and his notebook contains memoranda, Latin vocabulary and exercises. Its chance survival is a reminder that many monastic schools have left no record, and also of the loss of educational provision which the dissolution involved.[18]

Some monasteries also maintained guest houses or inns for the accommodation of both pilgrims and travellers. At Sherborne, the abbey built the New Inn as a hospice for visitors at the end of the fifteenth century, and similar inns were maintained by several monasteries including Glastonbury, Hinton Charterhouse, Hailes, Cleeve and Gloucester, while on the fine new gatehouse built at Cleeve by Abbot Dovell during the 1520s were inscribed the words *Porta Patens Esto, Nulli Claudaris Honesto* (Gate be open, Shut to no honest man).[19] A visitation of Somerset monasteries in 1526 revealed that all was not well at some houses, and these will be discussed later, but at Glastonbury, Athelney, Muchelney and Bruton only minor faults were noted, such as the complaint at Muchelney that the organist, a layman, disturbed the brethren, though whether by his personality or his playing is not stated; or the grumbles at Bruton that the ale was watery and weak.[20]

One final piece of evidence in support of the continuing appeal of monastic life is the fact that in many of the region's monasteries numbers were being maintained. At Tewkesbury, Sherborne, Winchcombe, the two Charterhouses and elsewhere, as well as in many of the nunneries, the numbers of religious occupants were maintained or declined only slightly during the final decades before their dissolution. At Glastonbury the numbers increased: there were forty-six monks present when Richard Whiting was elected abbot in 1525, and in 1533 and 1534 there were fifty-two monks in the house, while in 1538, shortly before the suppression, there were fifty-five. Inevitably, several monks died during these years, so that to account for the increase in numbers it has been calculated that at least twenty-two men must have joined the community.[21]

But if no major criticisms can be found of the majority of monastic houses in the region during the decades before the dissolution, there are others in which a scandalously bad state of affairs was revealed, and the notoriety of the few no doubt tainted the popular conception of all. At Malmesbury in 1527, a visitation revealed numerous failings. The abbot was said to be violent and ill-tempered, and the monks were undisciplined and rebellious; there was disorder and quarrelling in the cloister and the prior kept a pack of hounds in the monastery which roamed everywhere and disturbed the monks. Some monks were frequently drunk, others broke out at night and consorted with women of doubtful reputation, the services were neglected and the food was bad. Clearly, although the huge buildings of this ancient abbey dominated the town of Malmesbury and all the surrounding area, its spiritual influence was minimal and its reputation must have been deplorably low. In spite of the complaints about his rule and personality, however, the abbot, Richard Cam, remained in office for another six years until his death in 1533.[22]

An episcopal visitation of Somerset monasteries in 1526 also provides a list of abuses and scandals. At the nunneries of Barrow and Cannington there were said to be quarrels and dissensions, and at Cannington the elderly prioress, Cecilia de Verney, who had been head of the house since 1504, was critical of some of her nuns, although her complaints seem trivial enough. She complained that Elizabeth Bouchier did not attend the services in the church and that Juliana Burges was arrogant and conceited, *elatum habere animum*; otherwise all was well. At Woodspring, several of the brethren complained about the prior who was alleged to be tyrannical and given to bursts of rage, did not consult the brethren and was too much influenced by laymen. Worst of all was the Augustinian house of Keynsham which had been severely criticised in earlier visitations and was obviously in a shocking condition. The buildings were said to be filthy and in decay, a pack of hounds wandered at will through church and cloister, the services were neglected, there were insufficient service books, and the young canons were not instructed and were illiterate. Evidently the state of religious life at Keynsham was at a very low ebb and yet it is interesting to note that, of the fourteen canons questioned by the bishop's official at the visitation in 1526, no less than eight stated that all was well or complained only of minor deficiencies.[23]

In a few houses the numbers had either shrunk so low or the burden of debt was so heavy that a regulated monastic life could hardly have been maintained. For example, at the priory of St Mary Magdalen in Bristol, which had been founded in the twelfth century for Augustinian canonesses, the community was always very poor and by the 1530s was reduced to only two ladies, one described as 'impotent and aged' and the other as 'a young novice desiring continuance in religion'. They had two servants, a man and a laundress. There can have been little comparison between their life-style and that of the nuns in large wealthy houses such as Shaftesbury, Wilton or Lacock. The small house of Gilbertine canons at Poulton near Cirencester had

Roof boss from Keynsham abbey.
This fine twelfth-century roof-boss with its sophisticated carving is a reminder of the wealth and splendour of the Augustinian monastery at Keynsham, where the buildings have been totally demolished.

Floor tiles, Keynsham Abbey.
Late thirteenth-century tiled pavement in situ in the nave of Keynsham Abbey Church.

an income of only £20 in 1535 and consisted of a prior and two canons; it can have had only the vestiges of a regular religious life.[24]

At Stavordale near Wincanton, the small Augustinian priory founded in the twelfth century was another very poor house; by 1533 it was in such a bad state and the number of canons had fallen so low that it was taken over by the much larger Augustinian house at Taunton. In 1536 Richard Zouche wrote to Thomas Cromwell, claiming that his ancestors had founded Stavordale and asking for the lands and buildings. He described it as

> . . . a poor priory, a foundation of my ancestors, which is my lord my father's inheritance and mine, and by the reason of a lewd prior that was there, which was a canon of Taunton afore, brought it to be a cell unto Taunton, and now it is destroyed, and there is but two canons which be of no good living, and that is great pity . . .[25]

Zouche's request was evidently successful for his family was living there during the 1540s.[26]

The situation of some monastic houses in urban locations, where the abbey buildings and estates dominated the town and their influence was everywhere to be felt, also created friction and resentment. There had been notable fierce quarrels between monks and townsfolk during the fifteenth century at Cirencester, Shaftesbury, Bath, Sherborne and elsewhere. At Sherborne, in 1437, feelings had run so high that the townspeople had actually set fire to the abbey church – the reddened stonework is still clearly visible, 'the fossilized remains of a quarrel' – while at Edington in 1450, William Ayscough, Bishop of Salisbury, was dragged from the priory church while saying mass and brutally murdered; the Bonhommes' priory was then plundered.[27] In Bristol, discord between the town and St Augustine's Abbey went on throughout the early sixteenth century. In 1515 Thomas Wolsey himself was forced to intervene to prevent violence, and during the 1520s in another dispute the monks arrested some town officials and the mayor and corporation of the town imprisoned some of the abbey servants. The abbot, John Somerset (abbot 1526–33), stormed the prison in an unsuccessful effort to release them; the matter finally had to be referred to arbitration.[28]

Apart from these few bad examples of scandalous neglect and failure to observe the monastic Rule, there were other more insidious causes of disquiet regarding the condition of the monastic houses during the decades before the dissolution. In almost all the houses, with the notable exception of the Carthusians, there had been a gradual relaxation of monastic discipline and a tendency to adopt a more comfortable way of life. Almost everywhere the abbots and abbesses had withdrawn into their own richly-furnished private apartments with their own servants, kitchens and separate establishment.

For the monks and nuns private property, pocket money, regular breaks from the monastic routine, a more varied diet and separate cubicles in the dormitories had all become increasingly accepted as the norm. The massive programmes of building work on which almost all the monasteries of the region embarked during the later Middle Ages, and of which so much evidence can still be seen in the ruins which remain, pub an intolerable burden on the finances of some houses. More time had to be devoted to the management of estates and property, to dealing with tenants and with architects and builders, and to the handling of large sums of money. Abbots' lodgings like those at Muchelney, Forde, Milton or Cerne were extremely expensive to build, furnish and support, with a large separate establishment commensurate with an extensive country estate. Moreover, fine new cloisters like those at Hailes, Gloucester, Lacock, Forde, Muchelney or Glastonbury, or elegant new refectories such as those at Hailes, Cleeve or Milton, created a very different atmosphere, resembling more a comfortable country mansion than an establishment dedicated to spiritual progress through the denial of

Medieval carving of the parish priest from Muchelney.
In 1308 the Benedictine monks of Muchelney agreed to provide a priest to serve the parish church, and in addition to a house, the priest was to have each week loaves of bread, two gallons of the best monastic ale and a meal each day from the monastic kitchen. The carving shows the priest taking his bread and ale back to the charming medieval vicarage house which still survives at Muchelney.

worldly comforts. The new style of architecture, the sophisticated decoration and the domestic amenities, of which the elegant refectory at Cleeve is such a fine example, symbolised the acceptance of an improved standard of living and concern for creature comfort. It was a long way removed from the ideals of St Benedict or St Bernard. One other factor which led to a gradual retreat from high standards was the increasing involvement of noblemen, courtiers and local gentry families in the life of the monasteries, in managing the estates, controlling the finances and influencing the choice of abbot or abbess. The economic aspects of this involvement will be discussed in the next chapter, but its effects can be seen in the number of lay burials, monuments and chantry chapels which were to be found in monastic churches such as Tewkesbury, Gloucester and Bath by the end of the Middle Ages. The effects can also be seen in lay interference in monastic elections. The families of the founders and principal patrons of monastic houses had always felt able to take a close interest in the administration and affairs of particular establishments, and had expected the monks and nuns to pray for them. The founder's chapel and the wealth of tombs and chantries of the de Clares, Despencers and Beauchamps in Tewkesbury Abbey, and the arms of those families which appear in the stonework and medieval stained-glass windows of the church, leave no doubt as to the power, influence and generous patronage which these families had exercised in the monastery. The influence of the Berkeleys is very evident in St Augustine's Bristol and that of the Courtenays at Forde. The arms of numerous late-medieval Dorset families are carved over the abbey gatehouse at Cerne or appear in the pages of the incomparably beautiful Sherborne Missal of c. 1400. The letter of Richard Zouche to Cromwell in 1536 successfully requesting the grant of the site and lands of Stavordale Priory on the grounds that it had been founded by his ancestor was quoted earlier in this chapter; likewise, early in 1536 Humphrey Stafford wrote to Cromwell demanding to be granted Woodspring Priory which he claimed had been founded by his family.[29]

Numerous laymen also had great influence as stewards of monastic lands, receivers of rents, auditors and agents, and many of those who were to be the chief purchasers of monastic land and property were already very closely involved with the monasteries in the decades before the dissolution. Thus, Sir Edward Baynton of Bromham in Wiltshire was steward of the lands of Malmesbury and Stanley; Sir Thomas Hungerford of Farleigh Castle performed the same function for Edington and Hinton Charterhouse and the Earl of Shrewsbury for the nunnery at Wilton as well as eleven other monastic houses; and families such as the Arundells, Wadhams, Sydenhams, Horners, Berkeleys, Daubeneys, Horseys and many others who were to be the chief beneficiaries of the dissolution were already firmly installed in the administrative affairs of the monasteries for many years before the collapse came. Many monks and nuns were also the close relatives or friends of gentry families throughout the region; for example, numbered among the nuns at Buckland at the dissolution were members of several important gentry families of Somerset including the families of Sydenham, Popham, Hill, Maunsel, Dodington and Hymerford; the Augustinian canonesses at Lacock included members of such wealthy west-country families as Bridges, Benett, Wilson, Baynton and Maundrell.[30]

Some laymen and laywomen were also living in the monastic houses as 'corrodians', a corrody being an allowance of lodging, food, drink and other necessities granted in return for a payment in cash or land, or in return for some service to the monastery, or at the request of a founder, bishop, king or royal official. For example, at Forde in 1535, a corrody was granted to William Tyler, Master of Arts, which entitled him to a furnished chamber, food and drink, a broadcloth gown and an annual payment of £3 6s. 8d., in return for his services as a schoolmaster teaching grammar to the boys in the monastery and expounding Scripture to the monks in the refectory during their meals. This was in consequence of an order issued by Henry VIII in 1535 that all religious houses were to provide a daily lesson on the Scriptures, that it was to last one hour and that all the brethren were to attend. Likewise, at Forde in 1533, corrodies were granted to two married couples in return for a cash payment; they were to have accommodation, food and drink, 'as much as two monks of the monasterie receive'.[31] In 1515 John Tucke, Bachelor of Arts, was granted a corrody at St Peter's, Gloucester, in return for his services as a master at the grammar school and the song school; in 1538 Henry Edmunds was appointed to teach song and Latin grammar.[32] At Cleeve in 1535 Edward Walker, gentleman, occupied a suite of rooms which may still be seen there on the south side of the cloister under the monks' fine refectory. In return for a cash sum of £27 he had been granted for life 'a chamber under the east part of the fratry house' with an inner room for a servant, together with 'sufficient and holsome meat and drinke' at the abbot's table, food and drink for his servant, and a nightly allowance of bread and ale. If he fell ill or 'if it shall please the said Edward for his own singular mind and pleasure' he could have his meals delivered to his own room. At the same time there were other corrodians living in the abbey.[33]

At the nunneries numerous young girls from aristocratic and gentry families spent their time acquiring accomplishments suitable to their station. Writing of the Wiltshire nunneries, the seventeenth-century antiquarian John Aubrey noted that

young maids were brought up . . . at nunneries, where they had examples of piety and humility, modesty and obedience to imitate and to practise. Here they learned needlework, the art of confectionery, surgery, physic, writing, drawing, etc. . . . This was a fine way of breeding up young women who are led more by example than precept; and a good retirement for widows and grave single women to a civil, virtuous and holy life.[34]

The nunneries also provided a suitable and convenient home for ladies whose presence in the wider world might have caused embarrassment. For example, among the residents in the nunnery of Shaftesbury in 1535 was Cardinal Wolsey's daughter who was known as Dorothy Clausey. She was then twenty-four years of age; soon afterwards she became a nun at Shaftesbury and remained there until the dissolution when she was granted a pension of £4 *per annum*.[35]

During the decades before the dissolution there was increasing pressure upon the monastic houses from royal officials, courtiers and local gentry over the appointment of abbots and abbesses, and blatant attempts to secure the election of persons who, it was thought, would be favourable to the interests of those who had supported their elevation. There are so many instances of this sort of lay interference in monastic affairs that only a few examples can be cited here.

In 1528 Cecily Willoughby, abbess of the large and wealthy nunnery of Wilton, died and immediately the fifty nuns found themselves at the centre of powerful conflicting interests. Cardinal Wolsey, as papal legate, had the right of conducting the election and his agent at Wilton, the priest Thomas Benet, suggested that the cardinal should favour Dame Isabel Jordayn, the prioress, who was 'ancient, wise and discreet'. But in spite of Wolsey's backing for Dame Isabel, her candidature encountered an even more powerfully supported rival. This was another nun of Wilton, Dame Eleanor Carey, whose brother, William Carey, was Squire of the Body to Henry VIII; moreover William Carey had recently married Mary Boleyn, the former mistress of the king and the sister of Anne Boleyn whose favours Henry was then actively pursuing. Supporters and opponents of both candidates then produced numerous bitter accusations against the morals and suitability of each lady, and the nuns were driven first one way then another by the rival claims and counter-claims of the powerful protagonists. Eventually, under this pressure, Dame Eleanor was forced to confess to having had two children and, after protracted negotiations in which the king, Anne Boleyn, Wolsey and the powerful friends of both ladies were all closely involved, Dame Isabel was eventually confirmed as abbess.[36]

In 1525 Wolsey's agent, Thomas Benet, had also been active in securing the election of the cardinal's candidate as Abbot of Milton and, following the election, the monks wrote to Wolsey, 'We have elected John Bradley as abbot, according to your letters.'[37] The election of a new abbot for the Augustinian house at Bristol in 1525 caused great dissensions in the town, with armed supporters of the rival candidates only too ready for violence against their opponents.[38] When Abbot Sherborne resigned at Muchelney in 1532 rival factions formed among the local gentry to influence the choice of his successor.

Eventually Thomas Ynde or Ine, the candidate favoured by the powerful group led by the eminent lawyer, Sir Nicholas Wadham, was elected.[39] Likewise, when John Ryve, the rector or head of the house of Bonhommes at Edington, died in May 1538, the leading local landowner, Walter, Lord Hungerford of Farleigh Castle, wrote to Cromwell to recommend Paul Bush, the corrector or deputy.

> On Thursday night last, died the rector of the monastery of Edington. The Bishop of Sarum, diocesan there, has the power to admit one of three whom the brethren of the house shall present unto him. I desire your Lordship to write to the Bishop in favour of a friend of mine whom the brethren have nominated. His name is Sir Paul Busche, and he is also 'corrector' of the house.
>
> Farleigh 25 May 1538.

Shortly afterwards Lord Hungerford was appointed steward of the lands of Edington.[40] The extensive lands and property of Sherborne Abbey were of great interest to many people and, as early as December 1533, Sir Christopher Hales, a prominent lawyer who had been attorney-general, wrote to Cromwell from Gray's Inn; he suggested that if John Meere, the Abbot of Sherborne, should die then John Barnstaple, a monk of Sherborne, would be the most suitable successor, notwithstanding the fact that some influential local men supported John Dunster, the prior of the abbey. Clearly, the interests or opinions of the monks counted for very little. In the event Abbot Meere resigned early in 1535 and immediately Sir John Horsey, who lived in a large mansion at Clifton Maybank near Sherborne and who was the steward of Sherborne Abbey lands and Bailiff of Sherborne, made a secret offer to Cromwell of the large sum of 500 marks (£333 6s. 8d.) if John Barnstaple should be elected abbot, in spite of the strong support for the prior. Barnstaple was duly elected, and on 9 May 1535 Horsey wrote to Cromwell to thank him.

> I thank you for offering my friend, Dom John Barnstaple, to be Abbot of Sherborne on the resignation of Dom John Meere, late Abbot. The Monastery are well pleased with the appointment. I cannot come to you now, as I am appointed to look to the taxing of the clergy. I will come, however, shortly to make payment secretly between your mastership and me, unto you of 500 marks according to my promise.

A month later on 10 June 1535 John Barnstaple himself wrote to Cromwell to thank him, and from his letter it is clear that in order to secure his appointment he had agreed to a deal over the prior.

> Thank you for my preferment to be Abbot of Sherborne. According to your letter, I am content to permit the prior of the said house to enjoy the office of prior, and also to occupy two other offices generally seperated from the priorship. All these offices amount yearly to the sum of £40.

Four years later, John Barnstaple was to surrender the abbey to the Crown, and the lands and buildings including the great abbey church were acquired by Sir John Horsey. Such dealings were a long way removed from the ideals incorporated in the Rule of St Benedict or in the twelfth-century constitution of the Cistercians, the *Carta Caritatis*, which was written by Stephen Harding who had been a monk at Sherborne.[41]

In 1534 Henry, Duke of Richmond, an illegitimate son of Henry VIII, made no attempt to conceal his own interest in the election of a new abbot for the small Cistercian abbey of Bindon in Dorset. He wrote to Cromwell pointing out that the abbey's lands were adjacent to his own in the Isle of Purbeck and that he needed the goodwill of the abbey to protect his deer: 'the convent have agreed to take care of my deer . . .'[42]

The general impression that remains of the state of the west-country monasteries on the eve of the dissolution is that, with some notable exceptions, there were few houses guilty of gross depravity or serious abuse, but that there was little fervour in their religious life. The state of affairs was not nearly so bad as was claimed by Cromwell's commissioners in 1535–6, nor was it nearly so good as it should have been. Most monks and nuns continued the daily round of services, but, although the monasteries continued to function, they were no longer regarded as power houses of the religious life nor as performing any longer a valuable, spiritual function to the glory of God or for the well-being of the whole of society. With their large incomes and fine modern buildings, many religious houses of both monks and nuns had become little more than comfortable residences and were not highly regarded or held in esteem by the neighbouring communities. The two exceptions were the houses of the Carthusians at Witham and Hinton Charterhouse. Their life-style, which differed so much from that of the other orders, their perpetual seclusion and their continuing adherence to a strict, austere Rule, meant that no criticism was levelled against them and they continued to be looked up to as a spiritual force.

Few criticisms are found of the friars although, as will be shown in Chapter 5, at Marlborough in 1538 one of the Carmelite friars was accused of the rape of a young child. But it is notable that, with a few exceptions, the stream of bequests and gifts which had formerly been such an important part of the friars' income had largely dried up, and most of the friaries were suffering from severe poverty.

In spite of their wealth, their long traditions and their charity, most of the houses of monks and nuns apparently had little support in the West Country and were in no position to confront the religious changes of the 1530s or to withstand the determined assault of the Crown. The monasteries were vulnerable in too many ways for their own security in such rapidly- changing times. The gentry, many of whose ancestors had founded or endowed the monasteries and were buried and commemorated within them, stood to gain hugely by the dispersal of the monastic estates. To the townsfolk, they had become largely irrelevant and the religious life of the towns was focussed on the parish churches and chantry foundations. In the countryside, the monks and nuns were seen as landlords and tithe-collectors rather than as spiritual leaders. To those who favoured religious reform, the monasteries were part of an outdated and corrupt system, which depended upon concepts such as purgatory, prayers for the dead, pilgrimages and images, which they wished to see swept away. Even the one practical contribution to society at which the monastic houses had excelled, the copying of manuscripts and the production of books, had now been overtaken by the printing press.

Nonetheless, in view of their antiquity, the extent of their estates, their wealth and influence, and the splendour of their buildings and possessions, few would have been rash enough to predict in 1530 that within ten years all the monastic houses would be suppressed and that there would be no more monks or nuns, and that the friars who were such a familiar feature of life in the larger towns of the region would have been swept away. The following chapters will show the extent of the monastic wealth, the remarkable speed with which the institutions were suppressed, how the dissolution was accomplished and the fate of the religious, their estates, buildings and artistic treasures.

Chapter 2

The *Valor Ecclesiasticus* and the Economy of the Monasteries in 1535

It was because of their wealth that the monasteries were destroyed. Their spiritual value was questioned by many people during the century before the dissolution and with few exceptions their religious fervour was at a low ebb, while neither their scholarship, almsgiving and hospitality nor their educational, social and charitable work was sufficient to win them many friends; but above all, it was the combination of an impecunious monarch, a ruthless, determined and extremely able minister and the country gentry who coveted monastic lands that together brought about the rapid fall of these ancient and wealthy institutions. This chapter will consider the wealth of the west-country monasteries on the eve of the dissolution, their estates and properties, the sources of their wealth and the ways in which they disposed of their large incomes.

The first major challenge to the monasteries and the first clear opportunity they had to take a firm stand against religious change came in a complex series of political moves during 1533–34, culminating in the Acts of Succession and the Act of Supremacy. The Act of Supremacy was crucial for the progress of the English Reformation, for it declared that the king and not the Pope was supreme head of the Church in England. A requirement of the Acts was that all adults, including monks and nuns, should take an oath upon the Holy Scriptures that they acquiesced in the repudiation of Katherine of Aragon, agreed with the royal marriage to Anne Boleyn and that they would give allegiance to the children of that marriage as lawful heirs to the throne – as well as accepting the royal headship of the Church. There is no record that any member of a west-country monastic community refused to take the oath as required. No doubt many had great misgivings, especially among the Carthusians. As early as May 1533 Prior Edmund Horde of Hinton Charterhouse was reported to Cromwell for maintaining that he would never consent to 'so unjust and unlawful a deed' as the king's marriage to Anne Boleyn; while in 1534 all the Somerset Carthusians were said to be prepared to suffer martyrdom rather than support the royal supremacy. Evidently Edmund Horde was eventually persuaded to conform by Cromwell himself, for the prior wrote to Cromwell in March 1535 to apologise for his blunt speaking which 'rose upon mine untowardness in certain things which ye willed me to do concerning the King's Majesty'. Horde's high reputation among his fellow Carthusians seems to have led them also to take the required oath.[1]

Others doubtless saw no alternative in the face of royal power, or hoped fervently that time would change the difficult situation. None could have forseen the full consequences of their action. But, however reluctantly they may have bowed to the royal will, the fact that they had solemnly sworn to accept the royal supremacy left the monks and nuns with little defence against royal power during all the upheavals which were soon to follow.

Any description of the economy of the monasteries on the eve of suppression must depend very heavily on the *Valor Ecclesiasticus* which provides a detailed list of the annual income of each ecclesiastical benefice and of all the monastic houses. This remarkable source was compiled not only with great speed but also with remarkable thoroughness by commissioners appointed for each county, and the final returns were arranged under dioceses. The reason for the survey was that in 1534, as well as the Act of Supremacy which sealed the break with Rome and made the king supreme head of the Church in England, parliament also passed the Act of First Fruits and Tenths, which ordered that from 1 January 1535 the first year's income, or 'first fruits', of any ecclesiastical benefice or office should be paid over to the Crown, and also imposed an annual tax of 10 per cent on the income of each benefice. In order that this tax could be levied, it was therefore necessary to carry out a survey of all the ecclesiastical benefices in the country. To undertake this major task commissioners were appointed by the chancellor on 30 January 1535 and all monks, clergy and ecclesiastical officials were ordered to appear before them and give detailed information, on oath, of their income. In dealing with the monasteries, the commissioners were ordered to

> search and know the number and names of every abbey, monastery, priory, and house religious and conventual, as well as charterhouses as other, founded and edified within every deanery or elsewhere within the limits of this commission . . . and the number, names, and certainty of all the manors, lands, tenements, rents, farms, possessions, parsonages, portions, pensions, tithes, oblations and all other profits as well spiritual as temporal appertaining or belonging to every such abbey . . .
>
> And their whole and entire, distinct and several yearly values. And the true certainty of such annual or perpetual rents, pensions, alms, and fees for receivers, bailiffs, auditors, and stewards only, and none other officers, yearly given and paid out of the same . . . [1]

The compilation of the *Valor Ecclesiasticus* was an enormous undertaking and, not surprisingly, the commissioners did not accomplish their task by 30 May 1535 as had originally been planned. Most returns were complete by the autumn however, and by the end of the year only a few fragments of the great jigsaw remained unfilled. The commissioners' returns were arranged in the traditional accounting manner of the time, in Latin, showing all the sources of revenue of each monastery and its gross annual income, and deducting, as free of tax, all pensions, alms and fees which each house was obliged to pay under the terms of its foundation or of subsequent bequests. The whole account of the wealth of the Church which was thus compiled was finally assembled in London as the *Valor Ecclesiasticus*.[2] Modern scholars who have analysed the commissioners' work have been impressed by their general care and accuracy, and by 'the quite remarkable reliability of the returns as a whole'.[3] Not surprisingly, there are errors and omissions. In the West Country two major monasteries were overlooked by the commissioners and do not appear in the *Valor*. They are St Augustine's in Bristol and the Cistercian abbey at Kingswood. The income of both can, however, be calculated from other sources. Bristol was a county in its own right and, although part of the large diocese of Worcester, was far from the diocesan centre; it was presumably for this reason that it was missed by the commissioners. The omission of Kingswood is more easily explained, since although the site of this monastery was surrounded by south Gloucestershire it was actually situated in a small detached part of Wiltshire. The abbot later explained that the commissioners for Gloucestershire had refused to take details of the annual value of his monastery on the grounds that it was not part of their commission, and the commissioners for Wiltshire had also refused to come although they had been invited to do so.[4] A more general reservation about the returns is that they tend to undervalue some monastic assets and especially the lands which were directly farmed by the monasteries or for which the rents were paid wholly or partly in kind. Because of the nature of medieval tenure, income from rents fluctuated greatly from year to year; in a period of rapid inflation it was of course difficult to apportion realistic values to all parts of such large estates, or to property ranging from rough moorland grazing on Exmoor or heathland in Dorset to houses, inns and shops in Bristol, or from sheep pastures on the Cotswolds or Salisbury Plain to fisheries in the Somerset Levels or fulling mills in west Wiltshire. Moreover, the valuations were being compiled for the purposes of taxation and, even under oath, the temptation to understate rather than exaggerate income must have been great. Professor Knowles has suggested that for some monasteries this undervaluation and failure to include fully items such as cash-in-hand, crops, livestock, wool or payments in kind may have been as much as 20 per cent: 'Thus Glastonbury, with an income in the *Valor* of £3311 net, may easily have handled a sum much nearer £4000.'[5]

The commissioners were instructed to make 'a fair book after the auditors fashion'. This was divided into receipts and allowances, and the income itself was divided into spiritual and temporal. Here for the first time was disclosed just how wealthy the monastic houses really were. Naturally the imposition of a heavy tax on the clergy and the searching inquiry into all sources of clerical and monastic wealth created many rumours and anxieties, and there was talk of further confiscations of Church property by the Crown. Tudor governments, lacking a standing army or efficient police force, were always keen to be told of any indications of public opinion, and informers wrote to Cromwell from all over the country with reports of sermons, tales of ale-house gossip, political discussions or religious dissension. For example, in 1535–6 Cromwell was told of a chantry priest in Gloucester who had refuted the doctrine of purgatory and told his congregation that 'if the purgatory priests do pray with their tongues till their tongues be worne to stumps' it would not help the souls of the dead.[6] A preacher at Wotton-under-Edge had attacked 'foolish, lewd and beggarly ceremonies . . . full of idolatry and superstition'; and at Winchcombe the parish priest, Anthony Saunders, angered the abbot and monks by his preaching which they described as 'new learning and full heresy'. In south Gloucestershire, Sir John Walsh at Little Sodbury had sheltered William Tyndale, the translator of the Bible, and both Walsh and Sir Nicholas Poyntz of Iron Acton were active in encouraging the preaching of reform, bringing preachers to Iron Acton where they used the open-air pulpit which survives in the churchyard.[7] From Bristol, Cromwell was told of a preacher who had declared that trust in the monastic life or in religious ceremonies could avail nothing and that salvation could only come through faith, 'nor could a ship laden with Friars' girdles or a dung cart full of monks' cowls help to justification'.[8]

The rumours and unease caused by the enquiry into the wealth of the Church in 1535, and the speculation as to what would follow, are reflected in the conversations of some farmers in west Dorset which were overheard and reported to Cromwell by Sir Thomas Arundell of Chideock Castle, near Bridport, on 20 May 1535. One man had been overheard to complain of the stormy weather and to have said that

> . . . it was a heavy world and like to be worse shortly, for he had heard say that the priests would rise against the King . . . because they should pay so much money to the King's grace.

Another speaker, a very aged man, claimed that he had long ago been told by a well-learned man that the priests would rise in revolt and would rule the realm three days and three nights,

> . . . and then the white falcon should come out of the north-west, and kill almost all the priests, and they that should escape should be fain to flie and hide themselves and cover their crowns with the filth of the beasts, because they would not be known.[9]

That such conversations should take place, or that they should be thought worth reporting to the king's secretary, gives some indication of the stir that was created by the decision to impose a new tax on the Church and by the careful examination of its property, wealth and income.

The men chosen to serve as commissioners to conduct the enquiry were the bishops and the county gentry who were already closely involved with the monasteries and who, within a few years, were to be the main purchasers of monastic property. Thus in Wiltshire we find Sir Edward Baynton, Sir Walter Hungerford, Sir John Seymour, Edward Mompesson and others; in Somerset the names of Stourton, Powlett and Portman appear, while in Dorset and commission included Arundell, Strangways and Horsey.[10]

The bishops of each diocese generally acted as the leaders of each group of commissioners and supervised the compilation of their surveys. In Bath and Wells diocese, for example, the bishop, John Clerke, received his instructions on Palm Sunday, 16 April 1535, and assembled the other commissioners immediately after Easter to begin their work, complaining to Cromwell that 'The business will be long and laborious . . .' They found it impossible to complete the task by Trinity Sunday (30 May) as was originally envisaged, but the final survey for the diocese was compiled and sent to Cromwell on 17 September 1535. At the same time the bishop wrote to testify to the zeal of the commissioners, pointing out that they rode night and day, incurred great expenses and neglected their own private affairs, with the sole object of increasing the king's revenue.[11]

From the results of the commissioners' labours it emerged that the total gross income of all the monasteries, great and small, in the West Country in 1535, excluding St Augustine's Bristol and Kingswood, was as follows:

Dorset	£4431	2s.	4d.
Gloucestershire	£7171	19s.	6½d.
Somerset	£8993	3s.	10d.
Wiltshire	£4177	15s.	9d.
Total	£24774	1s.	5½d.

SPIRITUAL INCOME

On average about a fifth of the income of most monastic houses came from what was termed spiritual income, *spiritualia*. Most of this came from parish churches which had been taken over or 'appropriated' by a religious house, so that the institution became the rector of the parish and took a major portion of the tithes and offerings while appointing a vicar on a smaller stipend, or with rights to a portion of the tithes, to

Roof-boss from Hailes abbey.
This is one of several thirteenth-century roof-bosses found amid the ruins of the abbey and now displayed in the museum on the site.

undertake the care of the parish and the cure of souls there. Other spiritual income included rents for glebe lands in appropriated parishes and offerings at shrines. The small Cistercian abbey of Bindon in Dorset had, according to the *Valor*, a gross annual income of £236, of which the spiritual income accounted for £51. This was made up of revenue from the appropriated parishes of Chaldon Herring, £11, and Winfrith Newburgh, £33, together with rights to portions of the tithes from other parishes. At the larger Benedictine abbey of Milton Abbas the gross annual income was £715 and the gross income from spiritual sources was £127. This was made up of tithes and rents of glebe lands from the appropriated parishes of Milton, Stockland (Devon), Sydling St Nicholas, Osmington and part of the tithes of Milborne St Andrew and Holworth. It is noticeable that the spiritual income of Hailes Abbey included only £10 revenue from the offerings of pilgrims to the shrine of the Holy Blood. This may be an example of failure to declare the full total, since this shrine was an extremely popular centre of pilgrimage and the offerings of pilgrims had enabled the monks to rebuilt the cloisters and enlarge their church; its fame is referred to by Chaucer in the Pardoner's Tale: 'By the blode of Crist that is in Hayles'. Moreover as late as 1533 Hugh Latimer, who was rector of West Kington near Castle Combe and who was later, as Bishop of Worcester, to be foremost in the destruction of the shrine at Hailes, wrote with genuine distress and indignation of the crowds of pilgrims which he saw passing along the Fosse Way near his home on their way to Hailes.

> . . . you would wonder to see how they come by flocks out of the west country to many images, but chiefly to the blood of Hailes. And they believe verily that it was Christ's body, shed upon the mount of Calvary for our salvation.[13]

There may have been a similar failure to declare the full income at Cleeve where the monks possessed the Chapel of Our Lady at Cleeve situated a mile or so away from the monastery, close to the Bristol Channel. In the chapel was a renowned statue of the Virgin which attracted pilgrims from a wide area, for whose accommodation the monks had built an inn or hospice. As at Hailes, however, the income of the shrine is given in suspiciously round figures and was said to be no more than £2 0s. 0d.[14] Two years later, early in 1537, the Abbot of Cleeve was to complain that his house had been undervalued by the commissioners compiling the *Valor Ecclesiasticus*.[15]

In the collection of their spiritual income, as with their temporal, the monks and nuns relied almost entirely upon lay officials who were entrusted with the task of collecting parochial tithes, and often farmed out the tithes for a lump sum leaving the person who had leased the tithe to make what profit he could from their collection. The collection of tithe in kind was inevitably a complex and time-consuming business, involving innumerable opportunities for dispute and ill-feeling, and since many of the appropriated parishes were a long way from the monastic house it is understandable that the monks and nuns did not wish to undertake the tithe collection themselves. Nor could they leave it to the vicar in each parish who was entitled to some tithes (the 'small' tithes) himself and whose interests might lie more with the tithe-payers, his own parishioners, rather than with the tithe-receivers, the monks of some distant monastery. The unfortunate consequence was that the monasteries had little contact with their appropriated parishes and were seen by the parishioners only as the recipients of portions of their crops and livestock, and as doing little or nothing in the parish in return. The wealthy Augustinian house at Cirencester owned the grain tithes of Shrivenham in Berkshire and had let these in four lots to four different persons, all of whom would naturally have sought to collect as much grain as possible, so as to make a profit on the lump sum paid to the canons at Cirencester. For the parishioners at Shrivenham, therefore, the reality was direct pressure from the tithe- collectors to yield up more of their grain crops, while any connection between this and the monastery fifteen miles away at Cirencester must have been tenuous. More than half the income of Llanthony by Gloucester came from possessions in Ireland and these included the tithes of numerous appropriated churches in Meath, Louth, Drogheda, Dublin and elsewhere; the contact between

The Refectory, Cleeve Abbey.

The refectory of this Cistercian house was rebuilt on a new alignment during the decades before the Suppression. The dining hall is on the upper floor and beneath are kitchens and rooms for corrodians. The foundations and tiled floor of the earlier refectory can be seen at right angles to the present range of buildings.

The Cloister, Cleeve Abbey.

This is one of the best preserved monastic sites in the west country. The buildings were preserved to be used as barns, and only the church was demolished. The triple-arched entrance to the Chapter House can be seen, and to the right the monks' day stairs. The range above contained the monks' dorter or dormitory.

the monks and the Irish farmers who supported them with their tithes must have been virtually non-existent.[16]

TEMPORAL INCOME

The major part of the monastic income came from temporal sources such as the rents of lands and property, the income from demesnes farmed directly by the monasteries, the profits from sheep flocks, cattle, woodlands or fees for markets, fairs and mills. Some west-country monasteries had considerable urban properties – shops, inns, workshops and houses which were let to tenants. For example, Bath Abbey derived 11 per cent of its total income from urban properties, Llanthony by Gloucester 12 per cent; Malmesbury Abbey had 'divers tenements' in Bristol which brought it an income of £5 6s. 8d. per annum. It also received £4 for various houses and buildings at Holborn in London and a further 13s. 6d. for land and tenements in Fleet Street. Maiden Bradley had tenements in Kidderminster worth £26 per annum; Glastonbury had property in London worth £21 2s. 7d. per annum and property in Bristol worth £5 per annum. But these were unusual, and most west-country monasteries had few urban proper-ties. The *Valor Ecclesiasticus* gives few details about mills and most of those listed among monastic properties are undoubtedly corn mills, although some west-country monasteries owned fulling or tucking mills for the working of cloth and these were let out to tenants. Fulling mills are listed among the possessions of Maiden Bradley, Cirencester and Winchcombe. The customs of many manors compelled tenants to have their corn ground at the manorial mill and so the possession of such a facility by a landowner was often very lucrative. This is reflected in the annual value of some of the monastic corn mills. Llanthony by Gloucester obtained £9 2s. 0d. from this source, Keynsham £17 13s. 4d. Other west-country examples include

Tewkesbury	£18 10s. 0d.	Maiden Bradley	£4 0s. 0d.
Winchcombe	£6 19s. 4d.	Tarrant	£3 0s. 0d.
Glastonbury	£18 6s. 8d.		
Malmesbury	£8 19s. 8d.		

Some of these mills may have been used for both grinding corn and fulling cloth. For example, the Carthusians at Hinton Charterhouse are known to have had a fulling mill at Freshford, but this is not mentioned in the *Valor* although an income of £3 10s. 0d. from mills is shown. The income from mills is not always shown separately and their specific use is not always indicated. It is likely that the 'Wyneyards Mill' which belonged to Malmesbury Abbey and was worth £3 3s. 0d. per annum in 1535 was a fulling mill, since it was said to be in the occupation of William Stumpe; it was Stumpe, a wealthy clothier, who was to purchase the abbey buildings at Malmesbury after

The George Inn, Norton St Philip.
This medieval inn belonged to the Carthusians of nearby Hinton Charterhouse, and it was the place where much of the wool and cloth from their estates on Mendip and their fulling-mill at Freshford was sold.

the dissolution and use some of them for large-scale cloth production. There were undoubtedly numerous other mills the income from which is not mentioned separately in the *Valor*. It is clear from other sources that the nuns at Lacock had fulling mills at Bishopstrow and Hatherop, and a gig mill at Bishopstrow. They also possessed a coal mine in south Gloucestershire.[18] Other monasteries possessed profitable stone quarries. The Benedictine monks at Pershore had a quarry at Hawkesbury in the south Cotswolds which was worth 1s. 8d. per annum. Other quarries in the Cotswolds included Llanthony's quarry at Barrington worth 6s. 8d. per annum, Winchcombe's quarry at Enstone worth 10s. per annum, and the quarry at Upton (St Leonards) belonging to St Peter's abbey Gloucester worth 1s. per annum.

Other non-agricultural income of the monasteries shown in the *Valor Ecclesiasticus* included the rent of £3 which Cerne received from butchers for use of the shambles in Cerne Abbas, and 7s. which Malmesbury received as the rent for stalls in the market place. At Cirencester £3 0s. 6d. was received from merchants for stalls in the Bothehall, £1 for tolls in Ponder Lane and £1 from livestock traders. Other west-country monasteries which received income from market dues and tolls included.

Shaftesbury	£2 4s.	6d.
Sherborne	13s.	1½d.
Tarrant	£2 0s.	0d.
Winchcombe	3s.	0d.
Malmesbury	£2 0s.	2½d.

Malmesbury and Cirencester both received money, £2 per annum in each case, as dues from brewers or alewrights, and a unique entry for the Carthusians at Hinton Charterhouse shows that they received by royal grant the very large income of £31 6s. 8d. as a levy on cloth made in Wiltshire.

Several monasteries had fisheries which brought a small income, although most of the fish were no doubt eaten by the monks or nuns and their servants. For example, Malmesbury possessed a fishery on the River Wye at Tintern worth £1 6s. 8d. per annum, and Winchcombe had a fishery worth £4 per annum. There must have been many others which are not listed separately in the *Valor*. A reminder of the importance of fish in the economy of west-country monasteries survives in the form of the early fourteenth-century fish house at Meare which belonged to Glastonbury Abbey. The income from manorial or hundred courts is also listed as part of the income of some houses, although the amount received fluctuated a good deal from year to year. The Bonhommes at Edington are said to have received £7 0s. 10d. per annum from their courts; the numerous Glastonbury manors and its five hundred courts produced £132 2s. 8¼d. per annum; the courts of the nuns at Shaftesbury were even more profitable and produced £154 3s. 7d. per annum.[19] A further source of monastic income was derived from sales of timber and this became an important feature of the economy of some houses.[20]

INCOME FROM THE LAND

It was the agricultural income which was by far the most important component of the total wealth of most monasteries. There had been a great change in the management of their land by most monastic houses in the century or more before the dissolution. Most had ceased direct farming operations on the greater part of their lands, keeping only one or two nearby manors where the cultivation of the demesne lands was directly supervised by the monks or their officials; they then rented to tenants all the land on other manors including the manorial demesne which had earlier been farmed by the monks or nuns as lords of the manor, using the labour service which tenants provided as part of their rent. By the end of the Middle Ages these labour services had been changed to money rents. The result of these changes was that, as with the appropriated parish churches, the monks or nuns abandoned any direct involvement with the farmers on their manors, becoming merely collectors of rents, and since the task of rent-collecting was

The Fish House at Meare, Somerset
This fourteenth-century fish house belonged to Glastonbury abbey and stood beside the large monastic lake or mere. It served as a lodging for the fisherman and as a store house for his tackle and for the fish which he caught. The fish house is a reminder of the intensive way in which the monasteries exploited all the resources of their estates.

frequently part of the duties of the farmer to whom the demesnes had been leased, or was entrusted to a lay official, the relationship between the abbey and its tenants became even more remote. It was not the sort of relationship which could be likely to lead to violent protest by the tenants over any proposals to suppress the monasteries. Certainly the monks managed their estates like any other landowners and were no more or less benevolent to their tenants than were lay landlords.

Some west-country monasteries did retain their sheep flocks and their grazing lands even after they had let out all the rest of the land on a manor. This was especially the case in the Cotswolds and on the Dorset chalklands. Thus Winchcombe Abbey retained its sheep, flocks numbering in all some three thousand sheep, and the large areas of pasture in the manors of Frampton, Charlton Abbots, Snowshill and Hawling, together with the facilities at Sherborne (Glos.) which had for long been used to assemble, wash and shear all the abbey flocks in the late spring of each year.[21] The sheep flocks belonging to the Dorset monasteries were of such importance that they are listed in detail in the *Valor Ecclesiasticus*. The full figures are shown in Appendix III, but in total the seven major monasteries of Dorset possessed 24,959 sheep; Milton Abbey situated in the centre of the chalklands was the largest sheep owner with 1,775 sheep at Milton itself and a further 5,554 on outlying manors. Cerne came next with 6,029 sheep and the smallest flock, 885 sheep, was possessed by Sherborne Abbey, many of whose manors lay in the heavy clays of the Blackmore Vale or in west Dorset. Although they are not listed in the *Valor Ecclesiasticus* it is clear that other monasteries retained their large sheep flocks until the end. For example, in 1521 the Abbess of Wilton paid for vestments and copes of silk and velvet 'wrought with gold and powdered with archangels', with wool worth £180; and in 1535 the nuns of Wilton retained pasture for 1,000 sheep on their manor of Chalke.[22] Augustinian canonesses at Lacock had a flock of over 2,000 sheep on their manor at Chitterne, and there were other flocks at Shorwell and Bishopstrow; part of the tenants' duties consisted of washing and shearing the flocks, and bringing the wool to Lacock to be stored in the wool house. By 1535, however, the flocks and pastures had been let to tenants.[23] Most of the monastic land was let for money rents, but a few monasteries continued to receive rents in kind. For example, the nuns at Amesbury had let all their lands including the demesne at Amesbury to tenants and received money rents for 290 acres of arable, for pasture land for 374 sheep and even for their dovecotes and fishery; together this brought in rents of £11 12s. 5d. More valuable, but far more inconvenient for the Amesbury nuns, were the rents in kind which are listed as follows

Oblations and Tithes	£7	0s.	0d.
15 Weights of Wool	£5	5s.	0d.
Lambs	£1	16s.	0d.
Small pigs		4s.	0d.
Geese		1s.	½d.
300 eggs		1s.	3d.
20 quarters of corn	£5	0s.	0d.
30 quarters of barley	£5	0s.	0d.
8 quarters of oats		16s.	0d.
2 quarters of peas		10s.	0d.
12 loads of hay	£1	16s.	0d.
Total	£27	9s.	11½d.

A survey of Stanley in 1536 revealed that the abbey possessed 400 sheep on its estate at Berwick Basset and 400 on other manors. The nuns at Wilton continued to receive each year wheat, barley, 62 capons, 110 hens, 105 geese, 800 pigeons, one calf, woolfells, 1½ pounds of pepper and 8 loads of hay.[24]

Although the income of many west-country monasteries was very large, their expenditure was also considerable. Many had spent enormous sums on building work during the late fifteenth and early

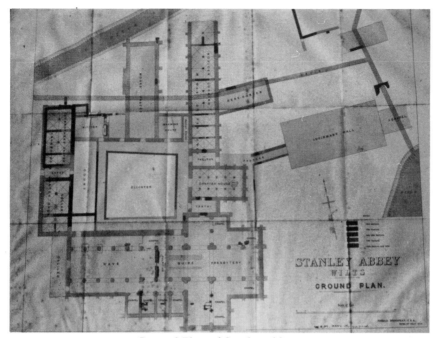

Ground Plan of Stanley abbey.
*Scarcely anything now survives above ground of this important Cistercian house,
much of which was demolished soon after the Suppression by Sir Edward Baynton who
used the stone on his new mansion at Bromham.*

sixteenth centuries, and the maintenance of their spectacular buildings
was a constant drain on resources. The separate establishments which
had been set up by the abbots of most houses, with fine apartments,
large kitchens, guest houses, stables and numerous servants were also
a heavy burden. Most houses also spent lavishly on the decoration and
furnishing of their churches, on vestments and ornaments, and on
many servants and lay officials. The consequence was that several
houses were in debt at the time of the dissolution, although in only a
few was the burden of debt very heavy; many of the debts are no more
than the sort of credit which might be expected by a large, ancient and
wealthy institution. Bath Abbey was said to be £400 in debt, though
this was not a large sum in relation to its annual net income of £617.[26]
The Cistercians at Cleeve had been in financial difficulties throughout
the reign of Henry VIII, in spite of several attempts to increase their
income, and at Muchelney the abbot and monks had pawned a
quantity of silver in 1534 to raise £100.[27] Most debt-ridden of all the
west-country monasteries was the Benedictine abbey of Athelney.
This had never been a wealthy house and its net annual income in 1535
was £209. The abbot seems to have allowed debts to accumulate until
the situation was very serious, and in April 1536 he was compelled to

write to Thomas Cromwell to beg for help in paying off the creditors, imploring him

> to be good master unto me and to my poor house concerning the payment of our debts, that I may be out of trouble and suit of law . . . worshipful master devise some means that this my petition may take effect and I am contented to abide your order in this behalf. I trust to order me and my house after such a strait fashion that I shall make payment of a hundred pounds every year.

The abbot lists his debts to no less than fifty-seven creditors and the total amount comes to more than £860. The debts range from £66 owed to the king, £90 owed to the Abbot of Glastonbury, £80 to the Abbot of Dunkeswell in Devon and £40 to Master Soper of Taunton, through to numerous small sums owed to individuals, clerics, gentry or tradesmen throughout the West Country. The abbot optimistically suggested to Cromwell

> If I could have a friend that would lend me four or five hundred pounds without any profit or lucre, [i.e. interest], I would gladly bind me and my house for the repayment of one hundred pounds yearly until the full sum be paid. . . .[28]

The full text of the abbot's remarkable letter and the complete list of his debts is given in Appendix V.

One feature of the economy of the west-country monasteries which emerges very clearly from the *Valor Ecclesiasticus* and from other sources compiled in the decades before the dissolution is the way in which, as uncertainties over the future grew, more and more leases of monastic property or monastic offices were granted to the members of the families of abbots or abbesses, or to men who were soon to be the purchasers of monastic lands.

Soon after William Dovell became Abbot of Cleeve in 1507 his family obtained leases of various monastic properties including a water-mill, houses, cottages and land. At Sherborne, Sir John Horsey, who was to acquire the abbey and its lands at the dissolution, was already intimately concerned with the administration of the abbey's affairs during the 1530s and acted as bailiff for its estates. Horsey was also one of the commissioners in Dorset for the compilation of the *Valor Ecclesiasticus*.[29] On the estates of Glastonbury in 1535 the *Valor* lists John Horner as tenant of its lands in Mells and Leigh-on-Mendip, where his family had lived for more than a century, and he also acted as bailiff for the abbey. At the dissolution he was able to find the enormous sum of £1,831 19s. 11¼d. to buy the estate. The Phelips family, who were to acquire the Cluniac priory at Montacute, were already closely involved with the administration of the lands both of Montacute and Muchelney.[30]

Mells Manor House and Church.
This view by John Buckler shows the fine, late-medieval parish church and the manor house which belonged to Glastonbury abbey. In 1543 the house, together with the Glastonbury lands in the district, was purchased by the Horner family who had made a sufficient fortune as tenants and officials of Glastonbury to be able to afford the huge price of £1,831 19s 11½d.

The Poyntz family of Iron Acton who acquired the lands of Kingswood were already stewards of the abbey and lessees of its land for long before the dissolution.[31] The family of Paul Bush, the last rector of the Bonhommes at Edington, acquired the lease of the manor of Dilton, and the rector's brother, John Bush, became steward of the priory lands in west Wiltshire. The last abbess of Lacock, Joan Temmse, granted an eighty-year lease of the manor of Shorwell to her brother Thomas, who also became auditor and steward of the monastic lands; another brother, Christopher, acquired a sixty-year lease of Hatherop; and her brother-in-law, Robert Bath, leased Bishopstrow for ninety-nine years. Thomas Chard *alias* Tybbes, Abbot of Forde, was also at pains to provide for his family, granting them numerous offices and emoluments from the abbey estates.[32]

Finally, we can obtain a good picture of the economy and administration of St Augustine's Bristol during the period before the dissolution since, although the abbey was not included in the *Valor Ecclesiasticus*, a good deal of other documentary evidence survives in the form of account rolls. These provide the information to enable us to see in intimate detail the working of a great institution, its income and expenditure and the way in which its affairs were organised.[33]

INCOME

A list of the sources of income of St Augustine's is given in Appendix IV where it will be seen that there was income from appropriated parish churches, in the form of tithes, offerings and the rent of glebe land. There was also property at eleven places in Gloucestershire, six in Somerset and one in Dorset. It is not easy to distinguish between the spiritual and the temporal income in the surviving accounts, but it is possible to classify the income under four main headings:

	1491–2	1511–12
1. Fees, offerings and oblations	£1 2s. 6½d.	£1 9s. 10½d.
2. Revenues from Bristol property and appropriated churches	£105 18s. 7½d.	£82 19s. 5½d.
3. Revenues from manors, rectories, and property outside Bristol	£595 3s. 10½d.	£577 13s. 2¼d.
4. Profits from trade	£65 16s. 2½d.	£65 19s. 8d.

The first source of income represented offerings made by visitors to the abbey and, since St Augustine's possessed no famous relic or especially venerated statue, only a small sum each year was obtained in this way. Moreover, there were eighteen parish churches crowded in and around Bristol, where local people were much more likely to have made their offerings. The revenues from Bristol property included part of the tithes of three appropriated churches, All Saints, St Nicholas and St Augustine the Less, although in both years for which the accounts survive the money due from St Augustine the Less was not collected by the abbey 'because the vicar's benefice is so much impoverished that the said pension has been remitted by the abbot and convent for the time being'. The appropriated churches both within and outside Bristol also involved expenditure by the abbey, since as rector it was liable to maintain the chancels of these churches. A much larger source of income was the Bristol properties including houses, shops, a water-mill, the hay grown on the Canons' Marsh, and the pasture and gardens along the banks of the Avon.

The third and largest source of income was derived from the numerous properties and churches outside Bristol which are listed in Appendix IV. These were rural, agricultural properties and the income came in the form of tithes, rents, profits of manorial courts, sales of timber and the like. Like most other monasteries and large landowners at the end of the Middle Ages, St Augustine's had given up direct farming of the demesne lands on most of these manors and let them to leaseholders for long terms. In a few manors (Canonbury, Blacks-

The Gatehouse to St Augustine's abbey,
Bristol.
*This fine building was the gateway to St
Augustine's, now the cathedral, in Bristol.
The lower part dates from the twelfth century,
while the upper stages were rebuilt by Abbot
John Newland or Nailheart, (1481–1515) and
much restored in the nineteenth century.*

The Cloister Bristol Cathedral.
*A surviving part of the cloister of the Augustinian abbey at Bristol, showing the triple-arched
entrance of the late-Norman Chapter House. The high quality of the architecture throughout the
medieval part of the former abbey is a reminder of its wealth and importance. The abbey was
surrendered in 1539 and became the cathedral of the new diocese of Bristol in 1542.*

worth, Cromhall and South Cerney) the demesnes were managed for the abbey by a bailiff. Similarly, the collection of the rectorial tithes and other dues in those parishes which were appropriated to the abbey were left to receivers, so that there was little contact between the abbey and those who contributed part of their tithes to its maintenance. In addition to the money rents, the abbey received payments in kind from some of its properties, and in particular from the home farm at Leigh, later to be called Abbotsleigh, where the abbot had a residence, and also from Portbury, whence a constant supply of produce was brought up the Avon to the abbey. Cattle and pigs, poultry, eggs, wool, wheat, barley and pease were all supplied. Also brought up the Avon were timber for building work and maintenance in the abbey, and brushwood and faggots for its fires. Finally, the profits from trade consisted almost entirely of those from the sale of malt produced by the abbey, using barley from its manors. A second, much smaller source of revenue came from the sale of second-quality bread from the abbey bakery. Although the abbey possessed quarries on Dundry, a rope-walk and mills, all these were let out for rent and so the income from them is not included under this heading.

EXPENDITURE

By the end of the Middle Ages, at St Augustine's as at most other monastic houses, the responsibility for the various aspects of the life of the house was shared out amongst various officers known as obedientiaries, each in charge of a particular sector and each controlling that part of the monastic expenditure. Thus the sacrist was in charge of the expenses for the furnishings of the church and the provision of the materials for the services; the vestiar looked after the clothing; the cellarer controlled the food and drink; the chamberlain supervised the manors and the manorial courts; and the treasurer paid for legal expenses, visitations, taxes, etc.

The expenditure of these and other monastic officers can be summarised under five headings

1. The abbot's allowance
2. Business expenses
3. Housekeeping
4. Expenses for spiritual duties
5. The personal share of the canons

Like the heads of other monastic houses, the abbot of St Augustine's maintained a separate household and lived in some style, as befitted such a rich and influential person. He was allowed £160 or some 20 per cent of the total income of the house, and in addition he drew on the abbey funds for his entertainment of guests and travel on abbey affairs. The second item, business expenses, included legal costs, travel by the abbot and prior, together with their servants and attendants, payments to the Pope and the Bishop of Worcester, the cost of the ordination of deacons, gifts to local or royal officials and messengers, the payment of taxes, etc. In 1491–2 the business expenses amounted to £217 13s. 0d. and in 1511–12 to £107 8s. 7d. The higher figure for 1491–2 was accounted for by an expensive legal dispute between the abbey and the townsmen of Bristol, which cost £40 0s. 10d., and by the payment of £112 15s. 9d. in taxation that year.

Housekeeping expenses included food, drink and clothing for the canons and other members of the household, wages to the abbey servants, fuel for the kitchen, guest house and infirmary, cost of horses and stable expenses, the upkeep of the abbey buildings and similar necessary expenditure. Small cash payments were also made to each of the canons for the purchase of items of clothing, spices, etc. The total sums spent under all these headings were as follows

	1491–2	1511–12
Regular cost of food	£120 2s. 6d.	£115 18s. 10d.
Supplementary food & drink	£7 2s. 6d.	£6 10s. 0d.
Cash allowance to the canons	£5 8s. 6d.	£5 13s. 0d.
Clothing for abbot & canons	£12 7s. 4d.	£12 3s. 6d.
Firewood	£10 13s. 2d.	£11 6s. 6d.
Upkeep of abbey buildings	£9 18s. 4d.	£4 15s. 3½d.
Household stores & equipment	£2 15s. 5d.	£2 0s. 6½d.
Stable expenses	£3 10s. 3d.	£4 10s. 10d.
Servants wages	£26 18s. 4d.	£25 19s. 0d.
Total	£198 16s. 5d.	£188 17s. 6d.

The fourth category of expenditure included the care of the abbey church, the cost of the services, vestments, wine, bell-ringing, cleaning and lighting, as well as the cost of almsgiving and the distribution of food to the poor. There were also the expenses involved in teaching choir boys, maintaining the grammar school and educating the novices. These were heavier in 1511–12 because there were then two scholars being maintained at Oxford. It is noteworthy that in both 1491–2 and 1511–12 only about 5 per cent of the net income was being spent on hospitality and alms, and that most of the alms were distributed under the terms of various benefactions and were not entirely voluntary offerings to the poor by the canons. On the other hand, there may well have been a substantial amount of charitable work, such as the distribution of surplus food or of discarded clothing and footwear, which would not appear in any financial account. It has also to be remembered that the purpose of those who founded monastic houses was to ensure a continuity of religious worship; they were not concerned with fostering the care of the sick, poor or destitute, however laudable such work might be. Moreover, there was a hospital, 'the Gaunts', on the other side of College Green from St Augustine's which was dedicated to such work, and there were several other hospitals and almshouses in late-medieval Bristol.

The expenses under the fourth heading were

	1491–2	1511–12
Care of the church & cost of services	£30 6s. 3½d.	£24 18s. 4½d.
Hospitality, alms, etc.	£32 13s. 2½d.	£35 17s. 2d.
Education	£18 13s. 10d.	£32 13s. 9d.
Total	£81 13s. 4d.	£93 9s. 3½d.

Finally, there was the late-medieval development whereby, in spite of earlier prohibitions and all condemnations of the practice, the canons were each given a regular allowance of money as well as gratuities on special occasions. The total amounts were

$$1491–2 = £33 0s. 7¾d.$$
$$1511–12 = £30 15s. 2½d.$$

Having spent many years in the careful, detailed examination of the late-medieval records of St Augustine's, Bristol, the late Arthur Sabin concluded that 'the abbey resources were carefully garnered and controlled' and that

> the abbey rose adequately to contemporary standards of correct conduct even if it did not soar very high in saintliness. It seems reasonable . . . to suppose that it was in the main expending its income according to the wishes of its founders.[34]

But by the 1530s few people were prepared to defend a system in which an annual net income of over £670 was used to support the prayers of just over a dozen canons, and when the dissolution came in 1539 no protest was heard from the townsfolk of Bristol.

Chapter 3

The Commissions of 1535–6

While the *Valor Ecclesiasticus* was being compiled during 1535, another visitation of the monasteries was being prepared by Thomas Cromwell. This started its work in August 1535 and during the next six months Cromwell's commissioners carried out visitations of many of the west-country monasteries. This visitation was carried out under the powers granted to Cromwell in January 1535 when he had been appointed the king's vice-regent in matters spiritual, and also under the powers which the king had been given by the Act of Supremacy in 1534. The purpose of this visitation was quite different from that of the earlier commissioners who had investigated the income of the monasteries and the sources of their wealth, and the results of their enquiries have to be viewed in a totally different light. The purpose of this second visitation was to examine the state of the monasteries and to produce evidence of laxity, scandal and abuses which could be used by Cromwell as grounds for at least a partial suppression and confiscation of monastic property. The commissioners employed by Cromwell for this task differed greatly in character and in their attitude to the monasteries, but it has always to be borne in mind that the evidence they produced, although colourful, lively and sometimes amusing, is hardly to be taken at face value. The commissioners' own interests were closely tied to those of their master, Thomas Cromwell, and to advance in his service and to ensure their own futures in a fiercely competitive environment, it was essential for them to provide him with the sort of evidence he required. As Thomas Fuller was to write a century later,

> They were men who well understood the message they went on, and would not come back without a satisfactory answer to him that sent them, knowing themselves were likely to be no losers thereby.[1]

Their reports were not always critical and occasionally they spoke well of houses or of some of the religious, but their main object was to provide material for an unfavourable report which could be used in the parliament of 1536. The need for haste meant they had little time for detailed enquiries. The commissioners who visited the west-country monasteries during the autumn and winter of 1535–36 included Richard Layton, who was an energetic, ambitious priest. He had been in the service of Wolsey and, following the cardinal's fall, had transferred his allegiance to Thomas Cromwell; he played a major part in the suppression of the monasteries. His numerous letters and lively reports to Cromwell show an entirely contemptuous attitude towards the monks, a fine aptitude for the discovery of gossip concerning moral failings, and for salacious stories combined with an apparent disregard for the truth of his charges. As a result of his work for Cromwell, Layton obtained a succession of lucrative ecclesiastical benefices and became Dean of York in 1539. He died in 1543 while on a mission to Brussels as ambassador.[2]

Another commissioner, John ap Rice, was a lawyer, a member of an ancient Welsh family, and as well as his investigation of the monasteries, he played an important part in the Tudor transformation of the government and administration of Wales. He was rewarded for his service with considerable monastic property in Wales, including the Benedictine priory of Brecon, where he retired to live as a country gentleman.[3] John Tregonwell, the Cornish lawyer, was a sober, careful observer, less critical of the monks and nuns than the other commissioners and ready to give praise where he thought it was deserved. He acquired the buildings and estates of Milton Abbey in Dorset and went to live there in considerable state. He remained a conservative in religious matters, obviously out of sympathy with the sweeping changes in the Church during the reign of Edward VI, and pleased with the restoration of Catholicism under Mary.[4] The fourth and last of Cromwell's commissioners in the west country during 1535–6 was Thomas Legh. He was a young lawyer who, from his letters, seems a very cold, pompous man, with little sympathy for the monks and nuns. He was disliked by the other commissioners who, as will be seen, complained of his brutal, overbearing manner in visitation, of his insistence that he should be greeted at each monastery with immense ceremony, of his large number of servants and of his unreasonable demands for large gifts of money from each of the houses he visited. He was also rewarded with monastic property and became a Master in Chancery. In 1544 he was knighted for his services, but died soon afterwards.[5]

The commissioners conducted their enquiries very much along the lines of an episcopal visitation. They carried with them a set of articles or questions to be put individually to each monk or nun interviewed in private. It can readily be imagined that under the determined questioning of legal men skilled in the ways of the court, overawed or frightened monks and nuns could easily be led to reveal details of gossip or rumour; the visitors might be told details of petty jealousies, squabbles and spite which had perhaps festered for years; facts about the abbot or monks, their attitudes to the royal divorce and remarriage, the Act of Supremacy and other religious changes; about the continuance of superstitious practices, veneration of images or the maintenance of popish ceremonies. The commissioners also brought with them injunctions or orders which were to be given to the monks and nuns, enjoining stricter observance of their Rule, forbidding them from going outside the precincts of their houses, excluding persons of the opposite sex, warning strongly against superstitious relics, images, pilgrimages and the like, and emphasising the royal

Bath Abbey.
This aerial view shows the former Benedictine abbey and the Roman Baths. The cloister covered the area to the south of the abbey. Following the Suppression, the abbey church fell into ruin, but was eventually purchased by the townspeople and restored as a parish church.

supremacy. No one under the age of twenty-four years was to be professed, and those below that age might be released from their vows if they so desired.[6]

The commissioners descended upon the west-country monasteries in August 1535. Their progress through the region was somewhat haphazard and some houses were visited twice, others not at all; sometimes they acted together, at other times independently. But in all their journeys, they sent back to Cromwell in London a stream of information about the monasteries and their inmates, which would soon provide him with the ammunition he needed to mount a parliamentary attack upon the religious houses.

Early in August 1535, Richard Layton conducted a visitation at Tewkesbury, from where he seems to have come straight to Monkton Farleigh and Bath. From Bath on 7 August he wrote to Cromwell giving a very unfavourable report on the small Cluniac priory at Monkton Farleigh.

> . . . the prior had but viii whores, and the rest of the monks some iiii, iii, ii, as they might get them . . . the truth is a very stews.

While at the much larger Benedictine abbey at Bath, Layton reported that

> . . . we found the prior a right virtuous man . . . a man simple and not of
> the greatest wit, his monks worse than any I have found yet, both in
> buggery and adultery . . . the house well repaired but four hundred
> pounds in debt.

Layton's verdict on William Holway or Holleway, the Prior of Bath,
was unjust and inaccurate, for he was far from simple or lacking in wit.
He was a man of good character and learning, with a reputation as an
alchemist; he also took considerable pains over the management of the
monastic estates and sheep flocks, was interested in the history of the
abbey and had spent large sums on the abbey church.

It is noticeable that, whereas earlier visitations had criticised various
monasteries for delapidated or dirty buildings, neglect of services or
similar failings, Layton concentrated his attention on sexual irregularities, and his accusations credit the monks with a totally incredible
energy. Layton also sent to Cromwell from Bath a collection of relics
which he had confiscated, including the fetters of St Peter from
Monkton Farleigh, a relic which was greatly revered, carried in solemn
procession by the monks and sent to women in labour who believed in
putting it around them they would have a short and safe delivery. He
also sent the combs of various female saints and, from the library at
Bath Abbey, 'a book of Our Lady's miracles well able to match the
Canterbury Tales, such a book of dreams as you never saw . . .' By the
same messenger the Prior of Bath sent to Cromwell a gift of three Irish
hawks, one of many gifts and favours Cromwell was to receive from
the heads of religious houses anxious to secure the favour of such a
powerful and important royal official. The full text of Layton's letter
from Bath is given in Appendix VI.[7]

Early in August 1535, Legh and ap Rice visited Winchcombe and
Malmesbury, and then proceeded to Bradenstoke, Stanley and Lacock.
From Lacock on 20 August ap Rice wrote to Cromwell apparently
disappointed that they had found nothing wrong. 'At Lacock we can
as yet find no excesses', but they complained that Dr Legh was too
strict in imposing restrictions on the religious houses they visited,
restraining even the abbots from going outside the precincts: 'I think
this over strict, for as many of these houses stand by husbandry they
must fall to decay if the heads are not allowed to go out'.[8]

Meanwhile, Legh had gone on to the Augustinian house at Bruton
where the abbot was understandably reluctant to allow him to conduct
a visitation, since Layton had been there only a few days before.[9] Left
on his own, ap Rice visited the small Benedictine nunnery at Kington
St Michael near Chippenham, where he allowed one of the nuns who
was under twenty-four years of age to leave the house, and then went
to the Bonhommes' house at Edington. From Edington on 23 August
he wrote again to Cromwell, giving further details about the Augustinian canonesses at Lacock, since he was obviously impressed by this
well-conducted house and by the fact that the ladies there continued to

Lacock abbey.
The nunnery church stood in the foreground of this illustration, and the tower and window were built by Sir William Sharington into what had been the north wall of the church.

The cloisters of the Augustinian nunnery at Lacock.
Although the church was demolished by Sir William Sharington, the fine cloisters, with their remarkable array of carved roof bosses, were converted into a house for his family.

use the Norman–French which had been the language of educated persons in the early thirteenth century when the nunnery had been established.

> So it is that we found no notable compertes [i.e. matters to report] at Lacock; the house is very clean, well repaired and well ordered. And one thing I observed worthy the advertisement here. The Ladies have their rule, the institutes of their religion and ceremonies of the same written in the French tongue which they understand well and are very perfect in the same, albeit that it varieth from the vulgar French that is now used, and is much like the French that the Common Law is written in . . .[10]

It is significant that, apart from an obviously unsatisfactory and dissatisfied novice, no specific complaints could be made about the other Bonhommes at Edington and that the rector or head of the house was obviously a good man.

By 24 August 1535, Richard Layton had reached Bristol having conducted visitations at Keynsham, Maiden Bradley, Witham, Bruton and Glastonbury. From the Augustinian monastery of Bristol he wrote to Cromwell to report that he could find nothing wrong with the austere, solitary regime of the Carthusians in their remote situation at Witham, and in a revealing phrase confessed also that he had been disappointed at Bruton and Glastonbury.

> At Bruton and Glastonbury there is nothing notable; the brethren be so strait kept that they cannot offend, but fain they would if they might, as they confess, and so that fault is not in them.[12]

At the Augustinian priory of Maiden Bradley, however, Layton had uncovered a great deal of scandal and rumour. He alleged that the prior had six children and that 'his sons be tall men waiting upon him, and he thanks God he never meddled with married women, but all with maidens, the fairest could be got . . .'[13] It seems likely that Layton's imagination had got the better of his accuracy concerning the prior, for a subsequent commission at Maiden Bradley reported only that there were six priests and two novices 'by report of honest conversation . . . desiring continuance in religion'. After the dissolution of Maiden Bradley, the prior, Richard Jennings, became rector of Shipton Moyne in Gloucestershire where he remained until his death in 1553.[14]

We can, however, without hesitation, believe Layton when he lists a further collection of relics which he has confiscated from the monasteries he visited. These included a piece of the Holy Thorn of Glastonbury, part of a seamless robe of Christ, a piece of Our Lady's smock, the girdles of Our Lady and Mary Magdalen, part of the Last Supper and a fragment of the stone manger in which Our Lord was placed as a baby in Bethlehem. On this last item the cynical Layton

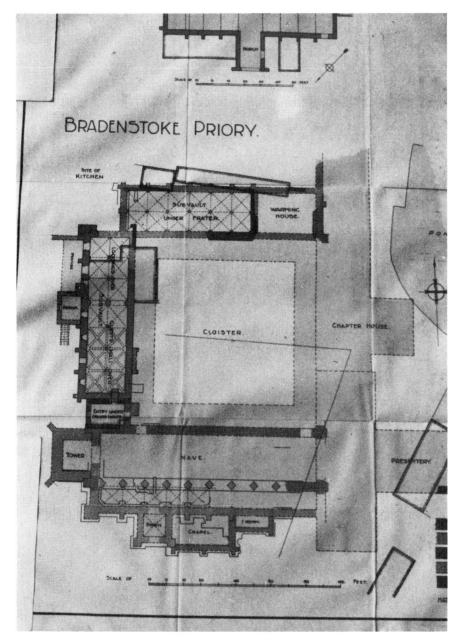

Bradenstoke Priory, Wiltshire.
This plan by Harold Brakspear was prepared after excavations on the site of this Augustinian priory.

commented, 'belike there is in Bethlehem plenty of stones, and some quarry, and maketh there mangers of stone.'[15] The full text of Layton's letter of 24 August 1535 is given in Appendix VII.

During the latter part of August 1535 Thomas Legh was conducting visitations of the Wiltshire nunneries and also of Tarrant in Dorset; on 3 September he was at Wilton.[16] His high-handed manner and attitude caused considerable disquiet to his fellow commissioners who complained to Cromwell about him, although apparently with little success. For example, on 16 October 1535 John ap Rice wrote to Cromwell protesting that Legh had behaved very insolently at Bruton, Bradenstoke, Stanley and Edington, and that

> Wherever he comes he handles the fathers very roughly, many times for small causes, as for not meeting him at the door, where they had warning of his coming. More modesty, gravity and affability would purchase him more reverence. . . .

It was also alleged that Legh went about in a fine velvet gown, with great pomp, accompanied by a dozen liveried attendants, and that he insisted upon large gifts from each of the monasteries he visited. An example of Legh's success in obtaining gifts and favours from the monasteries can be seen from his reception at Wilton, where the abbess and nuns were persuaded to grant him the next presentation to their benefice of Stanton St Bernard, 'to our beloved in Christ, Thomas Legh, doctor of laws, the first and next advowson or patronal right of the prebend of parish church of Stanton where it shall next fall vacant.' On another occasion the nuns at Tarrant were induced to make him a gift of £20 together with a further £4 to cover the costs of his visitation. One of his colleagues, John ap Rice, wrote of him 'The man is young and of intolerable elation of mind.'[17] John Tregonwell was much later arriving in the West Country than the other commissioners, having been visiting monasteries in Oxfordshire, but during November 1535 he conducted visitations of the Benedictine abbey at Athelney, where he found the house 'in metely good order', the Cistercian house at Cleeve and the small Augustinian priory at Barlinch near Dulverton, before going on to Devon and Cornwall.[18]

One effect of the commissioners' visitation of the nunnery at Shaftesbury was to reveal the presence there of Cardinal Wolsey's daughter, Dorothy. Evidently this wealthy nunnery had been considered an ideal situation for a young woman whose presence in the outside world might have caused great embarrassment. She had therefore, taken the name of Clausey or Clusey and had been compelled to enter the nunnery at an early age under the pretence that she was the daughter of a gentleman called John Clusey. In 1535 Dorothy Clausey, as she was known, was almost twenty-four years of age and had been at the nunnery for several years. Under the terms set down by Cromwell, however, all persons of less than twenty-four

Aerial View of Shaftesbury abbey, Dorset.
The abbey and its great church were demolished very rapidly after the Suppression, and this is all that remains of the most ancient and wealthiest of English nunneries.

years could leave monastic life, and the thought that Dorothy might leave the nunnery caused John Clusey to write to Cromwell to reveal the secret and to plead that she should remain in the nunnery.

> . . . My Lord Cardinal caused me to put a young gentle woman to the monastery and nunnery of Shaftesbury, and there to be professed, and

would her be named my daughter, and the truth is she was his daughter. And now by your visitation she hath commandment to depart, and knoweth not whither. Wherefore I humbly beseech your mastership to direct your letter to the Abbess there, that she may continue at her full age to be professed.

According to the letter, the young woman herself wished to remain at the nunnery; as a result she was allowed to do so, and remained there until the suppression of the house in March 1539.[19]

No sooner had the commissioners completed their investigations than complaints and protests began to reach Cromwell concerning the injunctions which the commissioners had delivered and the restrictions they had imposed, especially the order that the religious were not to go outside the precincts of their houses. Heads of religious houses also hastened to send gifts to Cromwell, hoping thereby to secure his favour in the attack which they sensed might be coming.

As early as 31 August 1535, the abbot of St Augustine's Bristol wrote to protest at the harsh injunctions and restrictions imposed by Richard Layton. He also asked for permission for the brethren to walk outside the precincts of the house in order to visit the abbey estates and for the benefit of their health

to walk, three or four together, the juniors with the seniors (refraining the town) about the hills and fields to recreate their minds and to lax their veins, whereby they may be more apt to continue both day and night in the service of God.

They also desired

to have some poor honest woman to keep us if any pestiferous plague or distress of sickness do fall among us, as it hath been there of long consuetude.[20]

Likewise from Wilton on 5 September, the abbess wrote asking to be allowed to visit the estates in company with 'two or three of the sad and discreet sisters of the house to supervise such things abroad as shall be to its profit.' She also added that the house was in debt and unlikely to improve unless its husbandry was carefully supervised.[21] A similar appeal was made by the Prior of Bath on 24 September, and by the abbots of Forde on 11 October, Glastonbury on 26 October, Athelney on 4 November and Cleeve on 8 November 1535, and an undated protest against the injunctions was sent to Cromwell from Winchcombe.[22] Meanwhile, the abbots were equally keen to win and preserve Cromwell's favour with gifts, perquisites and offices. On 26 August 1535 the Abbot of Glastonbury, Richard Whiting, sent him the advowson of the parish church of Monkton, and noted that this was the first time that such a gift had ever been granted by the abbey.

The Abbot's Gatehouse, Cerne Abbas.
This late-medieval entrance is the finest surviving fragment of the Benedictine abbey of Cerne. It is decorated with shields bearing the arms of various local families, and it survived the Dissolution by being turned into a dwelling.

I would it were a thing of such value as might do you singular pleasure, but as it is you have it with all my heart. And any thing that I have or may do you pleasure with at any time it shall be always ready at your will and commandment to the best of my power, as knoweth Almighty God who always have you in his blessed tuition with honour.[23]

From Tewkesbury on 24 October, Cromwell was sent the gift of a gelding together with £5 to buy a saddle.[24] While on 18 November, the small Augustinian house of Ivychurch near Salisbury appointed Cromwell as high steward of the abbey and sent him a year's fee for the office. The abbey at Bath sent Cromwell a gift of the works of Anselm and, from the Cistercians at Kingswood, Cromwell received a book written by the prior, Thomas Reading, in support of the royal supremacy over the Church, together with a letter in which the prior sought Cromwell's favour and begged him to: 'close up the eye of justice and open the eye of pity to me and the religious men of this house who have no succour except in your evangelical charity.'[25]

The work of the commissioners in visiting the monasteries, interviewing the religious and collecting evidence was not Cromwell's only source of information on the state of the monasteries, for he also received unsolicited statements and allegations concerning individuals and conditions in the monasteries from some west country houses. The most sweeping and wide-ranging assertions came from William Christchurch, an obviously disgruntled monk of Cerne, who earlier in 1535 had sent a long list of complaints to Cromwell. The complaints are directed principally at Thomas Corton, the abbot, as well as at some of the senior monks, and they may be summarised as follows:

Summary of the Allegations of William Christchurch against Thomas Corton, abbot of Cerne. [undated, but sent in 1535]

1. For keeping concubines in the cellars of the abbey and especially one Joan Postell or Bakers.
2. For letting the church and lands go to ruin.
3. For wasting the goods of the monastery on his concubines and children and giving them great gifts.
4. For giving sumptuous gifts to a son whom he had by a former concubine, Joan Gardeners, by whom he also had a daughter, now dead.
5. For maintaining another son called Harry whom he begat on Alice Roberts 'to the great slander of our religion' in the town of Cerne.
6. He had a man child by one Edith, servant to Nicholas Foway.
7. He openly solicits honest women in the town and elsewhere to have his will of them.
8. His concubines sit at table with him.
9. His brother and others of his kindred bear rule in the monastery, to the disquiet of the monks.
10. The abbot does not keep obits and doles.
11. He allows two of his monks who daily haunt queens (*i.e. prostitutes*) to celebrate mass without confession.
12. He allows some of the monks to play at cards all night and celebrate mass in the morning.
13. He has abolished some masses.
14. He allows women to stay with the brethren from noon to evensong.
15. He has several times imprisoned William Christchurch for writing and speaking against him.
16. He expelled William Christchurch from the monastery and sent him to the prior of Monmouth where he was very ill handled.[26]

Obviously, William Christchurch had a considerable grudge against the abbot and some of his allegations are hard to credit, but no doubt they all added to Cromwell's store of evidence to be used against the monasteries.

Another letter sent anonymously to Cromwell in 1535 made various accusations against Richard Hempsted, the prior of the Augustinian house of Llanthony by Gloucester. It alleged that 'the grossest immoralities' were practised there and that the writer had already informed Dr Parker, chancellor of Worcester diocese, of the state of the priory, but that, for a reward, he had been induced to ignore the matter. A canon of Llanthony and the schoolmaster were both said to have remonstrated with the prior, but he imprisoned the canon and dismissed the schoolmaster. The schoolmaster was said to be living near Ludlow and to be willing to give evidence. No action seems to have been taken as a result of this letter.[27]

Various irregularities were also said to be found at Abbotsbury and William Grey, a monk of the abbey, wrote to Cromwell during 1535 to report that the abbot disregarded the injunctions imposed by the commissioners, that he wasted the goods of the monastery, sold the woods, jewels, plate and treasure of the house, and also kept women 'not one, two or three, but many.'[28] As at Cerne, the allegations are obviously exaggerated and it is difficult to know how much to believe, but they at least provide evidence that all was not well.

Numerous complaints also reached Cromwell about the situation at Winchcombe. Cromwell himself had stayed there in July 1535 and appears to have personally conducted a visitation of the abbey and an examination of each of the monks. His visit seems to have totally unsettled the monks and thereafter Cromwell received several letters from one of the monks, John Horwood, who generally used his monastic name of Placet or Placidus. This monk wrote to Cromwell on 20 August 1535 asking for permission to seek out and destroy books about the Pope or about purgatory. Later, he wrote again asking to be excused from rising at midnight for Matins, 'considering my infirmity', and also to be excused from the frugal monastic diet.[29] In September 1535 another of the Winchcombe monks, who is referred to only as Peter, attempted to leave the monastery in order to go to Cromwell and complain about the abbot.[30] In December 1535 during Advent, two other monks insisted on eating meat contrary to monastic discipline and also completely refused to obey the abbot.[31]

A further unsettling influence at Winchcombe was the parish priest, Anthony Saunders. He had been appointed by Cromwell and ordered to preach 'the pure and sincere Word of God' to the monks of both Winchcombe and Hailes, supporting the King's claims to be supreme head of the Church and exhorting the monks to refrain from any thoughts of the Pope or of popish practices. Evidently his task was hard: the abbot not unnaturally resented this outsider who had been imposed upon them and he refused to discuss theological matters with him. Saunders complained to Cromwell

If the abbot favoured the Word of God as much as he hindered it, he might assist me, but what ever communication any man used in his company or monastery it may be allowed, so it be not the Gospel.

In November 1535, Saunders wrote to Cromwell complaining of the difficulties the monks at both Winchcombe and Hailes put in his way: 'I have small favour and assistance amongst the pharisaical papists.' He also asked Cromwell to compel the monks to leave their worship in order to attend his sermons and to come on time; 'they do not come in due time, they set so much by their Popish service.'[32]

Armed with the material about monastic inadequacies and scandals collected by his commissioners, as well as with the information sent to him by disgruntled monks and other correspondents, Cromwell was able to press forward early in 1536 with a Bill for the Dissolution of the Lesser Monasteries, defined as those with an annual income of less than £200. This was passed by parliament and its results in the West Country will be considered in the next chapter.

The Gloucester Candlestick.
This ornate twelfth-century candlestick was part of the possessions of St Peter's abbey, Gloucester. It serves as a reminder of how many similar objects of great beauty were destroyed during the Suppression.

Chapter 4

The Suppression of the Smaller Houses 1536

Before the visitations of 1535–6 were complete, and before Cromwell's visitors had investigated more than half of all the monastic houses, Cromwell had determined upon his course of action. Armed with the material already collected by his visitors, he presented a bill to Parliament early in 1536, whereby all religious houses with a net annual income of less than £200 were to be suppressed and all their lands, property, buildings and valuables given to the king. The preface to the bill, written by Cromwell himself, is a masterly condemnation of the smaller monastic houses, while giving every indication that the larger, better-ordered monasteries were not to be molested.

> Forasmuch as manifest sin, vicious, carnal and abominable living, is daily used and committed amongst the little and small abbeys, priories and other religious houses . . . [so that they] spoil destroy, consume and utterly waste . . . [their] farms, granges, lands, tenements and heredi-taments . . . and their goods and chattels, to the high displeasure of Almighty God, slander of good religion and to the great infamy of the King's Highness and the realm if redress should not be had thereof . . .
> In consideration whereof the King's most Royal Majesty, being Supreme Head in earth under God of the Church of England, daily finding and devising the increase and advancement, and exaltation of true doctrine and virtue in the said Church, to the only glory and honour of God and the total extirping and destruction of vice and sin, having knowledge that the premises be true, as well by the compts of his late visitations as by sundry credible informations, considering also that divers and great solemn monasteries of this realm, wherein, thanks be to God, religion is right well kept and observed, be destitute of such full numbers of religious persons as they ought and may keep. . . .
> the Lords and Commons . . . most humbly desire the King's Highness that he shall take into his possession all houses which have not . . . above the clear yearly value of two hundred pounds.[1]

Cromwell's skilful propaganda and the pressure he, and possibly the king himself, exerted on parliament, with the damning evidence of scandalous misconduct in numerous monasteries which the 1535–6 visitation had provided, as well as the generally low level of lay support for the monasteries, all ensured that the bill would rapidly pass through the Lords and Commons; it became law in mid-March 1536. In the West Country, a dozen houses were affected by the Act and were suppressed, but some whose income brought them within the provisions of the Act escaped by paying a fine. Thus the Cistercian abbey of Bindon in Dorset was reprieved by payment of £300, although its net annual income was £147, and the Augustinian canonesses at Lacock also paid a fine of £300 and were allowed to continue although their income was £168 per annum.[2] The whole of the Gilbertine order was also exempted from the provisions of the Act, perhaps through the influence of Robert Holgate, Master of the Order, who was president of the Council of the North and a chaplain to the king, with the result that the two small houses of Poulton and Marlborough were able to continue until 1539.[3]

There was also uncertainty over the position of the Cistercian abbey of Cleeve in west Somerset. In the enquiry which produced the *Valor Ecclesiasticus*, the surveyors had reported that the income of the monastery was £155 9s. 5¼d. per annum, which meant that the house was well within the terms of the Act of 1536, but subsequently, the abbot had protested that this had considerably under-valued the annual revenue. The royal official who had to cope with this problem was Sir Thomas Arundell, who had been a member of the commission compiling the *Valor Ecclesiasticus* at Cleeve in 1535. Like his fellow-Cornishman John Tregonwell, Sir Thomas Arundell remained conservative in his religious opinions in spite of the prominent part he played in the suppression of the monasteries, and notwithstanding the extent of the former monastic properties he acquired. His sympathies lay entirely with Catholicism and with the old order of things; he was out of sympathy with the changes of Edward VI's reign, and was executed for conspiracy against the Duke of Northumberland in February 1552. He was a member of a rich and well- connected family; the second son of Sir John Arundell of Lanherne in Cornwall, the foremost Cornish family of the time.

Sir Thomas Arundell's interests and estates included Chideock Castle in west Dorset and Wardour Castle in Wiltshire. He had been a member of Wolsey's household and was well-acquainted with Thomas Cromwell.[4] In 1536 Arundell was appointed to supervise the dissolution of the smaller religious houses in Somerset, Dorset, Devon and Cornwall, but found that Cleeve was omitted from his list; moreover, he was aware of the fact that the monks at Cleeve were well-regarded in west Somerset, providing employment, hospitality and charity in that remote area. It was also rumoured in that district that the abbey had been reprieved by the king. He therefore wrote to Cromwell to enquire what he should do and urging that Cleeve should be allowed to continue.

> I desire your Lordship in the behalf of all the honest gentlemen in that quarter . . . for the standing of the said house, wherein there is xvii priests of very honest life and conversation, and have kept always great hospitality to the relief of the country. . . .

Arundell went on to point out that the original survey had undervalued the house and that the abbot had subsequently sought to put this right. He also reported that if the house was reprieved the abbot and

The Gatehouse, Cleeve Abbey.
This was built as the entrance to the Cistercian abbey in the thirteenth century and greatly altered by the last abbot, William Dovell whose name appears on it. As well as a statue of the crucifixion, the gatehouse also bears a Latin inscription which in English reads:
   'Gate be open
   Be shut to no honest man'.

monks would pay 1000 marks to the king and that for Cromwell himself 'you shall have their continual prayer and the hearty good will of rich and poor thereabout abiding.'

Arundell also thought it prudent to point out that he looked for no reward for himself.

> . . . God is my judge, I do not look for any reward therefore, the house is not rich as I am sure ye know, and I would to God that the good King knew that I know in this matter and then were there no doubt but it should be as I would wish as Our Lord knoweth who send your Lordship good and long life]. . .[5]

In spite of Arundell's earnest and apparently quite sincere testimonial to their worth, the Cistercian monks were not allowed to remain in their attractive house in its pleasant site and the house was suppressed.[6] It may be that the Cistercian house at Stanley was similarly under-valued in the *Valor Ecclesiasticus*, but this also came within the terms of the 1536 Act and was suppressed.[7] A few other small houses such as St James' Priory in Bristol, Leonard Stanley, Deerhurst, or Holme in east Dorset, survived in 1536 because they were cells or off-shoots or larger, wealthy houses and were not regarded as separate establishments.

In order to deal with buildings, lands and property coming into the hands of the Crown as the result of the dissolution of the smaller houses, a new government department, the Court of Augmentations, was set up. This was designed to administer the former monastic property, since evidently at this stage it was envisaged that the new-found wealth would remain in Crown hands. Commissioners were appointed for each county, with instructions to visit each monastery which came within the terms of the Act, to make a careful survey and inventory of the goods of each house and to send a 'brief certificate' to the chancellor of the Court of Augmentations, Sir Richard Rich. The commissioners were also to report on the number of monks and nuns, on their religious life and reputation, the number of their servants and how many of them wished to have 'capacities' or licences releasing them from their vows of poverty and obedience and allowing them to depart to seek new lives in some other sphere. Inevitably, it took some time for the commissioners to deal with all the smaller houses, especially since, besides members of the local gentry, each commission had to include one of the receivers and one of the auditors from the Court of Augmentations, and only seventeen were appointed for the whole country.[6] In the West Country the receiver for Gloucestershire, Wiltshire, Bristol and Hampshire was Richard Paulet, and the receiver for Somerset, Dorset, Devon and Cornwall was Sir Thomas Arundell; William Berners was the auditor working with Paulet, and from 1536 to 1539 William Turner worked as auditor with Sir Thomas Arundell; after 1539 his place was taken by Matthew

Deerhurst Priory Church.
Throughout the Middle Ages this notable Saxon building was the church of a Benedictine priory.
The cloister extended into the foreground of the picture.

Colthurst. With these officials of the Court of Augmentations, various local gentlemen were also appointed to survey the smaller monasteries. In Wiltshire Sir Henry Long and John Pye acted as commissioners, and in Gloucestershire John Walshe and Edmund Tame.[7] Their task was not easy and could not be accomplished quickly, since not only were they required to make a survey and compile an inventory of the monastic possessions, they also had to supervise the administration of the property on behalf of the Crown, to arrange its surrender and final closure, and to ensure the departure of the monks and nuns and the proper treatment of the head of each house. The weeks and even months before the commissioners arrived and did their work were, therefore, a time of great uncertainty and anxiety for the inmates of each doomed monastery. Technically, everything now belonged to the Crown, but in practice the estates had still to be administered, the livestock tended, the crops sown, servants paid and the life of the house continued. Each monk or nun had also to make the difficult decision of either leaving the religious life or going as a stranger to a new, larger and possibly unwelcoming monastery.

The returns of the commissioners who carried out the Dissolution of the Smaller Houses survive for Gloucestershire, Wiltshire and Bristol, but not for Somerset and Dorset. A summary of the commissioners' report is given in Appendix VIII. The returns provide a great deal of interesting material about the west-country monasteries and are often in marked contrast with the scurrilous and salacious gossip of Richard Layton and Cromwell's other visitors of 1535–6. For example, at Ivychurch, an Augustinian monastery near Salisbury, they reported that the house was 'in very good state, with much new building of stone and brick'. Lacock they described as 'A head house of nuns of St Augustine's rule, of great and large buildings . . . set in a town. To the same and all other adjoining by common report a great relief . . .' They found the church, mansion and all other buildings at Lacock in good condition and reported that there were 17 nuns, all desiring to continue in religion, and 42 servants, made up of 4 chaplains, 3 waiting servants, 9 officers of the household, a clerk and a sexton, 9 women servants and 15 hinds or labourers. The house was out of debt, with jewels, plate, ornaments, etc. worth £104 9s. 2d. and stocks and stores worth £257 0s. 10d. Likewise, at the Cistercian house of Stanley not far from Lacock, the commissioners reported.

A head house of monks of the Order of Citeaux, of large and strong buildings, by report to all the country a great relief . . . Priests 9 Novices 1, by report of honest conversation, all desiring continuance in religion.[8]

On the other hand, the church at Flaxley had been burnt down and the house was said to be in ruin and decay, the bells melted with the fire and the metal sold to pay for rebuilding the church. Easton (Wilts.) and St Oswald's in Gloucester were also ruinous in their buildings, although the monks were 'of honest conversation' (i.e. local reputation). At Monkton Farleigh near Bath, where Richard Layton claimed in 1535 to have found all sorts of gross immorality, the suppression commissioners noted 'vi monks, all being priests, of honest conversation, wholly desiring continuance in religion.'[9]

The commissioners revalued the lands and property, including the demesnes, and generally put a higher annual value on them than the *Valor Ecclesiasticus*. Many of the smaller monasteries are shown as having a very large number of servants, but these figures can be misleading, since many of the servants were farm labourers employed on the monastic lands, while not all of the others were employed in the direct service of the monks and nuns. Moreover, large households of the Tudor period, secular and religious, were labour intensive and it was the common practice to employ a large number of servants. Thus at Stanley there were 43 servants, but they included a schoolmaster, 3 dairy women, 7 holders of corrodies and 18 hinds or farm labourers 'in divers granges'. Even so, the 14 remaining servants may seem a large number to care for 10 monks dedicated to a life of austerity and abstinence. Even the 4 poorly-endowed nuns at Kington, with an annual income of only £35 15s. 0d., had 11 servants, although these included a chaplain, a clerk and 4 hinds.

There were great contrasts in the ornaments, jewels, plate and

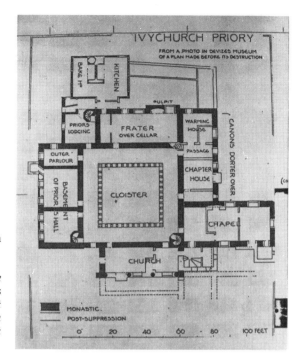

Plan of the former Augustinian priory at Ivychurch near Salisbury.
The Earls of Pembroke acquired the buildings, and little now survives above ground of this important abbey which had close links with the former royal palace at Clarendon.

possessions of the houses. At Maiden Bradley, the well-kept buildings and fine church were complemented by ornaments, etc. worth £40 13s 4d.; at Lacock and possessions of the house came to £360 19s. 0d. But the two nuns of St Mary Magdalen in Bristol had goods worth only £3 12s. 10d., although the house was said to be in good repair; and the possessions of the nuns at Kington were only valued at £17 1s. 0d., and this included corn and cattle on the demesne farm worth £12 19s. 8d. Above all, it was the bells and the lead on the roof of each monastery which were immediately saleable, and these were carefully valued by the commissioners. At Lacock the bells and lead were worth £100 10s.; at Llanthony where the house was newly-repaired they were worth £57 5s. 0d. At Flaxley, however, the lead and bells had been sold and at Easton and Kington the bells belonged to the parish church, while at St Mary Magdalen, Bristol, although the house was 'in convenient reparation', the lead and bells together were only worth 19s. 4d.[10]

During the period of uncertainty following the passing of the Act suppressing the smaller monasteries in the spring of 1536, and while the commissioners of the Court of Augmentations were pursuing their slow, careful enquiries into the affairs of each of the smaller houses, several monks took the opportunity to apply to the archbishop's office for 'capacities' or licences to leave the monastic life. Thus in November 1535 Richard Skidmore, a Benedictine monk of St Peter's Gloucester, was given permission to leave, to hold a benefice and to change his Benedictine habit for the dress of a parish priest. During the next few months more than a dozen monks from west-country monasteries obtained similar capacities. Such a decision was evidently not an easy one for many of the monks. At Flaxley, for example, where the house had already been severely damaged in a disastrous fire, four of the seven monks told the commissioners in September 1536 that they wished to continue in the religious life at some other monastery; however, by November 1536 most of the monks, including the abbot, Thomas Were, had applied for permission to change their habit and become secular priests. Since they were already ordained priests, the monks had little difficulty in finding posts outside the monastery, and obviously decided that this offered a better prospect than either the uncertainty of waiting until the commissioners finally closed the house, or of seeking a place in another monastery where they would be strangers and uncertain of their welcome. For the nuns, however, there were few, if any, possibilities in the outside world; many were elderly and, though they often came from good families and had wealthy relatives, the prospect of seeking shelter with them was not attractive. Most of the nuns moved to larger monasteries, not expecting that these would also be closed down within the next two or three years.[11]

The policy, which later became general, of paying pensions to dispossessed monks and nuns, did not apply to inmates of houses dissolved under the terms of the 1536 Act. Accordingly, it is difficult to find evidence of what happened to many of those who were forced to leave the smaller houses in that year. A few sought refuge in a larger house of the same order. Thus one of the Flaxley monks was received at Kingswood, as was also a monk from Tintern. Two Augustinian canons from Chirbury in Shropshire found shelter at Llanthony by Gloucester, and some monks from Stanley went to Beaulieu in Hampshire.[12] Thomas Matthew, a canon of Barlinch, transferred to the Augustinians at Taunton and three years later received a pension when the house was suppressed. Likewise, John Partridge and William Dunne *alias* Brynt of Woodspring were able to continue the monastic life at Keynsham and they received pensions when Keynsham was dissolved in 1539.[13] Two nuns from Cannington joined the much larger community at Shaftesbury and two others found shelter with the Benedictine nuns at Polsloe in Devon.[14]

As soon as the Act for the suppression of the Smaller Monasteries was passed, a stream of requests and petitions began to reach Cromwell from local gentry and others, who hoped for grants of monastic property or some other share of the spoils. Almost as soon as the legislation had gone through parliament, Sir Anthony Hungerford wrote to Cromwell asking for the small Gilbertine house of Poulton, between Cirencester and Fairford, and offering Cromwell '100 marks for your pains'; later Sir Edmund Tame, the wealthy clothier of Fairford, asked to be allowed to rent the estates of the house. In the event, both were disappointed, since the Gilbertine houses were reprieved until 1539.[15] Likewise, no sooner had the Act passed through parliament than Sir Humphrey Stafford wrote to Cromwell, in the fawning terms adopted by all Cromwell's correspondents, to ask for the house and lands of Woodspring, on the grounds that it had been founded by his ancestor, and also

> I am not able to do such acceptable service unto the King's Highness my Master, as my poor and true heart would and if I had wherewith to maintain it . . . And if it would please your mastership to be so good master unto me as to help me to Woodspring Priory I were and will be whilst I live your bedeman and always ready to (do) your mastership such poor service and pleasure as shall become me to do whilst I do live . . .[16]

A little later, Sir Henry Long, who was Sheriff of Wiltshire and one of the commissioners for reporting on the smaller monasteries to the Court of Augmentations, wrote to Cromwell, not to ask for one of the smaller houses, but with a request to be appointed steward of the lands of Hinton Charterhouse as a reward for his work. Long stated that he had received nothing for his work and claimed, somewhat incredibly, that unless he was granted this office he would be ruined.

> I am much more charged now than ever I was, unless the King's Grace be good and gracious unto me, I shall be fain to give over my house, and to get me into some corner. My special trust is in your Lordship, as one Lord knoweth who have your Lordship in his blessed keeping with long life and great honour . . .[17]

Sir John Tregonwell, who had been a diligent servant of Cromwell and had been involved in many affairs on Cromwell's behalf, including the visitation of the monastic houses in the West Country during 1535–6, also wrote to Cromwell and asked for some reward for his services from the monastic estates. Since Tregonwell was very familiar with the west-country monasteries, he helpfully included a list from which he hoped Cromwell might choose one with which to recompense him. In return, he promised both a financial reward and the assiduous prayers of his family.

> If it may stand with your mastership's pleasure to obtain of the King's Highness the farm of one of these under-written monasteries for your most bounden John Tregonwell, to be let to him at a convenient rent, whereby he may have some help towards his living, and finding of his wife and children, your kindness therein shall be considered with such reward as shall content your mastership and besides that you shall bind him and all his perpetually to pray to Almighty God for your prosperity and health long to endure.

Bindon	Wilts. [recte Dorset]
Dorchester	Oxon.
Brewerne	Oxon.
Bridgwater	Somerset
Cleeve	Somerset
Canonleigh	Devon
Polsloe	Devon
Maiden Bradley	Wilts.
Ivychurch	Wilts.[18]

Like the other applicants, Tregonwell was unsuccessful in his request at this time, although he was to be lavishly rewarded later by Cromwell. Another early applicant, also unsuccessful, was Sir Henry Capell, a Somerset gentleman, who in May 1536 asked Cromwell for the grant of the lands of the small Benedictine nunnery at Barrow Gurney in north Somerset, worth only £24 per annum.[19] One petitioner who was extremely successful was Sir Edward Seymour, later to be Duke of Somerset, who by grants of June 1536 and August 1537 obtained the house, site and many of the estates of the Augustinian priory of Maiden Bradley which had a net annual income of £180.[20] Flaxley in the Forest of Dean was granted to Edward Beauchamp on 27 May 1536.[21] The dispersal of the lands of the smaller religious houses and the fate of their buildings will be discussed in more detail in Chapters 7 and 8. While the protracted work of visiting, valuing and arranging the affairs of the religious houses and finally dissolving them went slowly forward during the summer and autumn of 1536, the work of the commissioners was interrupted by the outbreak of the risings, known as the Pilgrimage of Grace, in Yorkshire, Lincolnshire and elsewhere, early in October 1536. There is little indication of any violent or vehement protest against the suppression of the smaller monasteries in the West Country. They were few in number, widely scattered, and when the crunch came few of them, with the possible exception of Cleeve, could muster any influential friends to plead on their behalf. Most of their potential supporters were, in any case, too concerned not to miss the opportunities of personal profit which the dispersal of the monastic estates would bring. Nonetheless, the government remained wary and concerned to learn of any expressions of dissent or discontent, however insignificant, during the later months of 1536, when the smaller monasteries were being suppressed and while the Pilgrimage of Grace presented such a challenge to royal policy in the north and east of England.

Bristol had been a hotbed of dissension throughout the early 1530s, with rival preachers supporting and protesting against contemporary religious changes from the pulpits of the numerous churches in the town. Regular reports reached Cromwell concerning the religious controversies in Bristol and 'the infamy, discord, strife and debate'

The Refectory, Cleeve Abbey.
This refectory was rebuilt in the most opulent manner during the decades before the Suppression. With its superb masonry and woodwork and its beautiful decoration, it is a long way removed from the ideals of St Bernard.

which the preachers had created. In 1536 an eighteen-year-old Bristol boy, John Scurfield, was in trouble with the Church authorities for his letters in defence of the sacraments, and the vicar of Christ Church, John Keene, was reported by the mayor for attacking the religious changes and the reforming preachers.

> They say they have brought in the light into the world; no, no, they have brought in damnable darkness and endless damnation. Choose you to go to hell as ye will, for I will not be your lodesman.

Keene was also accused of calling his congregation heretics and new-fangled fellows, and of wishing to see Hugh Latimer, a leading reformer and now his diocesan bishop, burnt for heresy; even more significantly and dangerously, Keene preached in Bristol in support of the northern rebels during the Pilgrimage of Grace. John Rawlins, parson of St Lawrence in Bristol, was imprisoned in 1536 for similar sentiments regarding Latimer, and another priest, William Glasker-yon, was imprisoned for four days for saying that 'I trust ere I die to see him [the bishop] burnt', and for welcoming the Pilgrimage of Grace.[22] In Salisbury during 1536 and 1537 friction between religious conservatives and those who supported reform was caused by the preaching of the bishop's Scottish chaplain, John Macdowell, who was enthusiastic for changes in religion. The city was divided and violence was threatened by the adherents of both sides. Again, Cromwell became involved and ordered a judicial inquiry into the controversies.[23]

Potentially the most dangerous episodes of public unrest during 1536 were the Taunton riots and, while there is no evidence to link them specifically to the dissolution of the smaller monasteries or to other religious changes, the disturbances themselves and the government's alarmed response to them are symptomatic of the nervous atmosphere of the time. The riots seem to have been started in April 1536 by a food shortage, a 'scarceness and dearth of grain', and when some rioters had been put in gaol, an even larger mob assembled intent upon releasing them. The panicked response of the authorities, who were without adequate forces to quell even an ill-disciplined mob, illustrates the tensions of contemporary society. Eventually the rioters were persuaded to disperse and the ring-leaders were imprisoned in Nunney Castle, from where a dozen of them were later taken to Taunton to be hanged. A month later, in May 1536, letters were sent to Cromwell by Sir John St Loe of Sutton Court in north Somerset and Henry Capell of Wrington, reporting several people for spreading rumours about Thomas Horner who had taken and imprisoned the men who were executed, and suggesting that Horner was so unpopular in consequence that 'without some punishment therein, it will be to Horner's detriment, besides danger in case any like assembly should happen again'.[24] Sir Nicholas Wadham of Merrifield in south Somerset took advantage of what he termed 'our doings at Taunton in the repressing of the Rebellious that there of late were risen' to ask Cromwell for a reward for himself.

> Sir, I shall beseech you to be so good master to me as to move the King that I may have some thing to help me withall now in my later days of his gift whatsoever it shall please his grace.[25]

There is no indication that there is any direct link between these disturbances and religious controversies and the suppression of the smaller monasteries, but the widespread prevalence of heated discussion and debate, as well as the government's reponse to a comparatively small disorder at Taunton, are all symptomatic of the frantic spirit of the time and of the government's fear of revolt.

Chapter 5

Further Visitations and the 'Voluntary' Surrenders
1536–9

The Act for the Dissolution of the Smaller Monasteries of 1536 specifically excluded 'the great solemn monasteries of this realm wherein, thanks be to God, religion is right well kept and observed. . . .' Many of the inmates of the larger houses must therefore have felt that the danger was past and that their lives would continue along the familiar path. But such optimism can only have been short-lived, for even while the smaller monasteries were being suppressed, new pressures and fresh harassments were being experienced by the larger monasteries. Soon after the last of the lesser houses had been surrendered, a succession of distinguished, ancient and wealthy monasteries began to drop, one by one, into the hands of the Crown, until by the early months of 1539 only a tiny remnant survived. By early in 1540 all had succumbed and monasticism was at an end throughout England and Wales.

Before considering the successive surrenders of all the west-country monasteries to survive the suppressions of 1536, however, it is useful to look first at some of the increasing demands which were placed upon the monasteries during these brief, final years of their existence, and at the surviving evidence of the uncertainties and difficulties which these pressures created within the monasteries. Most marked is the increasing demand from royal officials and local gentry for leases, offices, pensions and other perquisites during the last years of monasticism, as well as lay interference in monastic affairs, notably in the election of abbots and abbesses. Shortly before their surrender to the Crown, the abbot and monks of Muchelney who, as was shown in Chapter 2, were already heavily in debt, were induced to grant a pension of £4 per annum to Thomas Cromwell, and pensions of £2 per annum to royal officers and local gentlemen including John Tregonwell, John Horsey, Amias Paulet, John Cuffe, William Portman and the brother of the Bishop of Bath and Wells, Thomas Clerke.[1] At Kingswood, the abbot and monks were persuaded to grant Cromwell a pension of £6 13s. 4d. per annum and smaller annual pensions to numerous other officials and influential persons, so that a total of £33 per annum was being spent in this way.[2] The Bonhommes at Edington granted Cromwell the advowson of their benefice at North Bradley and from Winchcombe he was presented with the sinecure high stewardship of the abbey lands; the abbot explained that, although the income from this office was only £5 per annum, Cromwell would also have 'a pretty manor' and could count on the service of '200–300 men at his commandment to serve the King'.[3]

Witham, Somerset.
The site of the Carthusian house at Witham, founded in c.1178. The precinct wall survives as do some of the fishponds; earthworks indicate the position of the church, cloister and domestic buildings, although the site has been greatly disturbed by landscaping and the creation of a formal garden. The London to Taunton railway line cuts diagonally across the precinct.

Such heavy annual payments put a severe strain on monastic finances and were a major reason for the growing practice of granting leases for years at low rents, but with large entry fines which was pursued by many west-country monasteries during the final years of their existence.[4] The Carthusians at Witham had granted numerous leases and pensions and, after great pressure from Cromwell himself, had provided him with the lease of one of their farms, called West Barn; in consequence they were in desperate need of money and during 1537–8 were obliged to sell church plate, cattle and timber and to borrow money in order to meet all the demands upon them.[5] From monasteries throughout the region there is evidence of cash being raised through the leasing of lands and, above all, through the granting of long leases in return for cash payments. In 1535 St Augustine's Bristol leased its valuable demesne lands at Leigh (Abbots Leigh) to its bailiff, John Collins, and later also leased him the pasture for 500 sheep there.[6] The last abbess of Lacock leased many of the nunnery lands to members of her own family, granting her brother, Thomas, a lease of the manor of Shorwell on the Isle of Wight for eighty years, another brother, Christopher, obtaining Hatherop in Gloucestershire for sixty years and her brother-in-law, Robert Bath, was provided with Bishopstrow (Wilts.) for ninety-nine years.[7] In 1538 the Abbot of Winchcombe, Richard Anselm *alias* Mounslow, completed a complex transaction with a relative, William Mounslow, mercer of London, and also Richard Rowndale, lawyer of the Temple, whereby they leased the London property belonging to the abbey.[8] At Wilton, lands which would earlier have been granted for life with a low fine were increasingly let during the 1530s for individual years with low annual rents but heavy cash payments as entry fines.[9] Similarly, the Abbot of Milton leased the abbey demesnes at Sydling St Nicholas for eighty-one years, the demesnes at Hewish near Milton for forty years and the manor of Chalmington, which had already been leased until 1560, for another sixty-one years thereafter.[10] A careful study of the monastic lands in Somerset has shown that the number of leases increased greatly in the years before the Dissolution and that, whereas before the 1530s most leases were for life, after 1536 few if any were granted except for years.[11] Early in 1539 John Tregonwell and other commissioners wrote to Cromwell about various west-country monasteries, including Bridgwater, Athelney, Buckland and Taunton, and complained about 'the great waste and many leases lately passed'.[12] In return for such leases, as well as for the offices, pensions and gifts which they distributed, the monks hoped to secure influential friends at Court and favour with the local gentry for the years ahead; in the event the effect was to provide those who were soon to be the major purchasers of monastic lands and the beneficiaries of the Suppression with an even closer contact and familiarity with the monastic estates.

The frantic wave of leasing, sales of monastic timber and the disposal of monastic property may well have led Cromwell to act more quickly in the Suppression of the monasteries than he might otherwise have done. It was also no doubt the reason that he wrote to the heads of the monastic houses early in 1538, urging them not to believe any tales of plans for their Dissolution and to conserve their property carefully, assuring them that the king 'does not intend in any way to trouble you or devise for the suppression of any religious house that standeth.'[13]

The interest of local families in monastic estates and property also extended to the election of heads of houses who might be expected to be compliant and generous. Thus Lord Hungerford was quick to intervene in the election of Paul Bush as head of the Bonhommes at Edington in May 1538, and a few months later, Lord Hungerford was appointed steward of the lands of Edington.[14] Although during the years 1536–9 most monastic communities were at pains to secure friends and to prepare themselves for an end which an increasing number of them must have anticipated as they saw the surrender of so many of their fellows, yet a few, secure in their wealth and antiquity, continued almost to the end to hope and expect that they would be allowed to survive. The Account Rolls of Glastonbury for the year

Edington Parish Church, Wiltshire.

This fine church was built for the college of Bonhommes founded by William Edington, bishop of Winchester, in 1351–2. The church was consecrated in 1361. Because the nave was used for parochial worship, the church survived the Dissolution in 1539, and continues to serve as the parish church.

Walter of Sevenhampton and two chaplains of Edington receive the church of Coleshill from Robert Wyville, bishop of Salisbury, in 1358 (B.L.Add.Ch.71759).

1538–9 show the abbey continuing to function as it had done for so many centuries: rents were collected, foodstuffs were brought to the abbey, charity was disbursed, the buildings were repaired, watercourses scoured and the regular round of services was maintained. Among the expenses were costly reconstruction work on tide mills at the mouth of the Brue and the charges for restocking the moors at Shapwick with livestock. There is no indication in the accounts that almost all the neighbouring monasteries had already been suppressed, or that the monks at Glastonbury itself were under constant pressure to abandon the religious life.[15] Evidence concerning the number of men joining the community at Glastonbury during its final years also suggests that the rapidly-approaching end was not suspected or anticipated. Dr Robert Dunning has calculated that, although death inevitably created vacancies in the community, the number of monks was maintained and that 'between 1525 and 1538, in fact, at least twenty-two men joined the house, eight of them after 1534.'[16] The Cistercians at Hailes were also among the last to surrender their house, and when they did so on Christmas Eve 1539, the royal commissioners led by Dr John London were impressed by the admirable state of the buildings and the demesne lands, and reported to Cromwell

> The father had his house and grounds so well furnished with jewels, plate, stuff, corn, cattle, and the woods so well saved as though he had looked for no alteration of his house. His arable land also was in like manner husbanded, no small number of acres ready sown with wheat, and the tilth seasonably ordered for barley . . .[17]

But while some abbots might choose to ignore the rapidly-approaching storm which was to sweep them away, the uncertainties of these final years can hardly have failed to affect the monks and nuns. The effects of this period when their future was increasingly in doubt can be seen in the findings of the last episcopal visitation of Glastonbury and Athelney. This was conducted by the Bishop of Bath and Wells, John Clerke, in July and August 1538. At Glastonbury on 15 July 1538 the elderly abbot, Richard Whiting, and his thirty-three monks were assembled in the chapter house and, after hearing a sermon by Richard Clerkson, each monk was examined by the bishop. The complaints which the monks made to him reveal a sorry state of affairs in which personal jealousies and petty spite predominate. The community of Glastonbury during the last months of its existence hardly seems happy or united, and it was certainly not a model of spiritual endeavour. The complaints were verbose and varied; the services were said to be too long and tedious, and 'the Convent is much grieved with many processions and other ceremonies'. There were no opportunities for study; many of the brethren were indignant that one monk, Brother Neot, had been at Oxford for nearly twelve

The Abbot's Kitchen, Glastonbury.
A remarkably well-preserved kitchen with four fireplaces. Its size and solid construction are an indication of the large, separate household maintained by the late-medieval abbots.

years, 'and yet can neither preach nor read'. The young monks were without instruction and were apparently denied access to the library. One stated that a lecturer was only appointed when a visitation was to be held and that 'against every visitation there is lectures, and when the visitation is done then the lectures do cease', and 'for lack of lectures and other teaching the brethren doth divers times play at dice and cards.' Money set aside for the poor was not distributed, 'and what cometh afterward of it no man can tell.' The abbot was said to be weak and to favour some monks more than others; and the junior monks evidently felt alienated from him and from their seniors. The best food went to the seniors and the inferior fare to the juniors. Only the abbot himself and nine of the monks reported to the bishop that all was well; the rest all took the opportunity of the visitation to voice their complaints and dissatisfaction. Although, as we have seen, the number of monks at Glastonbury did not decline during the final years, the state of the community was far from ideal.[18]

A month later, on 17 August 1538, Bishop Clerke conducted a similar visitation at Athelney where, as was shown earlier, the small community faced major financial problems. Only the statements of four of the monks survive and they also complained about the tedious services, which they said were too long, with too much singing and 'much rendering of the salter (psalter)', so that they had no time for study. They lacked a schoolmaster to instruct them, and instead had too many singing men who were moreover 'light fellows' and a disruptive influence. More seriously, the community life was evidently in danger and the monks had begun to have their meals in private rooms – 'the brethren doth dine and suppe in their chambres'. One alleviating factor must have been the fact that 'the brethren hath vii gallons of ale weekly apiece'.[19]

The final attack upon the monasteries began early in 1538. With the smaller monasteries already in the king's hands, and with the Pilgrimage of Grace and the Lincolnshire Rising safely suppressed, Cromwell could turn his attention to the large and wealthy monastic houses. Visitors were sent out to conduct further investigations of these and, if possible, to persuade the monks and nuns to surrender voluntarily. To add weight to their persuasions the visitors could use both a stick and a carrot. The stick with which they might chastise those houses who resisted suppression was the threat of yet more interference, of renewed investigation and of the stricter regulation of each house. The carrot was the offer of pensions, generous provision for the head of each house and generally adequate sums for the monks, though rather less so for the nuns. The precedent for pensions had been set by the voluntary surrender of the Cluniac priory of Lewes in Sussex on 11 November 1537; for whereas in the case of previous suppressions only the head of the house received a pension, on the grounds that the monks or nuns could, if they wished, continue the religious life in some other monastery, at Lewes all had received pensions. This provided a powerful incentive to voluntary surrender and for conforming to the royal wishes. The visitation in the West Country started early in 1537 when Dr Thomas Legh, who, as we have seen, had earlier been criticised by his colleagues for his high-handed and arrogant manner to the monks and nuns, visited Muchelney. Under its

Aerial view of the site of the Benedictine abbey of Muchelney.
The abbot's lodging and the home farm survive in the foreground, while the parish church and medieval vicarage house still stand, but only the foundations of the great monastic church and cloister remain.

Part of the abbot's lodging at Muchelney.
The scale and excellence of this building is another reminder of the opulent lifestyle enjoyed by late-medieval abbots and of the separate establishments which they maintained.

easy- going abbot, Thomas Ive, Muchelney had debts of more than £400 to set against its annual net income of about £450, and it was liable to pay fees and pensions to the value of £43 12s. 0d. per annum. The abbey was also impoverished by building work and by poor estate management, so that it had earlier been forced to raise £100 by pledging a quantity of silver goblets, crosses, censers, basins, candlesticks and bowls to two Exeter merchants, John Baker and Richard Radcliffe.[20] Because of their debts, the abbot and his ten monks were in no position to resist Legh's demands and on 3 January 1538 a group of local gentlemen gathered at Muchelney to witness the final surrender of the house to Thomas Legh. They included Sir Thomas Speke, John Sydenham, Richard Phelips and Thomas Phelips. Legh received the surrender, which was signed by the abbot and all his monks, and later wrote to Cromwell to inform him of the event, adding that

> I found the abbot very negligent, and also defamed of incontinency, and 10 brethren all very ignorant. After examination, they all subscribed to the instrument of their surrender, sealed it with their common seal, and delivered it in presence of divers knights and gentlemen.[21]

Inventories were made of the goods and property belonging to the house, and the bells and lead, the most easily saleable items, were described as good 'and much the better because they were not easy to be alienate, sold, or carried away'.[22] The monks were awarded pensions and dispersed, and the site was put in the charge of Richard Phelips. Shortly afterwards it was acquired from the Crown by Edward Seymour, Earl of Hertford, later to be Duke of Somerset.[23]

A month later, on 1 February 1538, a similar scene was enacted at Kingswood where John Tregonwell received the surrender in the presence of various local gentlemen. These included various members of the Poyntz family of Iron Acton, who were already stewards and receivers of the abbey and were soon to acquire the site and many of its estates. At Kingswood the abbot, William Bewdley, was awarded a pension of £50 per annum, the prior, Thomas Reading, received £6 13s. 4d. per annum, and the twelve monks each obtained pensions of £4 6s. 8d. or £4 per annum, except for a novice, John Stanley, 'being no priest', who was awarded only £2 per annum and a lay brother, Thomas Lawrence, who was sent to another unspecified monastery. Eighteen servants were paid off, including the butler, under-butler, cook, under-cook, brewer, ploughmen, dairymaids, laundry women, an organ player and even the abbot's mother who was apparently employed in the abbey. The practical side of the royal commissioners' work is made apparent by an entry in their accounts in which they allow 10s. to pay for a pair of balances and weights; these they had borrowed at Kingswood in order to weigh the silver and plate of the house and they had later been stolen.[24] On 10 March 1538 Llanthony

The gatehouse of Kingswood abbey.
This is all that survives of this Cistercian house, the rest was demolished by the Poyntz family and the stone was used to build a mansion at Ozleworth, or was taken for all sorts of building work in the locality.

by Gloucester surrendered to John Tregonwell, William Petre and John Freeman. The prior and twenty-four canons signed the deed of surrender; the prior, Richard Hempstead, was awarded a pension of £100 per annum, together with a house at Brockworth which was part of the monastic estate; the canons' pensions ranged from £8 to £4 per annum. A week later, on 17 March 1538, William Petre wrote to Cromwell to inform him that the canons at Llanthony had surrendered their house 'with as much quietness as might be desired'.[25]

THE FRIARS

During the summer of 1538 the houses of the various orders of friars were suppressed. A list of the principal friaries and of the number of friars in each is given in Appendix II. Unlike the monks, the friars had very little wealth and scarcely any property except their churches and friaries, since it was against the Rules of their respective orders to possess lands. But they were powerful preachers and were in close daily contact with many sections of the community in the towns, and they were accordingly feared by the government. Moreover, they had been in a special relationship with the papacy and their position following the Act of Supremacy of 1534 was accordingly anomalous;

numerous friars had fled abroad in order to avoid having to swear the
oath of succession and accept the royal supremacy over the Church.
They escaped visitation in 1536, but in the years before their final
extinction many friaries were in debt and many of the friars apparently
demoralised; with few exceptions, they offered very little opposition to
the pressure which they faced to surrender their houses.

The task of securing the 'voluntary' surrender of the friaries and
receiving their possessions on behalf of the Crown was entrusted by
Cromwell to Richard Ingworth, who had himself been a Dominican
friar and 'prior provincial' or head of the English Dominicans. Subsequently, he had been appointed as suffragan Bishop of Dover. So
rapidly did Ingworth go about his business, and so little resistance did
he encounter, that by the end of 1538 his work was complete, and all
the west-country friaries had surrendered their houses to the Crown.

On 23 May 1538 Ingworth arrived at Gloucester, having visited
friaries at Northampton, Coventry, Warwick, Droitwich, Worcester
and elsewhere. From Gloucester he wrote to Cromwell describing the
poverty of the friaries he had visited and asserting that

> . . . before the year be out there shall be very few houses able to live, but
> shall be glad to give up their houses and provide for themselves
> otherwise, for they shall have no living. As for Gloucester, where that
> now I am, I think there be ii houses that will give up their houses, for
> they have no living.[26]

In fact, the three orders in Gloucester, the Dominicans with seven
friars, the Carmelites with three and the Franciscans with five, all
surrendered their friaries into the king's hands. The manner in which
this was accomplished by Ingworth was described in a memorandum
written by the mayor and three of the aldermen of Gloucester on 28
July 1538. They wrote that Richard Ingworth, Bishop of Dover,
summoned the friars before him in the presence of the mayor and
aldermen, and offered them the opportunity of having their liberty
and abandoning their friaries. The bishop emphasised to them that he
had no authority to suppress them and that they could continue if they
wished, but the friaries replied that 'as the world now is' they were not
able to maintain their houses and continue, so that all three friaries
voluntarily handed over all their possessions to the Crown.[27] The full
account of the suppression of the friaries in Gloucester is given in
Appendix IX.

From Gloucester, Ingworth travelled to Marlborough and then to
Bristol. Again he found the houses poverty-stricken and badly in debt,
and wrote that, 'The substance in the more part of the houses is very
small; in divers places little more than the debts; and the clamour of
poor men to whom the money is owing is too tedious.'[28] He also
informed Cromwell that most of the friars were eager to surrender
their houses and become parish priests. At Marlborough, Ingworth

found that one of the friars of the small, poverty-sticken Carmelite house there had been put in prison for sexual assault on a child: 'in prison for a maid child of X or XI years of age, whom he used naughtily'.[29] The remaining four friars willingly surrendered their house, and Ingworth found that the total value of the delapidated buildings was only £9 6s. 3d., while the friars had debts of £4 7s. 7d., so little remained to be taken into the king's hands.[30]

Arriving in Bristol at the end of July 1538, Ingworth immediately received the surrender of the four Carmelite friars and noted of their house, which stood near the site of the present Colston Hall, that '. . . all that was in it is little more than paid the debts. It is a goodly house in building, meet for a great man, no rents but their gardens.'[31] The resistance of the Bristol Carmelites had been weakened by the fact that the prior and the sexton had both fled; the remaining friars could not continue since the charity of the townsfolk had dried up and the house was more than £16 in debt. A contemporary account of the suppression of the Bristol Carmelites is given in Appendix IX.

The three other Bristol friaries gave up less easily. Ingworth reported that both the Augustinians, whose house was at Temple Gate, and the Grey or Franciscan friars, whose friary was in Lewins Mead, were 'stiff' in their opposition, although both houses were in debt: the prior of the Augustinians was said to have sold the plate and the trees growing around the friary. On 10 September 1538, however, both the Augustinians and the Franciscans, together with the Dominicans or Black Friars whose house was in Broadmead, surrendered into the king's hands.[32]

During the autumn of 1538 all the remaining west-country friaries surrendered. Most went willingly and with apparent relief, having been plagued by poverty and ceasing to attract the charity of the laity. At Dorchester Bishop Ingworth encountered some difficulty, for the seven Franciscan friars there had an income from mills along the banks of the river Frome near the friary, as well as from tenements in Dorchester; moreover, the warden, Dr William Germen, had been there many years and was held in high esteem in the town. Nonetheless, on 30 September 1538, the Dorchester Franciscans were induced to sign the surrender of their house.[33]

The speed and ease with which the friaries were suppressed was remarkable and within a few months the whole process had been completed. The friars, who had been such a common feature of English towns, such popular preachers and such dedicated workers among the poor, had disappeared without any disturbance and without a voice raised in their support.

THE HOLY BLOOD OF HAILES

Meanwhile, Stephen Sagar, Abbot of Hailes, had become anxious about the object which had for long been the greatest treasure of his house, the shrine of the Holy Blood. In February 1538 he wrote to Cromwell, thanking God that he lived at such a period 'of light and knowledge, and is able to read the Scripture in English and come to the truth.' He raised the matter of the Holy Blood 'which had been reputed a miracle for a great season', and steadfastly denied that it was ever changed or renewed, in spite of the malicious rumours that it was regularly replenished with drake's blood. In the light of the government's condemnation of what it regarded as feigned relics and miracles, and in view of its opposition to pilgrimages, the abbot was understandably concerned about this relic, especially since it had for so long been a major source of income for his monastery. The abbot may have raised the matter with Cromwell because the Holy Blood at Hailes was being cited by popular, reforming preachers as a prime example of the way in which simple people were deluded into giving money to spurious relics. For example, in February 1538 John Hilsey, Bishop of Rochester, had denounced the Holy Blood in a sermon at St Paul's Cross in London. He had told his audience that twenty years previously a miller's wife from Oxford had confessed to him that the Abbot of Hailes had given her many jewels which had been offered at the shrine, and when she had been reluctant to accept them the abbot had said to her 'Tush, thou art a fool, it is but duck's blood.'[34] No immediate action was taken, but in August 1538, at the urging of his

Part of the cloister wall of Hailes abbey.
Although little survives of this wealthy and important Cistercian house, the site is of great interest in showing the layout of the monastery and the foundations of the church including the chancel where the Shrine of the Holy Blood was visited by so many pilgrims.

1555·
M. HVGH LATIMER
BISHOP OF WORST.

Æ. 74

Hugh Latimer, bishop of Worcester.
Latimer started his career as rector of the parish of West Kington, near Castle Combe and rapidly progressed to become one of the leading reformers. He was executed during Queen Mary's reign in 1555.

diocesan bishop, Hugh Latimer, who was fiercely opposed to any relics, pilgrimages or superstitious images, the abbot, Stephen Sagar, journeyed to London to consult Cromwell and seek his advice about the relic. It is an indication of the style and splendour in which late-medieval abbots lived, that the journey from Gloucestershire to London and return, accompanied by his numerous retinue of servants, cost the abbot no less than £140; he was obliged to sell his best mitre, best cross and other articles in order to pay for it.[35] The abbot's consultation with Cromwell was apparently inconclusive for, having returned home, he wrote again to Cromwell on 23 September 1538 expressing his concern at the continued existence of the shrine, which he feared would 'cause abuse to weak consciences', and asking permission to demolish it. Perhaps hoping that it would not be confiscated by the Crown, he added, somewhat incredibly, that the silver and gold with which the shrine was decorated was 'not worth £40 scarce £30'.[36] Permission to destroy it was duly given by Cromwell and on 28 October 1538 a commission headed by the energetic Bishop of Worcester, Hugh Latimer, opened the shrine, 'which was enclosed within a round berall garnished and bound on every side with silver'. They viewed the phial containing the 'Blood of Hailes', and, opening it in the presence of a great multitude of people, found it contained 'an unctuous gum-coloured' substance. 'In the glass it looked red, but taken out it looked yellow like amber.' The phial was duly sealed up again until the king's pleasure should be known. Later, it was sent to Cromwell in London and pronounced a fake.[37] Thus was destroyed the most famous of all the west-country relics, which had for long been an object of piety and veneration and a focus for pilgrimages from all over the country.

LATER SURRENDERS

The second half of 1538 provided a respite for most of the remaining monasteries of the west-country, but during the first three months of 1539 they fell thick and fast into the king's hands. (The list of the surrenders made during the period January–March 1539 is given in Appendix XII.) Not all surrendered willingly, but sooner or later all were obliged to succumb to the pressure exerted by Cromwell's visitors and surrendered as the only way to secure their own futures. The last days of Athelney illustrate the pressures which were put upon the abbots and monks, and the dilemma they faced in balancing their own future welfare against the continued existence of their ancient foundations. The following episode also shows the difficulty which the religious found in dealing with the wordly-wise agents of Cromwell. As is shown in Appendix V, Athelney was heavily in debt; moreover the community had shrunk to number only the abbot, Robert Hamlyn, and six monks. Successive visitations had failed to persuade the abbot into a voluntary surrender of his house, and on 2

November 1538 John Dycensen, the rector of Holford in the Quantock Hills, was sent to Athelney by Lord Audley, the Lord Chancellor, who was a major landowner in that part of Somerset. He took with him a letter for the abbot, evidently urging him to accept the terms being offered both for himself and for his monks. After his visit Dycensen wrote to Cromwell and described in detail his interview with the abbot.

Having read the letter from Lord Audley, the abbot asked Dycensen whether Audley was 'a man of the new set, or after the old sort', to which Dycensen's diplomatic reply was that Audley was 'after the best sort'. According to Dycensen the conversation about Audley continued in the same noncommittal fashion.

> 'Well', said the abbot, 'Do you think he doth not judge there will be another world shortly'.
> 'My Lord', said I, 'There will be another world when we be out of this world, but in this I think there was never so gracious a prince as the King's grace that now is, for he loveth virtue and will punish vice.'
> Wherewith the abbot shook his head. . . .[38]

Later the abbot called Dycensen into his private chamber to question him further and to hear the arguments in favour of the surrender of the house. Initially, one of the abbot's fears was for the well-being of the neighbouring district if his abbey was suppressed. 'Then', said he, 'Our house should be destroyed and all the country [i.e. neighbourhood] undone by that means, as it is about Muchelney.'

Dycensen was at pains to reassure the abbot, even suggesting that some of the monks might remain, and offering the abbot 100 marks [£66 13s. 4d.] and a prebend in the cathedral at Salisbury: 'Whereby you shall have a grey amice, and all your brothers shall be provided for, and shall have service and promotions as shall be meet for them.' Whereupon, the abbot replied that he would fast on bread and water for three days rather than take so little as 100 marks. The conversation ended with Dycensen suggesting that more money might be forthcoming and the abbot protesting that he did not know what to do or how to make the decision. Then, with a homely touch, Dycensen described how the abbot sat down in his chamber and 'Ate bread and butter, and made me eat with him . . .' before writing a reply to Lord Audley agreeing to follow his advice.

Afterwards, Dycensen went to visit an old friend, the steward of the abbey, and dined with him and with the monks who told him they would be glad to surrender the house, 'and thus we made merry together'. Athelney finally surrendered to the king on 8 February 1539. The abbot was granted the valuable prebend of Long Sutton and a pension of £50 per annum, and the six monks were also awarded pensions.[39]

The fate of the Abbess of Amesbury illustrates what happened to those who steadfastly opposed the royal policy. Repeated visitations by Cromwell's officials failed to persuade the abbess, Florence Bonnewe, voluntarily to surrender the house and she told them that 'If the King commanded her to leave the house she would gladly go, though she begged her bread, and she cared for no pension, and prayed them to trouble her no further.'[40] Eventually, and after constant pressure, she was persuaded to resign, apparently in poor health caused by the anxiety and harassment to which she had been subjected. Shortly afterwards, her successor, Joan Darrell, together with thirty-three nuns, resigned the house into the king's hands; Joan Darrell was awarded a pension of £100 per annum and the other nuns were all granted pensions. Florence Bonnewe also applied for a pension 'during the little time that it shall please God to grant me to live', but her name is absent from the pension list.[41]

The Abbess of Amesbury was not alone in her reluctance to surrender her monastery and abandon the religious life. There are only a few indications of the attitude and feelings of the monks and nuns, but enough survives to show that for some at least this period was one of intense mental turmoil, and that they were very reluctant to abandon their way of life or to surrender their houses and possessions to the Crown. The nuns at the ancient and wealthy Benedictine nunnery of Shaftesbury were willing to go to great lengths to avoid the complete suppression of their house and, in December 1538, they used the services of Sir Thomas Arundell in an attempt to persuade Cromwell to allow them to continue.

> They have most heartily desired me to write unto your good Lordship, to move their petition that it might please the same to move the King's Majesty that they may remain here, by some other name and apparel, his Highness poor and true Bedeswomen, for the which they would gladly give unto his said Majesty five hundred marks, and unto your Lordship for your pains one hundred pounds.[42]

Thomas Arundell also made a similar request on behalf of the Benedictine abbey at Cerne. The complete letter from Sir Thomas Arundell to Cromwell is given in Appendix X. Both requests were unsuccessful and, ironically, it was Thomas Arundell who was to be the principal beneficiary from the suppression of the nunnery at Shaftesbury.[43] The canons at Bruton and the monks at Montacute were likewise very unwilling to surrender their houses, and did so only after repeated visits, threats and persuasion from Cromwell's commissioners. Early in 1539 two of the commissioners, Hugh Pollard and William Petre, wrote to Cromwell to tell him of the difficulties they had encountered in persuading the prior of Montacute and the abbot of Bruton to surrender, and that they had been obliged to use 'as many persuasions for the setting forth of the King's graces pleasure in this behalf as we could devise.'[44]

Place Farm, Tisbury. *This shows the medieval gatehouse to one of the numerous granges belonging to the abbess and nuns of Shaftesbury abbey. Other medieval buildings at Place Farm include the farm house, and the largest barn in England, nearly 200 feet long with a huge thatched roof.*

In March 1539 Pollard and Petre wrote again to Cromwell complaining of the obstinacy they had encountered at Montacute and Bruton, and asking for instructions on how to proceed in the face of the refusal of both houses to surrender.[45] Montacute finally surrendered to John Tregonwell on 20 March 1539, but only after the prior, Robert Sherborne, had been granted a pension of £80 per annum, together with 'a mansion place in East Chinnock which he himself built'; the thirteen monks obtained pensions ranging from £12 down to £4 13s. 4d. per annum.[46] After two further visits from John Tregonwell, the Abbot of Bruton, John Elye, and his fourteen canons surrendered on 1 April. Another example comes from Christchurch which was then in Hampshire and just over the Dorset border. John Draper, the last prior, appealed to the king to allow the house to continue on the grounds not only that it supported 'poor religious men', but also that the church was used for worship by 1,500 people from the town and surrounding hamlets, while the poor, not only of the parish and town, but also of the country, are daily relieved and sustained with bread and ale, purposely baked and brewed for them weekly to no small quantities, according to their foundation, and a house ordained purposely for them, and officers duly given attendance to serve them to their great comfort and relief.[48]

The most moving illustration of the dilemma facing the monks and nuns, and especially the heads of the houses, comes from the Carthusian priory of Hinton Charterhouse. Here the prior was Edmund Horde, who was a distinguished scholar and deeply committed to the austere regime of the Carthusians. No scandal or irregularities had been alleged against the monks at Hinton; they wished to continue their spiritual life and saw no reason why they should not do so, in spite of the pressure and persuasions of Cromwell's commissioners. Early in 1539 the prior's brother, Alan Horde, who was a lawyer of the Middle Temple, had written to the prior urging upon him the folly of resistance and the advantages of a voluntary surrender of the house since this would ensure good treatment, a generous pension for himself and adequate pensions for his monks. The prior's reply to his brother, with his anguished and patently sincere defence of his priory, shows plainly the difficulty of a man torn between expediency and conscience, and is an eloquent summary of the conflicting pressures which all monks and nuns faced at this time. In this private letter to his brother the prior could freely express his deepest feelings without any subterfuge and he wrote on 10 February 1539 that he was unwilling to surrender the monastery.

which is not ours to give, but dedicate to Almighty God for service to be done to his honour continually, with many good deeds of charity which daily be done in this House to our Christian neighbours. And considering that there is no cause given by us why the House should be put down, but that the service of God, religious conversation of the brethren, hospitality, alms deeds, with all other our duties be as well observed in this poor House as in any religious house in this realm or in France; which we have trusted that the King's Grace would consider. But because that you write of the King's high displeasure and my Lord Privy Seal's, who ever hath been my especial good Lord, and I trust yet will be, I will endeavour myself as much as I may, to persuade my brethren to a conformity in this matter; so that the King's Highness nor my said good Lord shall have any cause to be displeased with us. Trusting that my poor brethren, which know not where to have their living, shall be charitably looked upon. Thus our Lord Jesu preserve you in Grace.

Edmund Horde.[49]

It was the requirement that they should *voluntarily* surrender their house that stuck in the throats of the Carthusians at Hinton, and they could more easily have accepted the suppression of their house had it

The gatehouse of the Cluniac priory at Montacute.
Although all the other monastic buildings were destroyed, this fine gatehouse built of Ham stone, survived because it was used as a farm house.

been forced upon them by royal edict or parliamentary act. In January 1539, after yet another visit from Tregonwell and Petre, and ever more pressure upon him to surrender, Edmund Horde had told the commissioners that if the king would take the house in spite of the objections of himself and his monks then he was content to obey, but 'otherwise his conscience would not suffer him willingly to give it over.'[50] Most of the Carthusians at Hinton supported their prior in his stand, but the commissioners did have one lever to use against them. One of the Carthusian monks at Hinton, Nicholas Balland, had been an outspoken critic of the religious policy of Henry VIII, having written and spoken against the royal supremacy over the Church and in support of papal power. The monks of Hinton could not have been unmindful of the recent fate of the London Carthusians, so many of whom had suffered terrible tortures and a hideous death for refusing to abandon views similar to those expressed by Balland, and fear of the consequences must greatly have weakened their resistance to Tregonwell and Petre. They cleverly excused Balland by telling the commissioners that he was mentally unbalanced: 'he hath been in times past and yet many times is lunatick.' As a result, Balland escaped prosecution and, when the house was suppressed, he was granted a pension like the other monks.[51] As his letter to his brother shows, the prior realised that there was no alternative but to bow to the royal will, and he finally persuaded his brethren to accept the same view. On 31 March 1539,

Edmund Horde and his sixteen monks signed the final deed of surrender.[52] There was an interesting sequel to the story of Nicholas Balland for three months after the suppression of Hinton he was obviously still in the area and still strenuously denying the royal supremacy over the Church. On 24 June 1539 Walter, Lord Hungerford, of nearby Farleigh Castle, wrote to Cromwell to inform him that Nicholas Balland had been one of a party of men drinking at a house in Hinton and that he had stoutly maintained that 'he would never take the King as head of the Church, but only the Pope of Rome.' Balland was arrested and imprisoned at Farleigh Castle, but again the fact that he was regarded as unbalanced saved him and he escaped the very severe punishment he might otherwise have incurred; 'he hath been distracted out of his mind, and as yet is not much better.'[53]

Most of the other west-country monasteries gave the commissioners far less trouble and, during the early months of 1539, in a great sweep through Somerset, Dorset and part of Wiltshire the commissioners received the surrender of one monastery after another. The detailed, chronological sequence of these surrenders is given in Appendix XII, but the remarkable speed and efficiency with which the operation was conducted can be illustrated from the career of John Tregonwell, one of the principal commissioners engaged in these suppressions. In receiving the surrenders, making all the complex arrangements for the buildings, valuables, plate, lead, bells, estates and servants at each monastery, as well as apportioning pensions and gratuities to the monks and nuns, Tregonwell was generally operating alone, though sometimes he joined forces with another commissioner, William Petre. Two further commissioners, John Smythe and Hugh Pollard, were also operating in the West Country at the same time. The number of monasteries which they suppressed is remarkable and the distance they travelled, across difficult terrain and through the worst months of the year, is amazing. On 17 January 1539 Tregonwell was at Bradenstoke in east Wiltshire, where he received the surrender of William Snow, the prior of this Augustinian house, and his fourteen canons. By 23 January he had travelled the thirty-odd miles to the Augustinian house at Keynsham, and from there he visited Bath on 27 January, and Wells, Bridgwater, Athelney and Buckland during the first ten days of February. On 12 February 1539 he received the surrender of the Augustinians at Taunton and from there rode on into Devon and Cornwall, urging his horse across the rough moors and high ground of Exmoor, Dartmoor and Bodmin Moor, through the February rain and snow, and every two or three days arranging for the final closure of another monastic house and the dispersal of its inmates. By March 1539, Tregonwell was in Dorset. On 10 March he received the surrender of Bindon and the next day suppressed the ancient Benedictine house at Milton. For his own fortunes Milton was by far the most important of all the houses Tregonwell dealt with, for a year later

The Chapter House of the Carthusian monastery at Hinton Charterhouse.
On the upper floor of this fine thirteenth-century building was the monks' library, and on the third floor is a dovecote.

he was to purchase the site and many of the estates of Milton and was to establish himself there as a country gentleman. But this was in the future, and in March 1539 Tregonwell could not linger over Milton but pressed on to suppress Cerne on 15 March and the great nunnery at Shaftesbury with its fifty-seven nuns on 23 March. The account of the surrender of Shaftesbury is given in Appendix XI. By 25 March, he was at the nunnery of Wilton and from there went on to Amesbury on 29 March, where, as already described, he encountered his only failure when the abbess, Florence Bonnewe, refused to surrender her house. Tregonwell did not stay to argue, but pressed on to receive the surrender of Hinton Charterhouse on 31 March 1539. Here his great tour through the West Country ended. He had ridden several hundred miles through the winter weather and had received the surrender of twenty-two rich monastic houses.[54]

At the same time, the other monasteries of the region were falling with equal rapidity. Others which surrendered during these early months of 1539 included Sherborne, Lacock, Athelney, Montacute, Forde, Edington and Bruton, so that by the early summer of 1539 only Glastonbury, Amesbury, St Augustine's in Bristol, Malmesbury and the monastic houses of Gloucestershire remained. There was a lull in the process of monastic dissolutions during the summer of 1539 while parliament was in session, and this gave a temporary reprieve to the Gloucestershire houses. But in December 1539, the remaining houses were swept away in a final trawl by the commissioners.

This process started on 4 December 1539 with Amesbury which had refused to surrender earlier, but where the new abbess, Joan Darrell, proved much more compliant and where the commissioners found the thirty-three nuns 'very conformable', although it may be significant that none of the nuns at Amesbury signed the deed of surrender.[55] It continued with the Augustinian abbey of Bristol which was surrendered on 9 December 1539, and followed on 15 December by Malmesbury, the last of the Wiltshire monasteries, on 19 December by Cirencester, 23 December by Winchcombe, and by Hailes on Christmas Eve 1539. After the Christmas festivities, St Peter's, Gloucester, was suppressed on 2 January 1540 and monasticism in Gloucestershire came to an end with the surrender of Tewkesbury on 9 January.[56] Since the suppressions occurred over so many months, it was obvious to most heads of religious houses that the end of their monastery would not be long delayed and, as has already been shown, many sought to acquire influential friends or to secure their own futures. Thus during the early months of 1539 the commissioners complained that in many houses they had 'found great waste, and leases lately passed'; at Lacock they found the demesnes all leased out' and at Montacute the demesne lands had likewise been 'all leased out to divers persons'.[57] There were only two exceptions, where the abbots do not seem to have anticipated the coming changes and continued to manage their houses and estates in the traditional manner. One was

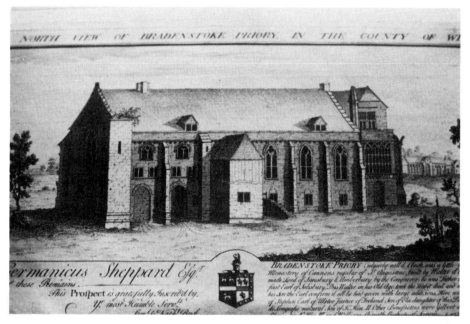

Bradenstoke Priory, Wiltshire.
Many of the buildings of this Augustinian house survived until the 1930s when they were purchased by a wealthy American, William Randolph Hearst, who took them to Wales. Little now survives on the site.

Malmesbury, where the commissioners reported in January 1539 that 'the house is well stored with cattle, the shrine well kept, and the demesnes all in their own hands.'[58] The other exception was Hailes where, at the time of its suppression on Christmas Eve 1539, the commissioners reported that the abbot and monks were 'very conformable', the house was out of debt and everything in excellent order.[59] The commissioners went on to suggest that the Abbot of Hailes should be suitably rewarded for his co-operation and the unusually careful way in which he had preserved the monastic estate. They also informed Cromwell that

> we have dispatched Hailes and Winchcombe and now be at Gloucester where we have taken the surrender . . . From Gloucester we go next to Tewkesbury, where we trust clearly to make a final conclusion of all our commissions for this shire.[60]

At Gloucester pensions were assigned to the abbot and thirty monks, of whom four were said to be students at Oxford; in addition no less than eighty-six monastic servants were paid their wages and dismissed, as well as twenty-three officers of the household, including cooks, butlers, bakers, porters, waiters, the barber, the groom of the

John Wakeman, the last abbot of Tewkesbury.
The monument commemorates the last abbot, although it dates from the mid-fifteenth century. In the fashion of the time the deceased is displayed as a corpse, crawled over by worms. John Wakeman actually lived until 1549, and in 1541 was chosen by Henry VIII to be the first bishop of the newly-created see of Gloucester.

horses, the master of the guest house and the verger. The clear yearly value of the possessions of the monastery was given as £1,952 10s. 11¾d.[61] At Tewkesbury this was calculated to be £1,063 8s. 10d., and the pensions were assigned to the abbot and thirty-eight monks. The commissioners noted that the nave of the monks' church was used by the parishioners of Tewkesbury and 'hath been ever a parish church to the inhabitants aforesaid.' The church, together with its bells and the lead on the roof, was valued at £453 and on 24 June [34 Hen. VIII] the church was sold to the parishioners for that sum.[62] The survey of Tewkesbury made early in 1540 can be found in Appendix XIV.

Most of this group of monasteries surrendered during 1539 with very little protest and little apparent reluctance; the only real difficulty encountered by the royal commissioners was at Glastonbury, where the process of dissolution met with much more stubborn resistance, the story of which will be told in the next chapter.

Chapter 6

The Suppression of Glastonbury and the Execution of the Last Abbot

Glastonbury was by far the greatest and most prestigious of all the west-country monasteries. Its wealth was immense and its estates spread across Somerset, Wiltshire, Dorset and far beyond; all visitors were impressed by its great buildings, superb treasures and lavish furnishings, as well as by the estates, manor houses, parks, barns and fish ponds which the abbot and his monks possessed. The long history of Glastonbury embraced some of the greatest figures in English monasticism – St Aldhelm, St Britwald, St Dunstan, Henry of Blois, William of Malmesbury and many others – while legends assiduously fostered by the monks linked it with the earliest days of Christianity and with King Arthur and his queen, with St Patrick, with Joseph of Arimathea and even with Christ himself. It was the burial place of early kings, richly endowed and visited by successive monarchs, and it remained a noted place of popular pilgrimage.

The buildings had been extended and made even more sumptuous during the final decades of the abbey's life, especially during the time

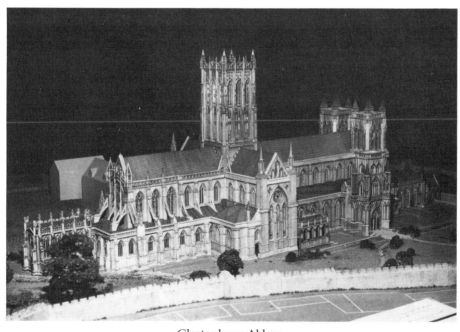

Glastonbury Abbey.
A reconstructed model of the abbey church at Glastonbury showing the splendid architecture which was lost with its demolition.

95

of John Selwood (abbot 1456–93), Richard Bere (abbot 1493–1525) and Richard Whiting (abbot 1525–39). The magnificent church was furnished with tombs, shrines, altars, tabernacles, screens, woodwork, stained glass, plate, rich vestments and jewels, and was decorated with paintings, colour, lights and carvings. Shortly before the Dissolution in 1539, the abbey was visited by John Leland, who left a notable description of the church and the many new buildings.

> Richard Bere Abbate buildid the new lodging by the great chambre caullid the kinge's lodging in the galery. Bere buildid the new lodginges for secular prestes and clerkes of our Lady. Abbate Bere buildid Edgares chapel at the est end of the chirch, but Abbate Whiting performid sum part of it. Bere archid on bothe sides the est parte of the chirch that began to cast owt. Bere made the volte of the steple in the transepto, and under 2 arches like S. Andres crosse, els it had fallen. Bere made a riche altare of sylver and gilt: and set it afore the high altare. Bere cumming from his embassadre out of Italie made a chapelle of our Lady de Loretta, joining to the north side of the body of the chirch. He made the chapelle of the sepulchre in the southe end *Navis ecclesie* whereby he is buried *sub plano marmore* yn the south isle of the bodie of the chich. He made an almose house in the north part of the abbey for vii or x poore wymen with a chapel.[1]

Leland also spent some time in the monastic library at Glastonbury and at first was so overwhelmed by the number and antiquity of the books, 'scarcely equalled by any other library in all Britain', that he was awestruck and hesitated to enter.[2] Even Cromwell's experienced, cynical and essentially practical surveyors became enthusiastic and almost lyrical in their descriptions of Glastonbury, both of the abbey itself and of its estates. For example, three of the commissioners, Richard Pollard, Thomas Moyle and Richard Layton, wrote to Cromwell from Glastonbury on 22 September 1539

> We assure your Lordship it is the goodliest house of that sort that ever we have seen. We would that your Lordship did know it as we do; then we doubt but your Lordship would judge it a house meet for the King's Majesty, and for no man else. . . .[3]

And on 28 September, they wrote again to Cromwell

> The house is great, goodly, and so princely as we have not seen the like; with 4 parks adjoining, the furthermost of them but 4 miles distant from the house; a great mere, which is 5 miles compass, being a mile and a half distant from the house, well replenished with great pike, bream, perch, and roach; 4 fair manor places, belonging to the late abbot, the furthermost but 3 miles distant, being goodly mansions; and also one in Dorsetshire, 30 miles distant from the late monastery.[4]

Likewise, surveys of the abbey possessions made in the months

The Abbey Barn at Pilton in an illustration of *c.*1840 by J.C. Buckler.
This barn together with the surrounding estates was another of the widespread possessions of Glastonbury abbey.

The Abbey Barn, Glastonbury.

following the Dissolution are fulsome in praise of the estates and properties. The Somerset landholdings included parks stocked with deer at Northwood, Wyrrall, Sharpham and Pilton, the large lake stocked with fish at Meare, lands, manors and manor houses spread across Somerset, including Glastonbury Moor which was sixteen miles in compass, and the common at West Pennard, fifteen miles in compass. The manor house at Pilton contained a hall, chapel, dining room and eight chambers, as well as a kitchen, buttery, cellar, stables and outhouses. There were similar manor houses at Shapwick, Sharpham, Weston, East Brent and Houndstreet, while at Meare the surveyor's description of the manor house, fishery and other buildings reads like the prospectus of a modern estate agent, listing

> A faire house adjoining the churchyard, a fair hall, five chambers, chapel, pantry, buttery, kitchen, garden and orchard.
>   A pretty house for the fishers to drink in adjoining the same house. Two other faire orchards, a pretty house of stone with a little hall, chamber and orchard. Three ponds, an old thatched house to store their fishing boats, and a goodly fishing mere being four or five miles in compass.

The survey goes on to mention the attractive views or prospects over the mere from the manor house, the excellence of the fishing, and the many swans, herons and pheasants to be found there.[5] Other estates, manor houses, tenements, mills, quarries, woodlands and possessions were to be found in London, Bristol, Berkshire, Wiltshire, Dorset, Devon and Wales. One example of an outlying property was Ashbury Manor in Berkshire which was built on the Glastonbury lands there by Abbot Selwood (1457–93) and has been described as 'probably the most important stone house in Berkshire'. It included a fine hall, well-appointed chambers and an excellent timber roof, all built in the Somerset tradition and comfortably furnished.[6] The income of Glastonbury in the *Valor Ecclesiasticus* was given as the huge sum of £3,508 13s. 4¾d. per annum, and the surveyors in 1539 calculated it at the even higher figure of £4,085 6s. 8¼d. per annum. The visitations by Cromwell's agents during 1535 and 1536 had failed to uncover any major scandals at Glastonbury, and the number of monks was maintained or even slightly increased during the years before the Dissolution; there were more than fifty monks in the house during the 1530s.[7]

Notwithstanding the foregoing pages emphasising the wealth and splendour of Glastonbury, it must not be supposed that all was well with the abbey. The complaints made by some of the monks during the visitation of 1538 have been quoted in Chapter 5, and there seems no doubt that there were numerous petty quarrels and jealousies among the brethren. The junior monks felt isolated and neglected by their seniors, and the administration of the abbey with its great buildings, army of servants and vast estates diverted the attention of many monks from spiritual concerns. Above all, the last abbot, Richard Whiting, does not seem to have exercised a strict control nor presided over a particularly happy community during the final years. There is little definite information about the origin, career or personality of Richard Whiting and even his date of birth is uncertain. He was ordained deacon in 1499, priest in 1501 and became Abbot of Glastonbury in 1525; he must have been well over sixty years of age by 1539.[8] Contemporary witnesses speak of him as an old man and there is no doubt that he was greatly troubled by illness. On 7 April 1539 he wrote to Cromwell asking to be excused from attendance at parliament on account of his infirmities.

> My good Lord, the truth is this, as knoweth our Lord God, I have been greatly diseased with divers infirmities more than half a year, in so much that for the more part of the time I have not been able to labour forth of my house, and I cannot ride, neither yet go well but with the help of my staff, in very great pain; by reason whereof I am not able to do my most bounden duty unto the King's Majesty as with all my whole heart and will I would do, and that right much grieveth me, as knoweth God. . . . But if the King's pleasure be so, I will be gladly carried thither in a horse litter to accomplish his Grace his pleasure and commandment, rather than tarry at home . . .[9]

Bench End from Brent Knoll, Somerset.
This late-medieval carving is one of three bench-ends which depict the abbot of Glastonbury, the owner of the parish, as Reynard the Fox. With all sorts of satirical allusions, he is shown preaching to the birds, then in the stocks being tried, and finally being hung by geese. How the parishioners got away with such a thinly-disguised attack on their landlord is a mystery.

This was the parliament of April–June 1539 which passed the Second Act of Dissolution, giving the authority of statute law to the monastic surrenders which had already taken place and granting to the king 'all other monasteries, abbacies . . . which shall hereafter happen to be dissolved, suppressed . . .'[10]

Like most late-medieval abbots, Whiting had become divorced from the daily routine of the monastery and lived in great style in his own separate establishment, with numerous servants and retainers. It was this separation which gave rise to many of the criticisms by the younger monks in the visitation of 1538. The abbot's kitchen, which is the sole building to survive intact on the abbey site, gives some indication of the lavish manner in which the last abbots lived. Whiting was frequently absent from Glastonbury and many of his surviving letters were written from one or other of his manor houses in Somerset, from Sturminster Newton in Dorset or from the opulently-furnished house at Ashbury in Berkshire.[11]

Evidence of the administration at Glastonbury, and also incidently of the separation of the abbot from the monastic routine, is provided by the depositions in a law suit. John Watts, a former monk at the abbey, deposed that he had witnessed the payment of £10 in gold, part of a debt of £40, to the abbot by John Lyte in the abbot's little parlour in January 1539, 'immediately after the said abbot had dined, so that the abbot's gentlemen and other servants were in the hall at dinner'. The following summer Watts had also witnessed the settlement of the outstanding part of the debt by John Lyte. The payment was made in gold to the abbot in his garden whilst he was seated in 'an arbour of bay in the said garden', and while in the nearby abbey church the monks were singing High Mass. The episode also explains how the arms of so many of the late-medieval abbots are still to be seen on buildings in the former monastic estates.

> At that time the abbot asked of the said master Lyte whether he would set up the said abbot's arms in his new buildings that he had made. And the said master Lyte answered the said abbot that he would; and so at that time the said abbot gave unto the said Master Lyte eight angels nobles . . .[12]

Another view of the administration of Glastonbury during the last year of its existence is provided by the Account Rolls for 1538–9. These show that although all the neighbouring monastic houses had already been suppressed or were undergoing the final stages of dissolution and destruction, the monastic life at Glastonbury continued as it had done for so many centuries. The officials continued their careful oversight of the estates and properties, rents were collected, building work on farms and mills was undertaken, repairs were carried out on the church and buildings at Glastonbury, materials for the services

The chair of John Arthur.
*The two monk-treasurers of Glaston-
bury, John Arthur and Roger Wilfred
were executed with Richard Whiting,
the last abbot.*

were purchased, additional foodstuffs, sugar, fish, wine for the monks
were bought, the ancient round of feasts and festivals continued, alms
were provided for the poor, and men were paid to scythe the nettles
around the chapel of St Michael on the Tor where, before the year was
out, the abbot and two of his monks would be executed.[13] Abbot
Whiting was evidently hospitable to visitors. John Leland was
impressed by his hospitality and described Whiting as '*Homo sane
candidissimus et amicus meus singularis*' (A most honest man and my
particular friend). Sadly, when the abbot fell foul of Cromwell and was
executed, Leland thought it prudent to cross through these words in
his manuscript.[14]

Cromwell's agent, Richard Layton, although certainly no friend of
the monks, was none the less favourably impressed by Richard
Whiting and, shortly before the abbot was arrested, praised his good
qualities both to Cromwell himself and to the king. The episode
provides a good illustration of Cromwell's attitude to his commissioners and of the reliability of their so-called 'evidence'; for Layton
received a furious rebuke from his master and was forced into a
grovelling apology and total withdrawal of his good opinion of
Richard Whiting.

16 September 1539

. . . ye much marvel why I would so greatly praise to the King's Majesty
at the time of the visitation the abbot of Glastonbury, which now
appeareth neither then nor now to have known God neither his prince,
neither any part of a good christian man his religion, so that my excessive

and indiscreet praise that time unadvisedly made to my Sovereign Lord must needs now redound to my great folly and untruth, and cannot be well rebutted but much diminish my credit towards his Majesty, and even so to your Lordship whom I most humbly beseech to consider that I am a man, and may err and cannot be sure of my judgement to know the inward thought of a monk, being fair in wordly and outward appearance, and inwardly cankered as now by your discreet inquisition appeareth. And although that they all be false, feigned, flattering, hypocrite knaves, as undoubtedly there is none other of that sort, I must therefore now at this my necessity most humbly beseech your Lordship to pardon me for that my folly then committed . . . From henceforth I shall be more circumspect whom I shall commend either to his Grace or to your Lordship.[15]

Richard Layton, like all those who were employed by Cromwell, knew that his well-being and fortune rested entirely upon Cromwell's good opinion of him; he and his colleagues prepared to go to any lengths to flatter him or to agree with his views.

Just as the earliest beginnings of Glastonbury are obscured by the mists of antiquity and legend, so likewise there is considerable mystery about the precise sequence of events leading to the end of this great monastery.

During the 1530s Richard Whiting, like the heads of so many other religious houses, had accepted the royal supremacy over the Church and had gone to some lengths to secure and keep the favour of Cromwell and of influential local gentry by presents and the gift of offices and perquisites. It is not clear how Glastonbury escaped closure in the great sweep of west-country monasteries during the early months of 1539. Whether this was because of the resistance of its abbot and monks, or because its great wealth and importance meant that the house was dealt with separately, is uncertain. Nor is it known how far most of the monks supported the determined stand of their abbot. But the abbey survived until September 1539, resisting all the attacks and persuasion of Cromwell's agents.

Having failed to obtain a 'voluntary' surrender of the abbey, Cromwell's commissioners were obliged to look for evidence of religious or political views expressed by the abbot which could be used to bring a charge of treason against him. They also proceeded to harsher measures and much rougher treatment of the abbot and monks in order to compel them to surrender the treasures and possessions of the abbey. Some of the major letters which give details of the events surrounding the final suppression of Glastonbury are given in Appendix XIII. On 19 September 1539, three royal commissioners arrived unexpectedly at Glastonbury and demanded to interview the abbot. They were Richard Pollard and Thomas Moyle, who were both lawyers, and John, Lord Russell, a member of a prominent west-country family who had recently been appointed president of the Council of the West. Richard Whiting was at his manor of Sharpham, two miles from the abbey. There the commissioners found the old man and proceeded to question him. Failing to get the answers they wanted, they brought him back to the abbey and that night thoroughly searched his study, looking for evidence of treasonable writings or correspondence. Their search was rewarded, for they found, hidden away, a book of arguments against the king's divorce of Katherine of Aragon, a life of Thomas Becket and various papal documents. Armed with this material, the commissioners proceeded to examine the abbot again, and in particular to question him about the treasures of the abbey which he had concealed from them. In their account to Cromwell they claimed that the abbot's answers to their questions revealed

> his cankered and traitorous heart and mind against the King's majesty and his succession, as by the same answers, signed with his hand and sent to your Lordship by this bearer, more plainly shall appear. And so, with as fair words as we could, we have conveyed him hence into the Tower, being a very weak man and a sickly. . . .[16]

Having dispatched the abbot as a traitor to the Tower of London, the commissioners devoted themselves to a diligent search of all the monastic buildings at Glastonbury, in order to find the treasures which the abbot and his monks had hidden. They immediately found more than £300 in money, as well as 'a fair chalice of gold, and divers other parcels of plate, which the abbot had hid secretly from all such commissioners as have been there in times past; and as yet he knoweth not that we have found the same . . .'[17]

A few days later, on 28 September 1539, the commissioners wrote again to Cromwell to inform him of the success which had attended their searches. They told him that almost everything of value had been hidden by the monks.

> At our first entry into the treasure-house, and vestry also, we neither found jewels, plate nor ornaments sufficient to serve a poor parish church, whereof we could not a little marvel . . .

Diligent search had, however, revealed great quantities of valuables.

> We have daily found and tried out both money and plate, hid and mured up in walls, vaults and other secret places, as well by the abbot and others of the convent, and also conveyed to divers places in the country. And in case we should tarry here this fortnight, we do suppose daily to increase in plate and other goods by false knaves conveyed.

The commissioners also reported to Cromwell that they had assigned pensions to the monks and sent them away.

> We find them very glad to depart, most humbly thanking the King's

majesty of his great goodness most graciously shown on to them at this time, as well for his Grace's regard as for their pensions . . .

They had paid each of the servants a half year's wages and dismissed them, but had committed to jail two of the monks and two laymen, who were responsible for looking after the treasures and who had refused to reveal the hiding places. It was for their concealment of the goods of the abbey and refusal to surrender their treasures to the king's commissioners rather than for the charge of treason that the abbot and two of the monks were to be executed.[18]

Thus the long history of the greatest of all the English abbeys came to an end, and while the monks were being expelled, and the monastic buildings ransacked for hidden treasure, the elderly, sick abbot, Richard Whiting, was imprisoned in the Tower of London. Here he was subjected to much further questioning and examination on his religious opinions, but presumably insufficient evidence could be obtained; after many weeks, Whiting was sent back to Somerset, to stand trial at Wells on the curious charge of stealing from his own abbey, following Cromwell's well-known 'remembrance' – 'The abbot of Glaston to be tried at Glaston, and also executed there with his complices'.[19] The trial took place in Wells on 14 November 1539, and Lord Russell wrote to Cromwell to assure him that all was conducted properly and before a huge crowd of people,

> And I do send your Lordship enclosed the names of the inquest (jury) that passed on Whiting the said abbot, which I assure you my Lord is as worshipful a jury as was charged here these many years. And there was never seen in these parts so great appearance as were here at this present time, and never better willing to serve the King.[20]

Any hope that the abbot may have had that the local gentry would support him or refuse to find him guilty proved to be vain. Although they and their families had for many generations been tenants of the abbey lands and officers of the abbey estates, and although many had received gifts, perquisites and offices from the abbot, none the less they now knew that Glastonbury, like all the other local abbeys, had ceased to exist; the lands would soon become available for purchase or lease and it was from the Crown that offices, perquisites and favours could now be expected. Richard Whiting no longer had anything to offer. He and his two monks John Thorne *alias* Arthur and Roger James *alias* Wilfred were, therefore, found guilty and condemned to death 'for the robbing of Glastonbury church'.

Perhaps to ensure that no sympathy for the abbot and his monks should develop in the large crowd which was assembled, the executions, for which preparations must have already been made, were carried out the next day, 15 November 1539. By a final ironic touch, they were performed on top of Glastonbury Tor, overlooking the

Glastonbury Tor with the ruined chapel of St Michael at its summit.
*It was here on 15 November 1539, overlooking the abbey, that the last abbot, Richard Whiting,
and his two monks, John Thorne* alias *Arthur and Roger James* alias *Wilfred, were brutally
executed for their refusal to surrender the goods of the abbey.*

now-deserted abbey and with stupendous views across the Somerset
landscape, so much of which had belonged to the monks. In separate
letters to Cromwell written on the following day, Lord Russell and
Richard Pollard both described the executions. The abbot was taken
from Wells to Glastonbury and from there was drawn on a hurdle to
the top of the Tor, where he and his two monks were executed.
Cromwell was told that all three took their deaths 'very patiently', but
refused to incriminate anyone else or reveal the hiding place of any
more gold and silver. Immediately after his execution, Richard Whiting's body was divided into quarters and his head was cut off; one
quarter was displayed at Wells, another at Bath, the other quarters at
Ilchester and Bridgwater, while in this final macabre display his head
was set over the abbey gateway at Glastonbury. The whole of
Somerset was thus informed of the fate which awaited those who
opposed the will of the king or of Thomas Cromwell.[21]
     No useless sympathy with the late abbot or his two unfortunate
monks diverted Lord Russell or Richard Pollard from the main focus of
their concern, which was the lands and wealth of the former monastery and the developing struggle amongst those who sought their own
profit in the downfall of the monasteries. Lord Russell included with
his letter a list of the jury which had passed sentence on Whiting,

while Richard Pollard did not miss the opportunity to bring the names of his friends and of various local gentlemen to Cromwell's attention. Thus he used his letter to ask for the surveyorship of Glastonbury for 'my brother Paulett' who had been 'very diligent . . . to serve the King at this time, according to his duty and right. So was Nicholas Fitzjames, John Sydenham and Thomas Horner, your servants.'[22]

Even before the execution of the abbot, Cromwell had received the treasures of the abbey and noted the receipt of

> The plate from Glastonbury – 11,000 ounces and odd, besides gold.
> The furniture of the house of Glastonbury
> In ready money from Glastonbury £1,100 and odd
> The rich copes from Glastonbury
> The whole year's revenue of Glastonbury.[23]

Because of the manner in which it was suppressed, no formal deed of surrender survives for Glastonbury, nor is there any list of the pensions granted to the fifty or so monks who were members of the community at the dissolution. An account of the pensions still being paid to former monks of Glastonbury during the reign of Queen Mary gives twenty-five names, of whom six had recently died.[24] The fortunes of the monks and the fate of the monastic buildings at Glastonbury and the other west country monasteries will be considered in the following chapters.

Chapter 7

The Effect of the Suppression upon the Monks and Nuns and the Fate of the Monastic Buildings

The abbot of Glastonbury and his two unfortunate monks were quite exceptional in their steadfast refusal to bow before the royal will. Whatever their feelings or innermost thoughts, the great majority of west-country monks and nuns, from the heads of houses down to the most recent recruits, accepted the pensions and gratuities offered and left the monasteries without protest. Some, no doubt, abandoned the religious life with relief, others with sorrow, especially the nuns for whom the possibilities of profitable employment were negligible and whose pensions were small; but there was no open resistance. For the heads of the houses, the prospect offered by Cromwell's commissioners of a generous pension, a good house and an assured comfortable future, could hardly fail to be a powerful inducement and few displayed any reluctance in their acceptance. The terms varied according to the wealth of each house, but for the heads of the richer houses they were extremely generous and tempting. For example, the abbot of Cerne, in spite of the charges of immorality which were levelled against him, was awarded a pension of £100 per annum.[1] Paul Bush, the rector or head of the Bonhommes at Edington, received £100 per annum, together with the manor house at Coleshill in Berkshire, which had formerly belonged to the monastery.[2] The abbot of Malmesbury received a pension of £66 13s. per annum together with 'one tenement in the high streete within the towne of Bristowe', and 'one garden lying in the suburbs of the said town against the cross called Red Cross'.[3] Abbot Hamlyn of Athelney presided over a house which was badly in debt, but none the less he received a pension of £50 per annum and also obtained the prebend of Long Sutton as well as two parochial benefices.[4]

Thomas Chard, the last abbot of Forde who had been responsible for so much elegant work on the abbey buildings, obtained a pension of £80, the nearby benefice of Thorncombe and forty wain-loads of firewood each year from the woods of the former abbey.[5] Morgan Gwilliam, the last abbot of St Augustine's, Bristol, had only been in office for four months at the time of the suppression, but he received a pension of £80 per annum together with the comfortable manor house, garden, twenty loads of firewood yearly and a fine estate at Abbots Leigh.[6] The prior of Montacute, Robert Whitlocke, had the foresight to build a manor house in the nearby village of East Chinnock shortly before the suppression of his house, and he was awarded a pension of £80 per annum 'and he to have for his dwelling house for time of life a mansion place with the garden adjoining set and being in East

Chinnock, which the said late prior of late builded.' He lived for over twenty-one years in his house at East Chinnock and died in 1560. In his will he renounced the world and its troubles, saying that

> the life of man is like to a flower of the field that groweth today and tomorrow is cast into the furnace to be burnt. . . . I utterly forsake and renounce this miserable world and all things contained in the same. . . .

He left legacies to several neighbouring parish churches and to three vicars who had been monks at Montacute. His possessions included stills and a brass pot for making *aqua vita*, as well as 'all such books as I have of Physicke and Surgery'.[7]

Abbot Stephen Sagar of Hailes did even better. He received an annual pension of £100, a fine house on the abbey estate at Corscumbe (Coscombe) in the parish of Didbrook, Glos., with a garden, forty loads of firewood a year and other perquisites. He soon also acquired the rectory of Avening in Gloucestershire and the rich rectory of Adel in his native Yorkshire, becoming a chaplain to the king and a prebendary of York Minster. The income from these various offices made him so rich that he was able to lend money to the king himself, and in 1546 a debt of £66 13s. 4d. was repaid to 'Mr Segar late abbot of Hailes' from the royal treasury.[8] Similar examples could be multiplied from all over the region. Likewise the abbesses were generously and sympathetically treated by the royal commissioners. The Abbess of Wilton, Cecily Bodenham, was granted an annual pension of £100 and a pleasant house on the former monastic estate at Fovant, with orchards, gardens and meadows along the sheltered valley of the chalkland stream, and a cartload of firewood each week from the nearby woodlands. At the last moment the commissioners almost had second thoughts about their generosity when they found that the abbess had recently granted several long leases of lands at Fovant, South Newton, Chalke and Washbourne to her friends and relations, but eventually she was allowed to retain her pension, house and perquisites on the rather dubious grounds that she was 'without father, brother or any assured friend'.[9] At Amesbury, Joan Darrell had only been elected abbess in August 1539, having replaced Florence Bonnewe who refused to agree to Cromwell's demands, but none the less at the dissolution in December 1539 Joan received the handsome pension of £100 per annum, no doubt in consideration of her readiness to surrender the house. The commissioners described the abbess and her sisters as 'very honest and conformable'.[10]

The pensions granted to the heads of houses and to the monks and nuns were at the discretion of the commissioners who received the surrender of each house, and accordingly varied with the wealth of the house, the readiness of the religious to surrender and the skill of the abbot or abbess in negotiating favourable terms. Thus the abbot of the righ Augustinian house at Cirencester, which had an annual income in

General View of Forde Abbey.
The tower and left side of the illustration were part of the opulent abbot's lodging built by the last abbot, Thomas Chard (1521–1539). To the right are the surviving remains of the cloisters which were incorporated into the house at the Dissolution. The abbey church occupied the area on the right of the picture.

Forde Abbey.
The stonework of the cloisters shows the high quality and superb workmanship which survives at this former Cistercian house.

the *Valor Ecclesiasticus* of over £1,000, received £200 per annum and a house at Fairford; while the abbot of the ancient, rich house at Malmesbury was awarded an annual pension of £133 6s. 8d. Thomas Ware, the last abbot of the poor house at Flaxley which had been destroyed by fire, was granted a pension of only £15 per annum, and Thomas Bewdley, last abbot of Kingswood, received £50 per annum; likewise William Snow, prior of the Augustinian house at Braden-stoke which had an annual income of just £212 per annum and thus had only just escaped suppression under the Act of 1536, was allocated an annual pension of £60. In contrast, the last abbot of the rich Benedictine monastery at Winchcombe received £140 per annum, together with 40 loads of firewood each year. The Abbess of Shaftes-bury, which was credited in the *Valor* with an annual income of £1,166, received a pension of £133 per annum; while at Lacock, which had an annual net income of only £168 and had been obliged to purchase exemption from the Act of 1536, the abbess received a pension of only £40 per annum.

With their pensions, houses and other perquisites, some former heads of houses were able to live in considerable style and comfort for many years. Richard Hart, the last prior of Llanthony by Gloucester, had a pension of £100 per annum and a house at Brockworth just outside Gloucester, where he lived until his death in 1545 and to which he had evidently conveyed numerous possessions from the priory. At his death his bequests included most of the library of the former priory.[11] Even more comfortably off was Margaret Russell, the former abbess of the Cistercian nunnery of Tarrant. According to the *Valor Ecclesiasticus*, her nunnery had a net annual income of £214 in 1535, and at the dissolution in 1539 she was awarded a pension of £40 per annum. She moved to Bere Regis where she continued to live in a lavish style as befitted a cousin of the Duke of Bedford, and she remained there for nearly thirty years, dying in 1568. In her will, she described herself as sometime abbess of the late dissolved monastery of Tarrant, and she left a great quantity of silver plate, cups, chalices, cruets, rings and other valuables, many pieces of furniture, coffers, cupboards, bedsteads, candlesticks, bedding, brassware and linen, and most notably a collection of elegant, fashionable clothes, far removed from a nun's sombre habit, including

> my best gown of silk chamlett, my kirtle of satin, my scarlet petticoat and my best bonnet of velvet, six cushions whereof two covered with sarcenet one with green velvet wrought with gold, and the other three wrought upon cloth with needlework . . . my second best gown of grogroame, and my kirtle of silk chamlet . . . one coverlet of white wrought with red and green branches, a red coverlet with roses . . . three of my every day cushions and three of my holy day cushions. . . .

The ex-abbess had obviously devoted much of her time to needlework

Tarrant Crawford Church, near Blandford Forum, Dorset.
This is the parish church which stood at the gates of the wealthy Cistercian nunnery. Nothing now survives of the nunnery which was established in this remote situation in 1230 by Richard Poore, Bishop of Salisbury. The bishop's regulations by which the nuns' lives were governed provided much practical advice on their daily routine and devotions, and one of the rules ordered, 'Ye shall not possess any beast, my sisters, save only a cat.'

and her house was filled with embroidered cushions, pillows and coverlets.[12]

At least two and possibly more of the nuns of Shaftesbury continued after the dissolution to live together in a house near the site of their former nunnery. A survey of the monastery precincts made in 1562–7 lists two tenements by the house's cemetery which were rented by Margaret Mayo and Edith Maudlen, previously nuns of Shaftesbury. There may well have been more such ladies who combined their small pensions to continue living a semi-communal life, but of whom no record survives.[13]

The pensions awarded to former religious only ceased on death or if the recipient was appointed to an office of equal or superior value. Thus it was in the interest of the Crown that ecclesiastical preferments should be given to persons in receipt of pensions, and soon after the dissolution several former abbots as well as countless monks were appointed to ecclesiastical benefices. Paul Bush, the former head of the Bonhommes house at Edington, was appointed as the first bishop of the newly-created diocese of Bristol in 1542, and William Snowe, who had been Prior of Bradenstoke, became the first dean of Bristol Cathedral.[14] John Wakeham, Abbot of Tewkesbury, had been granted the very large pension of £266 13s. 4d. per annum at the dissolution in January 1540, but in September 1541 he was created bishop of the new see of Gloucester. William Jennings, former Prior of St Oswald's, Gloucester which was dissolved in 1536, became the first dean of Gloucester, and there were several ex-religious among the canons.[15] John Bradley, the last Abbot of Milton, became suffragan Bishop of Marlborough and also held the rich livings of Fittleton and Bradford-on-Avon.[16] The former Abbot of Athelney was presented to the prebend of Long Sutton in Wells Cathedral and the former Abbot of Kingswood became vicar of Hawkesbury where he died in 1548 leaving a wife and daughter, while the former abbot of Bruton became rector of Pucklechurch. The Prior of Maiden Bradley, Richard Jennings, who had been accused of gross immorality by Richard Layton and was said by him to have had six children, became rector of Shipton Moyne in Gloucestershire after the dissolution and remained there until his death in 1553. His later career was not devoid of controversy, and while at Shipton Moyne he may have married, since he was called before the ecclesiastical court to answer unspecified charges in 1540.[18]

The former Abbot of Sherborne, John Barnstaple, received an annual pension of £100 and in March 1541 he was presented to the rectory of Stalbridge, previously part of the possessions of Sherborne Abbey. His new office was secured through the influence of Sir Giles Strangways and Sir John Horsey, to whom he had earlier owed his promotion as abbot. Sir John Horsey had acquired the site, buildings and many of the estates of Sherborne Abbey at the dissolution and was duly remembered by the former abbot in his will of 1560. Sir John Horsey was left a silver and gilt standing cup, and bequests of jewelled rings were left to members of other local gentry families.[19]

THE MONKS AND NUNS

It is far easier to trace the subsequent careers of the abbots than it is to follow the varied fortunes of the monks and nuns. There has been much argument over the adequacy of the pensions awarded to the religious and they were certainly given far less than the very generous provision made for the heads of the houses. This reflected the fact that the abbots and abbesses were regarded as the owners of their monasteries and of the lands and estates; they lived in great style, separate from the monks and nuns, and in the manner of the richest of their lay neighbours. The pensions awarded to the monks varied according to the wealth of their houses, and their own age and seniority within the monastery, but they averaged about £5 per annum, an adequate though far from generous pension. The monks, however, could and did find alternative employment and sources of income as parish clergy, chantry priests, chaplains or in other ecclesiastical offices. The real sufferers were the nuns, most of whose pensions were considerably lower and for whom there were few alternative avenues of employment. For many of the monks and nuns

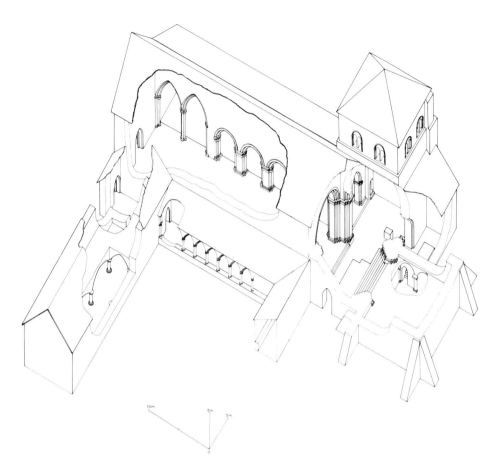

The Priory of St Oswald, Gloucester in the thirteenth century.
This cut-away drawing is based upon excavated evidence and shows the cloister and west range lying to the south of the church. Two taller, pointed arches have been added to the late Norman nave arcade. The Norman north transept tower survived, as did the late Saxon crypt under the choir.

alike, however, pensions and perquisites could hardly have compensated them for the total destruction of their ordered way of life, the disappearance of their security and the disregard of their religious vocations.

The careers of the former monks in Gloucestershire and Bristol have been traced with great care and in detail, and almost all are shown to have secured positions as parish priests or curates, as canons of the new cathedrals at Gloucester and Bristol, or as chantry priests until the chantries were dissolved in 1547.[20] For example, of the eleven ex-canons of St Augustine's Bristol, five became parish priests, three were curates, one was a chantry priest at Berkeley, another served the chantry at Winterborne in South Gloucestershire; the abbot, accompanied by one canon, departed with his pension of £80 for the Isle of Wight.[29] For the younger and more energetic monks there can have been few problems in obtaining other ecclesiastical offices, and many may even have welcomed the opportunity to escape from the narrow confines of the cloister. For the older monks and nuns, moulded by a lifetime of ordered monastic routine, the difficulties were infinitely greater and the dissolution must have appeared as a disaster.

An examination of the subsequent careers of the Benedictine monks of Sherborne illustrates both the possibilities and the problems faced by the monks. As already stated, the abbot became rector of the former monastery parish of Stalbridge and took with him William Vowell, the former infirmarer of the abbey, to act as his curate. John Dunster, the former prior, received a pension of £12 per annum and lived on in Sherborne where soon after the dissolution he was able to show John Leland the library. Later, Dunster became vicar of nearby Oborne, where he remained until his death in 1570. He may have continued to live in Sherborne, for the churchwardens' accounts for 1570 record that the great bell of the former abbey was tolled when the news of his death became known. The sub-prior, Thomas Capel, also stayed in Sherborne and became chaplain of the almshouse situated beside the former abbey. He died in 1563. Other monks became vicars or curates of nearby parishes, Bishop's Caundle, Chetnole and Lillington. Of the rest of the sixteen monks who signed the deed of surrender in March 1539 nothing is known, and presumably they left the district in search of employment elsewhere.[21]

Not all found it easy to settle to a new life in what was for them a completely changed world and some, evidently not knowing where to go, stayed near the former monastery. As mentioned in Chapter 5, when pressure was being exerted by Cromwell's commissioners on the Carthusian monks at Hinton Charterhouse in order to encourage their 'voluntary' surrender, one of the monks who narrowly escaped trouble for his outspoken comments on contemporary religious and political matters was Nicholas Balland. For his treasonable speeches Balland was imprisoned by Lord Hungerford in his castle at Farleigh, but his reputation as a harmless lunatic seems to have saved him from the horrendous fate he might so easily have suffered. His mental condition cannot have been helped by the fact that already the church and buildings of the monastery had been destroyed and all its treasures taken away. In Mary's reign Balland was one of those Carthusians who joined the new Charterhouse at Sheen, and on Mary's death he left England for Bruges where he died in 1578.[22] Men who had spent long years in the seclusion of the cloister were often unsuited to the state of matrimony and ill-equipped to undertake the notoriously pitfall-bestrewn task of choosing a wife. Richard Bragge, an ex-friar of Gloucester, was described as married in 1563, but his choice had evidently been ill-judged, 'which woman is ungodly, proud, envious and a common scold with other like'. Henry Wakeman, monk of Tewkesbury, secured the vicarage of Preston by Ledbury, but was deprived in 1554 because of his marriage.[23]

The subsequent careers of many monks can be traced through parish and diocesan records, since so many of them became parish priests or curates, but it is far more difficult to discover anything about the fortunes of the nuns after the dissolution. Many came from wealthy local families and no doubt returned to their family home as welcome or unwelcome guests. Abbesses like Elizabeth Zouche of Shaftesbury, Cecily Bodenham of Wilton, Margaret Russell of Tarrant or Joan Temmse of Lacock were able to live comfortably and in some style on their generous pensions. We know that Margaret Russell set up house at Bere Regis, Cecily Bodenham had been granted a house at Fovant; Mary Denny, the prioress of Kington St Michael went to Bristol and lived there until her death more than fifty years later in 1593.[24] She was buried in St Mark's, the former chapel of the Gaunt's Hospital. But of the nuns we know scarcely anything. Their pensions were generally significantly lower than those granted to the monks and the possibilities of other careers, apart from marriage, were non-existent. For example, at Amesbury the abbess received £100 per annum as her pension, but the average pension awarded to each of the thirty-three nuns was about £4 10s. Twenty-seven years later in 1555–6, twenty-one former nuns of Amesbury were still receiving pensions.[25] At Shaftesbury, the pension awarded to the abbess was £133 6s. 8d., the prioress had £20 per annum and, of the 47 other nuns, three had £6 0s. 8d., nine had £6, twelve had £5 6s. 8d., three received £5, eleven £4 13s. 4d., six £4, and three £3 6s. 8d.[26] This, however, was the generous provision for the well-connected ladies of England's wealthiest nunnery. Most nuns got less; for example, at Buckland near Taunton the prioress was awarded a pension of £50 per annum, two other nuns received £4 13s. 4d. and £4 6s. 8d. respectively, and the other eleven nuns each received an annual pension of £4. William Maudesley, the nuns' confessor, was also granted an annual pension of £4.[27] Twenty-seven years later in 1556, pensions were still being paid to eight of the former nuns of Buckland.[28]   Most of the former

religious, having acquired some benefice or other ecclesiastical prefer-
ment, ended their days there; but a few brief examples will serve to
illustrate the varied fortunes of some others. John Rastall had been a
canon of St Augustine's Bristol and was aged thirty-two at the time of
the dissolution. He was not a particularly devout religious and, as was
shown in Chapter I, he was accused of large-scale gambling, card-
playing and dicing in the abbey during the months before the
dissolution; he may even have welcomed the chance to escape from
the monastic life. He was awarded an annual pension of £6 13s. 4d.
and became a chantry priest at Winterborne in south Gloucestershire,
where no doubt he enjoyed a much freer life; but that came to an end
with the suppression of the chantries in 1547. Rastall then returned to
Bristol and was appointed curate of St James' church and later vicar of
St Nicholas. He died in 1563.[30]

William Tybbott had been sub-prior of the Augustinian house at
Keynsham and after the dissolution obtained the rectory of Cameley
in north Somerset. His parishioners included some who held strongly
Protestant views, and Tybbott may well have shared these feelings,
for he was deprived of the benefice early in Mary's reign. On the
accession of Elizabeth he was re-instated and remained as rector of
Cameley until his death in 1575.[31] William Newport *alias* Vaughan
was a monk of St Peter's Gloucester, and at the suppression in 1540
he received an annual pension of £6 13s. 4d. He remained in the town
and later became vicar of St Owen's Gloucester. In 1551 he was tried
before the Consistory Court for using sorcery to discover a thief. He
was said to have put a key into a book 'of written hand with certain
circles' and tied it with string. Then, in the chancel of the church he
held the book and, after prayers, named various suspects. When the
guilty party was named, the key and the book turned. He was
temporarily suspended from celebrating divine service and ordered to
perform public penance during service time in the parish churches of
St Owen, St Nicholas and St Michael in Gloucester.[32] This was not the
end of his troubles, however, since during the reign of Edward VI he
had taken advantage of the new order to get married, and early in the
reign of Mary he was accordingly deprived of his benefice and we
hear of him no more.[33]

Perhaps the career most remarkable for its dramatic changes of
direction was that of Paul Bush. He was born in around 1490 and
educated at the Bonhommes house at Edington. He joined the
community of the Bonhommes and was sent by them to Oxford,
where he studied at the Augustinian college. He graduated in 1518
and remained at Oxford, acquiring a reputation as a scholar, author
and poet. In *c*. 1530, he returned to Edington, no doubt expecting to
spend the rest of his life in that quiet situation, under the shelter of
Salisbury Plain. When the 'rector' or head of the house died in 1538,
Paul Bush was elected as his successor and had to face the pressures
from Cromwell's commissioners. In March 1539 he and his brethren

surrendered the house; Bush himself received the generous pension of £100 per annum together with the former monastic manor house at Coleshill in Berkshire. Here he could live comfortably and in the quiet seclusion of a wealthy country gentleman with scholarly and poetic tastes. But he did not long enjoy this pleasant retreat, for in 1542 he was chosen by Henry VIII to be the first bishop of the newly-created diocese of Bristol, which consisted of Bristol itself and some neighbouring parishes, together with the county of Dorset which had been detached from Salisbury diocese. Paul Bush was consecrated bishop in June 1542.

In Bristol Bush faced all the difficulties of establishing the new and oddly-constituted diocese, setting up the cathedral in the church of the former Augustinian abbey, and all the controversies of the sweeping changes in religion during the reign of Edward VI. He did take advantage of one of these changes, however, and married a woman called Edith Ashley, bringing her to his bishop's palace in the house of the former abbots of St Augustine's. With the accession of Queen Mary and the restoration of Catholicism in 1553, a married bishop could not be tolerated, so Bush resigned and retired to become rector of Winterbourne. Here too, he would have been in difficulty as a married priest, but his wife died shortly after the move to Winterbourne and Bush continued to live in considerable state and with several servants at Winterbourne until his own death in 1558. In spite of his marriage, he evidently remained a conservative in religious matters and during his retirement he composed a defence of the Mass and of the authority of the Church against the 'rash fantastycall myndes of the blynde and ignorante'. In his will he left a great many possessions and remembered his relations and friends as well as old servants from Edington. He was buried beside his wife in Bristol Cathedral. Like so many of his fellow religious, his career had taken many twists and turns which would have seemed inconceivable to him when he first sought the ordered life and apparently timeless security of the Bonhommes house at Edington.[34]

Understandably, many of the former monks and nuns cherished the hope that times would change and that their communities would be restored once more. But, as will be shown later in this chapter, this desire was dashed by the speedy demolition of many of the buildings, especially the former monastic churches, as well as by the dispersal of the monastic estates and endowments. The call of the monastic life remained alive with some of the former religious until the restoration of the Catholic faith in 1553 under Mary, and four of the monks from Glastonbury joined the revived community at Westminster Abbey. In addition, the Westminster community included monks from Sherborne and Richard Edy who had been a vicar-choral at Wells, rector of North Petherton and a canon of Salisbury.[35] The former Glastonbury monks were John Phagan, John Neott, William Adelwold and William Kentwyn, and in 1557 the four petitioned the queen for a restoration of

Glastonbury Abbey. They asked for no endowment and even offered to pay rent for the buildings.

> We ask nothing in gift to the foundation, but only the house and site, the residue for the accustomed rent, so that with our labour and husbandry, we may live there, a few of us in our religious habits, till the charity of good people may suffice a greater number; and the country there being so much affected to our Religion, we believe we should find much help amongst them, towards the reparations and furniture of the same; whereby we would happily prevent the ruin of much and the repair of no little part of the whole. . . .

They went on to emphasise the antiquity, spiritual life and splendour of Glastonbury and the unjust manner in which it had been suppressed: '. . . not surrendered, as other, but extorted, the Abbot preposterously put to death, with two innocent, virtuous monks with him.'[36] But Mary died before any action could be taken to meet their request. Evidently a scheme for the restoration of Glastonbury was being discussed, however, for when Thomas Shackell, rector of Hinton St George, made his will in July 1557, he left £2 'to the edifying of the Abbey of Glastonbury, if it be not paid in my lifetime'.[37] Likewise, when Richard Dovell, a Glastonbury yeoman whose relative Thomas Dovell had been a monk at Glastonbury, made his will in March 1557 he expected the monastery to be re-established, and inserted the clause

> I commend my soul to the merciful hands of Almighty God, and my body to be buried in the monastery house.[38]

At Montacute an attempt was also made to re-establish the Cluniac priory during Mary's reign. In a dispute over lands at Montacute in 1617 depositions were taken from elderly residents, and some of them could remember a time when the priory had owned the lands. John Rodberd, husbandman, of West Chinnock 'aged one hundred years or thereabouts,' stated that he was born and bred in the district and 'was often in and out of the said Abbie or Priory before the dissolution.' He could remember that the Prior of Montacute had kept a flock of sheep on Hamdon Hill. Another witness, Robert Eglin of Odcombe, a carpenter aged seventy-six years, also remembered the time when the prior 'was restored to the Priory and took possession thereof againe in the time of Queene Marie. . . .'[39]

Some of the Carthusians from Witham and Hinton who had fled abroad at the time of the dissolution returned in 1555 to the revived Charterhouse at Sheen in Surrey. They included the former Prior of Witham, John Mitchell, and Nicholas Balland, from Hinton, who had so stoutly maintained his belief in Catholicism and in the authority of the Pope. The re-established Charterhouse did not last long, however, for with the death of Mary and the accession of Elizabeth the brethren were forced once more to seek sanctuary on the Continent.[40]

There is no contemporary evidence to support John Aubrey's story of the return of the nuns to Wilton, in spite of the detail which he gives and notwithstanding the fact that Aubrey was well acquainted with the Earl of Pembroke and his family. In this instance it seems likely that Aubrey's love of a romantic legend got the better of historical accuracy, though it does indicate the attitude of later generations to the nuns.

> In Queen Mary's time, upon the return of the Catholique religion, the nunnes came again to Wilton abbey, and this William, earl of Pembroke, came to the gate (which lookes towards the court by the street, but now is walled up) with his cuppe in his hand, and fell upon his knee to the lady abbesse and the nunnes, crying *peccavi*. Upon Queen Mary's death, the earle came to Wilton (like a tygre) and turned them out, crying 'Out ye whores, to worke, to worke, ye whores, goe spinne.'[41]

THE FATE OF THE MONASTIC BUILDINGS AND TREASURES

The work of demolition, and the business of selling or converting as much as possible of the monastic buildings and their contents into cash, began almost immediately after the formal deed of surrender had been signed. Any vacant or demesne land was rented out as soon as possible and sheep, cattle, corn and implements were sold. From Glastonbury, immediately after the execution of the abbot, Richard Pollard wrote to Cromwell to inform him that all the cattle were being sold and the lands let.[42] Likewise, at St Oswald's Gloucester the commissioners immediately sold livestock and implements of husbandry for £89 6s. 6d. Included in the sale were 22 pigs, 207 sheep, 342 ewes, 160 lambs and 18 milking cows.[43] The valuables such as plate, jewels or rare books were sent to the royal treasury, while other saleable items were disposed of locally. An example of the treasures, buildings and possessions of Tewkesbury is given in Appendix XIV. The long lists of plate and other treasures from the monastic houses which were confiscated by the Crown do not always specify the monastery from which each piece came, but some indication of the size of the haul and of the wealth and variety of gold, silver, jewels, chalices, ewers, plates, images, censers and other objects which came from Glastonbury alone can be seen in the lists of valuables received by John Williams, master of the king's jewels, in the summer and autumn of 1539, while Abbot Whiting was being interrogated in London and before the abbey was formally suppressed. Among the vast quantity of treasure arriving in London from monasteries all over England, the following articles were specifically listed as coming from Glastonbury

A superaltar, garnished with saphire a gilt and part gold, called the great Saphire of Glastonbury.
A great piece of Unicorne horn, as it is supposed
A piece of Mother of pearl, like a shell.
Eight branches of fair coral
Divers parcels of gilt plate, 2,600 ounces
Divers parcels of gilt plate brought by Richard Pollard and Thomas Moyle, from Glastonbury and Reading 1,247½ ounces.
Delivered from Glastonbury and Reading divers parcels of gilt plate, 449 ounces.

Cromwell's personal memoranda show that over 11,000 ounces of gold and silver were received from Glastonbury, as well as copes, vestments, furniture, etc., and £1,100 'in ready money'.[44] From Tewkesbury early in 1540 there was sent to the royal treasury

Jewels reserved to the King's Majesty, Two Mitres garnished
Plate of silver reserved to the King's Majesty 1431 ounces.
Ornaments £194 8s. 0d.[45]

There were innumerable other consignments of valuables of all sorts; and so much treasure was removed from each house that, in 1540, William Wodlow of Winchcombe found himself in trouble for spreading the story in Gloucestershire that the king had already taken two horseloads of plate from Winchcombe Abbey and that soon all mens' goods would be taken for the royal use: 'Sirs, now beware and take heed, for all will be away.'[46] The libraries of manuscripts and printed books were also dispersed soon after the dissolution of each house. Some went to the royal library and a few found their way into other collections, like some of the books from Cirencester which were taken by the royal commissioners and were later deposited in Hereford Cathedral library and at Jesus College, Oxford, or the books from Llanthony which were taken to his residence at Brockworth by the last prior, Richard Hart; these eventually found their way to the archbishop's library at Lambeth and to the Bodleian Library. Some, like the incomparable Sherborne Missal, were smuggled abroad.[47] But many beautifully illuminated missals and service books were systematically destroyed during the Protestant purges of Edward VI's reign, or perished as a result of the Act against Superstitious Books and Images of 1550, which ordered that all popish books should be 'utterly abolished, extinguished, and forbidden for ever to be used or kept in this realm or elsewhere within any of the king's dominions.' More than a century later, John Aubrey recounted the story he had been told by his grandfather of the parchment leaves of illuminated manuscripts from Malmesbury Abbey blowing through the streets of the town, and being used by brewers as stoppers for their casks and by glovers and cobblers as linings for their products, by school-boys to cover their books and by soldiers to clean their guns.[48]

Gloucester Abbey, now the Cathedral, from the east.
The Abbey, founded 679–81, was rebuilt by Serlo in 1089, dissolved but saved from destruction by its conversion to a Cathedral College in 1541.

The east walk of the cloister at Gloucester cathedral.
This was the cloister of the Benedictine abbey of St Peter, and has some of the earliest fan vaulting in England, dating from c.1360. The wealth which came to St Peter's from pilgrimages to the shrine of Edward II, enabled building work of the most lavish kind to be carried on throughout the fourteenth and fifteenth centuries.

The demolition of the monastic buildings, and especially the churches, provided an easy, instant source of ready cash, and also ensured that it would be difficult ever again to re-establish the religious communities. In particular, the lead from the roofs of churches and cloisters commanded a ready sale, as did the cut ashlar stone, the fine timbers and the metal from the bells. The work of destruction began the instant the monks and nuns departed, and it is remarkable that local people accepted the ruin of so many hallowed places and so much fine architecture with such apparent equanimity. The Carthusian house at Hinton Charterhouse provides a good example of rapid demolition. Prior Horde and his sixteen monks, after much mental anguish, surrendered their house to John Tregonwell, the king's commissioner, on 31 March 1539, and Tregonwell arranged for the site and buildings to be purchased by Walter, Lord Hungerford, of nearby Farleigh Castle. Less than three months later, however, on 24 June Lord Hungerford wrote to Cromwell to complain that, during his absence in London, another royal commissioner, Sir Thomas Arundell, had been at Hinton and

> . . . he dispoiled and carried away a great part of the church and buildings I had paid for to the King's visitor, Dr Tregonyon (Tregonwell). This will be to my great loss, unless you direct him to recompense me.

He also complained that another local gentleman, Harry Champneys of Orchardleigh, had been to Hinton with various companions and had broken down the door of the prior's cell and stolen papers, surveys and 'evidences'.[49]

At Muchelney and Montacute, the monastic churches were demolished soon after the dissolution, and at Montacute the parishioners purchased five of the priory bells for their own church.[50] The four bells and clock from the priory of Leonard Stanley were sold to the parishioners for the sum of £30.[51] The churches at Lacock, Wilton, Athelney, Abbotsbury and many other houses were likewise demolished very rapidly or the lead was stripped from the roofs, the saleable timber and good-quality stone removed, and the rest allowed to tumble into ruin. The site and buildings of the nunnery at Shaftesbury were acquired by Sir Thomas Arundell immediately after the dissolution and, since he already had a residence nearby at Wardour Castle, the lead was taken from the roofs of the nunnery buildings and they quickly became ruins. A survey of the property made in c. 1548, which includes a small sketch, shows the buildings completely ruined and they are described as 'aedificia jam prostrata sunt'.[52]

Evidence for the rapid demolition of the buildings at Cerne Abbas comes from a protracted law suit over the lands there during the 1570s. Statements were taken from elderly witnesses who had known the lands before the suppression of the abbey. They included monastic servants and others who had attended the monastery school; Henry

The Guest House, Cerne Abbas.
This fifteenth-century buiding stands on the edge of the abbey precinct and was used for the accommodation of travellers and for visitors to the abbey.

Williams stated that he had lived in the former gatehouse of the abbey for twenty years after the dissolution, while William Dyer had been a monk at the abbey and was still receiving a pension of £5 6s. 8d. per annum in 1575. All the witnesses stated that the abbey church, cloisters and domestic buildings were 'razed' or demolished, that the buildings had been used as a quarry for stone, and that the lead from the roofs had been taken away. They spoke of great quantities of stone and timber being removed from the site 'by gentlemen of the country'. The south-west gatehouse, which still exists, escaped destruction by being turned into a dwelling. The south gate was destroyed in riots during the reign of Edward VI when 200 men of Cerne rose in protest against enclosures evidently attempted by the new owners of the lands, and 'tore down the hedges about Cerne and did break or shake in pieces the south gate.'[53]

The site and buildings of the nunnery at Amesbury were acquired by Sir Edward Seymour, then Earl of Hertford and later Duke of Somerset on 22 April 1540. These included the park, gardens, orchards and fishponds, together with the great monastic church with its side chapels and huge lead roof surmounted by an octagonal steeple, sixty-one feet high, covered with lead; also the cloisters, the nuns' dining room or 'frater' and dormitory, the abbess's lodging and all the domestic buildings. Almost immediately many of the buildings were systematically destroyed for the sake of the valuable lead on their roofs, which amounted to no less than 230 fodders, or fothers, (each fodder weighing 19½ cwt.). In April 1541, during the Thursday and Friday in Easter week, gunpowder was used to bring down the spire, so that the lead could be easily removed, and within a short time most of the buildings were in ruins. The lead was sold to buyers in Salisbury, Southampton and London. Expenses included payments to William Nottingham of Amesbury for melting and casting the lead, a task which occupied him for ten weeks, payments to William Bawdewyn, for acting as night watchman to guard the valuable lead, and sundry costs of which the following provide some examples.

31 MARCH, 1541

For 2 lb of gunpowder bought at Sarum, to fire the great timber of the steeple	2s. 8d.
For 2 line cords, the one to fire the gunpowder in the steeple and the other to make fast the great gable	1s. 0d.
For the hire of Mr Bundye's horse to ride to Easton (near Pewsey) to speak with Mr Berwyk about the pulling down of the steeple	4d.
For an ox hide to make a pair of bellows to melt the lead ashes	6s. 8d.
For a load of charcoal to melt the same ashes	8s. 0d.

Stone, timber, paving slabs, gravestones, glass, doors and windows were also sold, and men were paid for demolishing the roofs of the church and other buildings.[54]

The site of Stanley Abbey was acquired by Sir Edward Baynton, who took the stone to build his large mansion some five miles away at Bromham. The abbot's house on the site was spared for a time and was still there in 1555 when it was searched for counterfeit coin-making equipment, but soon after that it too was demolished. Sir Nicholas Poyntz, who acquired the site and buildings of Kingswood Abbey, used some of the stone to build his new mansion at Newark nearly three miles away in a dramatic situation on the Cotswold escarpment. The demolition of such huge buildings and the transportation of such enormous quantities of stone and timber was a major undertaking, and at Stanley at least one man was killed in dismantling the former abbey buildings.[55]

At Winchcombe, the royal commissioners who accepted the surrender of the abbey in 1539 ordered that the abbot's lodging, with its kitchen, buttery, pantry, bakehouse and other buildings, should

Ozleworth church.
This little church on the Cotswold escarpment, with its long and complex architectural history, was one of the possessions of St Peter's abbey at Gloucester, while the lands in the parish belonged to the monks of Kingswood. At the Dissolution Ozleworth passed into the hands of the Poyntz family of Iron Acton, who used some of the stone from Kingswood abbey to build a fine mansion called Newark at Ozleworth.

remain undefaced; all else, including the monastic church, cloister, chapter house, library, dormitory and infirmary, was deemed superfluous and the lead was immediately stripped from the roofs, amounting in all to 121 'fodders'. The ten bells from the church were also sold, together with all the monastic sheep and cattle.[56]

Likewise at Hailes, the commissioners declared that the church cloisters and other monastic buildings were 'superfluous' and ordered their destruction. Sixty-nine fodders of lead were removed, five bells, jewels and 894 ounces of gold and plate, as well as vestments, copes and tunicles which were taken to London.[57] Hailes provides a good example of the sort of scramble that occurred to secure anything of value from the site of a former monastery. In 1542, the commissioners of the Court of Augmentations who had charge of the site at Hailes complained that people from all over the district, including many of the local clergy, were carrying away everything they could from the abbey buildings, including glass, iron, lead, timber, stone, locks, hinges, and woodwork. 'There be many divers spoils daily done within the said late monastery to great substance over and above these above written, but by whom it is yet unknown.'[58] One local woman, who was a servant to Robert Acton, Sheriff of Worcestershire and tenant of some of the former lands and buildings of Hailes Abbey, told the commissioners that she had seen someone come by night to her master's house bringing certain locks from the former abbey; she had rebuked her master, saying 'Alas, why do you receive this stuff?', and he replied, 'Hold thy peace, for it is there now catch that may catch.'[59] A similar situation existed at Muchelney and, when the royal commissioners surveyed the buildings immediately after the departure of the abbot and monks early in 1538, they noted that the bells and lead were valuable and 'much better because they were not easy to be alienate, sold or carried away'.[60]

The lead from the roofs of many monastic churches and cloisters was melted down into blocks and sold by the royal commissioners before the site was sold or leased by the Crown, and numerous accounts survive of the lead and bells sold or transported to Bristol and elsewhere during the months following the dissolution. Richard Paulet, the receiver of revenues for the Court of Augmentations, listed many fodders which had been taken from various monasteries. From Malmesbury came 127½ fodders which were sold for £433, from Maiden Bradley 18 fodders were sold for £60. Stanley produced 16 fodders worth £61 8s. 4d., and the small nunnery at Kington 8 fodders which sold for £5 13s. 8d. Sir Edward Baynton bought 133 fodders for his new house at Bromham; the Marquess of Northampton had 119 fodders from Hailes and 121 fodders from Winchcombe. Part of the lead from Malmesbury was purchased by the inhabitants of Poole in Dorset for covering the roof of a tower at the end of the harbour.[61] At Cirencester, all the lead from the Augustinian abbey was stripped and melted into sows in 1541, and 220 sows were delivered to Nicholas Sprake to be kept for the king's use. This was 'all the lead being sometime covered of and upon the church, cloister, and chapter house, with the aisles of the church, Our Lady Chapel, and all the gutters and covering of windows appertaining to the late dissolved monastery of Cirencester'.[62] A great deal of lead from monastic houses came down the Severn and was stored at Bristol under the charge of John Scudamore, an officer of the Court of Augmentations. More was brought overland to be stored at Bristol Castle, and some was exported to France and Spain by Bristol merchants who already dealt in small quantities of lead from the Mendip lead mines. In 1546 one of the wealthiest of the Bristol merchants, John Smythe, sold his ship *The Trinity* to the king to be used in the war against France and received in payment 100 fodders of lead.[63]

As soon as the lead was removed from the roofs of churches, cloisters and other monastic buildings, and they were exposed to wind and weather, deterioration was rapid. Local people helped themselves to stone, timber and any other useful items, so that before long even the largest and most splendid structures were turned into ruins. The bells were also a valuable item and many were taken for the Crown. Late in the reign of Henry VIII Richard Paulet still had fifty-five bells from various monastic churches, and many others had been sold and broken up for their metal.[64] The way in which the ruined abbeys and friaries rapidly became a source of stone, tiles, paving slabs and other materials can be seen in the churchwardens' accounts of churches in Bath and Bristol. At St Michael's, Bath, the churchwardens took quantities of material from the abbey over many years for the repair of the church; and in Bristol during the reign of Queen Mary, when stone altars and other furnishings which had earlier been destroyed had to be replaced in churches, numerous items were obtained from the former friaries which were now derelict and ruinous.[65]

In a few places, churches and other buildings survived because alternative uses were found for them. The abbeys at Bristol and Gloucester were converted into Cathedrals in 1542 and were consequently saved from destruction, although at Bristol the nave was undergoing reconstruction at the time of the dissolution; the work ceased in 1539 and was not completed until the late-nineteenth century. The church at Milton Abbas survived as a private chapel and the cloisters were converted into a house. Tewkesbury and Edington survived as parish churches. The survey which was made of all the buildings at Tewkesbury in 1540 shows just how splendid the whole complex was, and how much was lost with the destruction of the cloisters and other monastic buildings.[66] The church at Edington had been used both by the Bonhommes and by the parishioners, so it survived as the parish church; the monastic buildings also survived as a dwelling house until the 1590s when most of them were demolished.[67] At Bath, the king's commissioners offered the abbey church, which had recently been so splendidly reconstructed, to the mayor and citizens for 500 marks £333 6s. 8d.), but they refused to purchase it. All the glass, lead and iron was then sold and the fabric of the church was completely stripped. The skeleton which remained was sold to Humphrey Colles in 1542, and soon afterwards he sold it to Matthew Colthurst, whose son Edmund later presented it to the mayor and citizens of Bath for a parish church. After Queen Elizabeth's visit to Bath in 1574 the church was restored.[68]

At Sherborne, the townspeople bought the great abbey church from Sir John Horsey, who had acquired it at the dissolution, and they then demolished the much smaller church of All Hallows which joined the west end of the monks' church. The parish register for 1540 records the transaction; it was written by the parish priest, John Chetmill, who now found his situation transformed: whereas previously he had been a lowly figure subservient to the abbot and monks, now he alone remained, and he conducted his parochial services in the great abbey church. John Chetmill was to survive all the subsequent religious changes and remained as vicar of Sherborne until his death in c. 1566.[69] Chetmill wrote that

Woodspring Priory.
The substantial remains of the Augustinian church at Woodspring shown in a nineteenth-century illustration by J.C. Buckler. The church was converted into a house at the Dissolution, and thus remains complete with the tower. Some of the domestic buildings and the priory barn also survive.

The Feast of the Annunciation of Our Lady, . . . the year of our Lord 1540 . . . the monks being expelled and the house suppressed by the King's authority, Master John Horsey, Knight, councillor to the said King's Grace bought the said suppressed house to himself and to his heirs in fee for ever; and then the said Master Horsey, knight, sold the said church and the ground to the Vicar and parish of Sherborne for one hundred marks (£66 13s. 4d.) to them and their successors for ever, and the said vicar and parish took possession on the same day and year above said

per me Dom John Chetmill, vicar.[70]

Some monastic buildings also survived because they were turned into houses by those who acquired the property from the Crown, or they were used as farmhouses and farm buildings by tenants. Thus at Milton Abbas, Lacock, and Forde considerable parts of the monastic buildings survive. At Stavordale the church became a house, and at Woodspring the church was turned into a dwelling which survives complete with its central tower. Ivychurch was also converted into a mansion by the Earl of Pembroke and remained until 1888 when it was demolished. It was in the quiet seclusion of Ivychurch that Sir Philip Sydney is said to have composed his *Arcadia*.[71] Finally, a few monastic buildings survived because they were converted to other uses. At Cleeve and Bradenstoke the churches were demolished, but the cloister and other buildings were used as farm buildings. At Muchelney the abbot's lodging remained as a farmhouse, as did the gatehouse at Montacute, while the cloister at Sherborne became a school. The best-known example is Malmesbury, where the site and massive buildings of the abbey were purchased by William Stumpe, a wealthy clothier. This ancient Benedictine abbey was one of the most magnificent in the west of England. John Leland in *c*. 1542 described the great church and its spire which had only recently fallen.

> The abbey church, a right magnificent thing, where were 2 steeples; one that had a mightie high pyramis [steeple] and fell dangerously 'in hominum memoria' [within the memory of man], and since was not re-edified. It stood in the middle of the transeptum of the church, and was a Marke to all the country about. The other yet standeth, a great square tower, at the west ends of the church.[72]

The lead, bells and plate from Malmesbury were reserved to the king, but the suppressed abbey itself had been placed in the custody of Sir Edward Baynton, whose daughter was married to Stumpe's eldest son, James. William Stumpe was thus able to purchase the abbey together with many of its former properties from the Crown for £1,517 15s. 2½d. It was due to Stumpe that part of the nave of the huge abbey church became the parish church, to replace the old church of St Paul to the south-west of the abbey which was in a bad state of repair. The rest of the abbey church was allowed to fall into ruin, a process which would have started immediately, following the removal of the lead from the roofs.[73] Meanwhile, Stumpe himself took up residence in part of the conventual buildings, formerly part of the abbot's lodging, and, according to John Leland's well-known description, used the cloisters to house his looms.

> The whole lodgings of th'abbey be now longing to one Stumpe, an exceeding riche clothier that bought them of the King.
> This Stumpe's son hath married Sir Edward Baynton's daughter. This Stumpe was the chief causer and contributor to have th'abbey church made a parish church.
> At the present time every corner of the vast houses of office that belonged to the abbey be full of looms to weave cloth in, . . .[74]

Another clothier, Thomas Bell, similarly purchased the site of the Black Friars at Gloucester and converted the buildings into workshops for cloth manufacture. His action was particularly commended by contemporaries for the employment he provided: 'Master Bell . . . doth much good work in that town among the poor people, setting

Malmesbury abbey.
*Although the cloisters and domestic buildings have disappeared, and only part of the church has
survived, enough remains to show the size and splendour of this ancient monastery.*

many on work, above 300 daily. . . .'[75]

Meanwhile the destruction of a major house such as Glastonbury
with all its huge buildings could not of course be accomplished
quickly, and an interesting pause in the process of demolition occurred
between 1550 and 1553. Through the personal interest and interven-
tion of the Duke of Somerset, the remaining buildings at Glastonbury
were used to accommodate a party of Flemish weavers who, as
Protestants, had fled to England to escape religious persecution. More
than two hundred people arrived at Glastonbury and were encouraged and helped to set up a weaving factory in the former abbey
buildings. Sir Thomas Dyer of Westonzoyland, a gentleman of the
king's household, together with other local gentlemen, was ordered to
ensure the welfare of the Flemish weavers and to see that the buildings
were suitable for them. This interesting experiment ended abruptly
with the death of Edward VI in 1553 and the return of Catholicism
under Mary. The Protestant Flemings had to flee once more and left
Glastonbury for Frankfurt. Under Mary a proposal was made to
re-establish the monks at Glastonbury, but as was shown earlier, this
scheme did not reach fruition before the death of Mary restored the
Protestant faith in England.[76]

Chapter 8

The Dispersal of the Monastic Estates

It was not the original intention that the Crown should rapidly dispose of a substantial part of the lands of the former monasteries, and Thomas Cromwell's often-quoted boast that he would make Henry VIII the richest monarch in Christendom suggests that he envisaged the monastic estates being kept together. But the Crown's pressing need for money, especially to meet the enormous expenses of the French war of 1543–46, as well as the necessity of satisfying innumerable suitors, claimants and influential persons, made it impossible to adhere to the original policy. Professor Joyce Youings has neatly summed up this change in policy over the monastic lands.

> . . . the same combination of political and financial motives which led to their confiscation in the first place, very soon led to their alienation in return for political services or ready money.[1]

The Act for the Dissolution of the Smaller Monasteries of 1536 also set up the Court of Augmentations to control and administer the former monastic lands on behalf of the Crown, and to arrange and supervise sales or leases.

In spite of the long-winded and difficult process which the Court of Augmentations developed for the alienation of monastic properties – a process fraught with opportunities for bureaucratic delay, infuriating and often expensive for the prospective buyer – none the less by the time of Elizabeth I's death, little more than sixty years after the dissolution, a very small proportion of the former monastic lands still remained in the hands of the Crown.

Extensive research during the last few decades, especially the work of Professor Youings on the dispersal of the monastic lands in Devon and Dr Katherine Wyndham's work on Somerset, has given the lie to the traditional view that the monastic properties were either given away or sold very cheaply, and that the potential wealth which might have been derived by the Crown was wantonly squandered.[2] The notion of reckless extravagance by the Crown and of vast fortunes acquired by favoured courtiers was already a popular view by the end of the sixteenth century. The Cornish historian, Richard Carew, wrote during the reign of Elizabeth that 'the golden shower of the dissolved abbey lands rained well-near into every gaper's mouth'; and the seventeenth-century divine, Thomas Fuller, described how 'the King's servants to the third and fourth degree tasted of his liberality.'[3] In fact, it has been conclusively demonstrated that, apart from some gifts, beneficial leases or sales at bargain prices to royal servants or influential political figures whose goodwill the Crown had to ensure, most of

Edward Seymour, Duke of Somerset

The brother of Jane Seymour and thus the uncle of King Edward VI, Edward Seymour was the virtual ruler of the country during the early years of the young King's reign. A curious mixture of high ideals and sharp practice, Seymour's zeal for a reformation in religion allowed him to obtain wide-spread lands and properties following the suppression of the monasteries and chantries. He was executed in 1552.

the lands were disposed of at or near the prevailing market price. The real loss to the community was felt not so much in the substitution of gentry families for the monastic landowners, as in the failure of the Crown to use the proceeds of the sale of monastic lands for beneficial purposes. Thus, apart from the creation of six new dioceses, including Bristol and Gloucester, the opportunity for extending and improving religious provision was lost, as were the many possibilities for increasing educational endowments, or providing alms and charity for the poor. However inadequate or haphazard the monastic provision of education or alms had been, it was at least better than nothing. For the tenants of monastic lands, most of which were already leased by farmers or were administered by laymen (often by the very persons who were to acquire them at the dissolution) the change in ownership can have made little difference, and their liability for rents and tithes continued as before. Two principal sorts of people were especially well-placed to acquire former monastic lands and were the major beneficiaries of the dissolution. They were the courtiers, councillors, office-holders, royal servants and gentlemen of the King's household who had earned royal favour by their service; and secondly, gentry families, merchants, lawyers and officials in each locality who had amassed sufficient fortunes to invest in property, and many of whom were already leasing monastic lands or acting as stewards, bailiffs, auditors or receivers of rent for the monastic houses. Because of the large number of those who acquired the former monastic lands in the region during the years following the dissolution, it is not possible to refer to all of the grantees, but the following pages will attempt to give representative examples of those who profited most by the dispersal of the monastic estates. Among the first group, those close to the centre of power, one of the foremost beneficiaries was Sir Edward Seymour, successively made Earl of Hertford and Duke of Somerset. In the early 1530s he was already favoured by Henry VIII and a gentleman of the Privy Chamber, and when his sister, Jane, became queen in 1536 and he subsequently became uncle to the future Edward VI, Seymour had manors, estates and honours heaped upon him. Following the suppression of the smaller monasteries he acquired numerous manors in Wiltshire which had been part of the estates of Maiden Bradley, and the site of the abbey became the principal seat of the family.[4] Later he was granted the sites and many of the lands of Muchelney and Amesbury, some of the lands of Stanley, the estates of Easton, Monkton Farleigh and numerous other west country properties.[5] By the time of his downfall and execution in 1552 he had been granted property worth more than £2,700 per annum in Somerset alone.[6]

Sir William Herbert was also a royal servant and courtier, who rose to great wealth, power and influence through his marriage to Anne, the younger daughter of Sir Thomas Parr, controller of the household of Henry VIII. In July 1543, when Anne's elder sister Katherine became the sixth queen of Henry VIII, William Herbert became the recipient of numerous estates and honours; in 1542–3 he received the site and extensive lands of the former nunnery at Wilton, where he demolished the monastic buildings in order to erect his grand new mansion. Later he also acquired the former Augustinian house at Ivychurch as well as numerous estates in Somerset; he was knighted in 1543, made a gentleman of the Privy Chamber in 1546, and created Earl of Pembroke in 1551.

At Wilton, the ancient nunnery buildings were demolished very rapidly and a magnificent new residence was erected in their place. In 1552 the young King Edward VI was entertained at the new mansion at Wilton during his summer progress through Hampshire and Wiltshire, and early in Queen Mary's reign the Spanish ambassador praised 'the handsomeness commodyteys of Wylton, with the good appointment and good furniture thereof', as well as being greatly impressed by the lavish life-style and large number of servants and retainers who were kept. Notwithstanding his involvement with the religious changes of the reigns of Henry VIII and Edward VI, Sir William Herbert remained politically pliant and like many of those who profited from the dissolution he readily conformed to each successive change in government policy over religious matters. Thus he did not scruple to acquire former monastic land and took an active part in the suppression of the Cornish rebels in 1549; but he retained the favour of Queen Mary and was one of the four peers who gave her away at her marriage to Philip of Spain in Winchester Cathedral in 1554. Under Elizabeth he again followed the prevailing religious policy of the time.[7]

The site and many of the estates of the Augustinian canonesses at Lacock were purchased for £783 in 1540 by Sir William Sharington, who destroyed the church and carefully converted the cloisters into a dwelling house. Sharington is a good example of the clever, ruthless opportunists who achieved success and wealth by steering a skillful course through the potentially lucrative, but fearfully dangerous, conditions of his time. Coming from a Norfolk family, he greatly increased his wealth by a succession of three fortunate marriages and, as a courtier, administrator and royal servant, he was rewarded in 1546 by being made vice-treasurer of Bristol mint. In this highly-profitable position he narrowly escaped disaster when, early in the reign of Edward VI, he became involved in the power struggle between Thomas Seymour and his brother Edward, the Protector Somerset. Sharington supplied Thomas Seymour with fraudulently-produced coins below the proper weight in gold, and in 1549 he was arrested and imprisoned. Thomas Seymour was subsequently beheaded, but Sharington was released after the payment of a heavy fine. His pardon is preserved at Lacock. It is a measure of Sharington's abilities that he was able to make a convincing display of contrition, and he was even held up by Bishop Hugh Latimer in a sermon on covetousness as an example of sincere penitence.

Master Sharington, an honest gentleman, and one that God loveth. He openly confessed that he had deceived the King, and he made open restitution. . . . It is a token that he is a chosen man of God, and one of his elected.

Few who fell foul of Tudor monarchs, or who were so closely implicated in political intrigue and financial fraud, were so fortunate as Sharington. He was a man of high aesthetic standards, much interested in all the latest developments of Renaissance architecture; he retained many of the original buildings at Lacock and adroitly added elegant work of his own, including an octagonal tower containing a small banqueting room. He was also consulted by other wealthy builders in the region, including Sir John Thynne, who was engaged on far more elaborate building work on the former priory site at Longleat. Sharington died in 1553 and is buried in Lacock parish church under one of the finest early Renaissance tombs in England. Another courtier, royal servant and local administrator, Sir Edward Baynton, bought the site of the Cistercian house at Stanley near Chippenham, together with the demesne lands of the abbey in June 1537, and quickly demolished the church and most of the monastic buildings, using the stone for his new mansion some four miles away at Bromham. Among several other offices, Baynton had been vice-chamberlain to Jane Seymour during her brief period as queen, and he remained a prominent figure at Court. For long before the dissolution he had been closely involved in the administration of the estates of both Malmesbury and Stanley, and was in an ideal position to secure grants of monastic estates from the Crown. His daughter was married to the eldest son of William Stumpe, who secured the site and demesnes of Malmesbury at the dissolution.[9]

In June 1540, Forde Abbey was granted to Richard Pollard, a west-countryman who was surveyor-general of Crown lands in the west and who had been an energetic royal servant for several years. He had been greatly involved in supervising all aspects of the dissolution on behalf of the Crown, including the destruction and confiscation of the rich shrine of Thomas Becket at Canterbury, the trial and execution of Richard Whiting, Abbot of Glastonbury, and the seizure of the lands and treasures of Glastonbury and of numerous west-country monasteries on behalf of the Crown. His work for the Crown had brought him considerable wealth, and his reward was to purchase Forde Abbey and its lands worth some £42 per annum for the bargain price of £400.[10]

Another royal official, William Petre, obtained the site of Montacute in 1539.[11] Likewise, as will be shown later, royal servants such as John Tregonwell and Thomas Arundell were respectively rewarded with the abbey sites of Milton and Shaftesbury. A royal servant and courtier of a very different sort, but equally ruthless, determined and opportunist, was Sir William Kingston of Painswick. He had risen in royal favour through his skill at tournaments and jousting and his prowess as a military commander. In 1522 he had been appointed constable of St Briavel's Castle to oversee royal affairs and peace-keeping in the Forest of Dean, and in 1530 he became constable of the Tower of London where he arranged the execution of Anne Boleyn in 1536. He was granted the site and buildings of Flaxley Abbey in March 1537, and demolished part of it to enlarge the abbey grange at Littledean and create a mansion there. Later he also acquired the lands of the Benedictine priory at Leonard Stanley.[12] Sir Maurice Berkeley, a member of an ancient landholding family, was a gentleman usher of the Privy Chamber and king's standard bearer. As an influential courtier he was able to acquire the site and surrounding lands of the Augustinian abbey at Bruton. Likewise, another courtier, soldier and royal official, Ralph Hopton, obtained the site and some of the lands of the Charterhouse at Witham, and later also purchased the former Glastonbury manor of Ditcheat.

A remarkable feature of the dispersal of the monastic lands in the West Country is the number of estates which were acquired by courtiers, royal servants or office holders, who, in spite of their zeal in helping to carry out the suppression of the monasteries, nonetheless remained essentially conservative in their religious outlook. This point can be most readily illustrated by three notable examples: William Paulet, the Marquess of Winchester; Sir Thomas Arundell; and Sir John Tregonwell.

William Paulet was one of those who benefited most from the dissolution. He obtained a great estate, most of it in Hampshire, but including a grant in 1550 of the site and lands of the Bonhommes at Edington. He remained, however, conservative in his religious views and openly stated that he took the willow, not the oak, for his emblem, bowing to the prevailing winds and reaping a profit where he saw the opportunity.[13] Paulet had risen rapidly in the service of Henry VIII, holding many offices and becoming successively Master of the Wards, Controller, and later Treasurer of the Royal Household. Under Edward VI he became Lord Treasurer, and in 1551 was created Marquess of Winchester. He was involved in the harsh punishment of those who took part in the Pilgrimage of Grace in 1536 and in the persecution of those who refused to abandon Catholicism under Edward. Remarkably, however, he retained the favour of Queen Mary and of Mary's closest adviser, the Catholic Bishop Gardiner of Winchester, and entertained Mary and her husband Philip of Spain after their marriage in Winchester Cathedral in 1554. Even more surprisingly, Paulet managed to retain his office as Lord Treasurer under Elizabeth, and apparently without difficulty adapted his religious views to those of the new regime, remaining a trusted courtier until his death in 1572 at the age of 87. The Paulet family were to remain Catholics and Sir William Paulet's great mansion, Basing House in Hampshire, became a Catholic stronghold; it was sacked by the Parliamentary army during the Civil War, after a protracted siege.[14]

Sir William Paulet, first Marquess of Winchester.
Notwithstanding his religious conservatism, Paulet acquired a huge estate based on former monastic land, and openly stated that he took the willow not the oak for his emblem, and bowed to the prevailing wind. In spite of all the religious changes, he continued to hold high office under Henry VIII, Edward VI, Mary and Elizabeth.

Sir Thomas Arundell was the second son of Sir John Arundell of Lanherne in Cornwall and a member of the foremost Cornish family. He became a lawyer and rose to prominence at Court through service in the households of Wolsey and Sir Thomas More. Active in government service throughout the 1530s, he played an important role in the dissolution of the west-country monasteries. He married a sister of Queen Catherine Howard and was appointed to the highly-lucrative office of surveyor and receiver of the Court of Augmentations. By family ties and marriage he was linked to many of the peerage and the court circle, and through his family he acquired the Arundell estates around Chideock in Dorset and Wardour Castle in Wiltshire. He made the most of the many opportunities for profit which came from his various offices and commissions, and amassed a great fortune, so that he was well-placed to purchase large tracts of former monastic land, including many of the widespread lands of the nunnery at Shaftesbury. In 1544 alone, he made an enormous purchase of manors and rectories in Wiltshire, Somerset and Dorset for £2,609 1s. 1d. The following year he bought the former Shaftesbury Abbey manor of Fontmell and large areas of land around Sixpenny Handley for £1,147 3s. 7d., and in 1545 he spent £1,097 17s. on former monastic land.[15] By 1550 Arundell had over- reached himself, and found himself on the wrong side in the changing religious and political scene during the reign of Edward VI; in particular he could not sympathise with the increasingly Protestant changes in religion and could hardly conceal his support for the Cornish rebels in 1549. As a result he was executed in 1552 and his vast estates were forfeit to the Crown; they were, however, restored to his widow and son, Matthew, during Mary's reign, and the Arundell castle at Wardour remained a bastion of the Catholic faith through all the subsequent persecutions.[16]

The third example, Dr John Tregonwell, was also a Cornishman, though of a far less exalted family than Arundell. Tregonwell's career illustrates the way in which an intelligent and dedicated young man could rise from humble origins, through a university education, to a prominent position in the royal service. After schooling in Cornwall, probably through a monastic school such as that at Crantock or Glasney, Tregonwell studied law at Oxford during the years 1516–22. He then entered the service of Wolsey and became a member of that brilliant circle of young men who gathered round the all-powerful cardinal. After Wolsey's fall, Tregonwell was extensively employed upon the royal service in England and abroad, including taking a prominent role in the royal divorce proceedings during the early 1530s. He was employed by Cromwell as one of the monastic visitors during 1535, and thereafter for the next five years he was heavily involved in receiving the surrenders of monastic houses throughout the West Country. In this service he was able to secure a considerable fortune for himself, and by 1540 he was well able to afford the £1,000

The former abbey church and cloisters of Milton Abbas.

In 1540 the buildings were acquired by Sir John Tregonwell, who retained the church and converted the cloisters into his dwelling-house. Until the eighteenth century the site was surrounded by the town of Milton Abbas.

St Catherine's Chapel, Milton Abbas.

This Norman chapel stands on the hill overlooking the abbey church, and is a good example of many similar chapels built on hill-tops above numerous west-country monasteries.

which he paid for the site and estates of Milton Abbey, and subsequently to buy a good deal more monastic land in Dorset and Devon. At Milton he converted the cloisters into an elegant dwelling and established himself there as a country gentleman, living in considerable style. In 1557 he was granted a licence 'to retain during his life 30 gentlemen or yeomen over and besides those who daily attend him in his household or serve him in any office.' In spite of the fact that his fortune was based so firmly on the ruin of the monasteries, Tregonwell remained essentially conservative and Catholic in his religious sympathy. He clearly disapproved of the religious changes during the reign of Edward VI and played little part in national affairs during the reign. He retained the favour of Queen Mary, in spite of having taken part in the divorce proceedings against her mother, and he was knighted at Mary's coronation. He entered parliament in 1553 and became a member of the Queen's Council in 1554. With the accession of Elizabeth, Tregonwell retired once more to his Dorset estate and remained there until his death in 1565 when he was buried in the splendid church of the former abbey beneath an old-style altar-tomb. Many members of the wealthy family he established in Dorset remained throughout successive generations loyal to the Catholic faith in spite of all religious persecution.[17]

Although many of those who served Cromwell in suppressing the monasteries and disposing of their lands were richly rewarded, it should not be supposed that such benefits were acquired easily or without long and diligent service. Tregonwell's labours were eventually to be amply recompensed, but there were many times when he despaired and felt that he was being poorly rewarded for his endeavours. As early as February 1536, he petitioned unsuccessfully for some reward from the monastic lands now coming into the hands of the Crown and there were to be several other disappointments. In his letters to Cromwell, he lost no opportunity of reminding his master of his diligence, long journeys and arduous tasks, and of the fact that he had received little remuneration. Some of his complaints are no doubt exaggerated and there was ample opportunity for him to acquire offices, gifts and perquisites from the monastic houses he visited, but nevertheless it was only after several years of anxious waiting and repeated application that Tregonwell's endeavours were eventually crowned with the jewel of Milton.[18]

The second major group of men to secure large parts of the former monastic estates and to profit greatly from the dissolution was the many local gentlemen who were already closely involved with the administration of monastic lands, as lawyers, auditors or receivers of rents, who were already leasing monastic estates, or who had acquired sufficient wealth through trade or the professions to be able to buy land from the Crown. Many of these men were also active in the royal service at local level, as justices of the peace, mayors, aldermen, administrators or local officials. There was a large number of such men

1. The West front of Sherborne abbey.
This shows the position of the former parish church of All Hallows. When the great abbey church was acquired by the townspeople in 1540, the parish church was demolished.

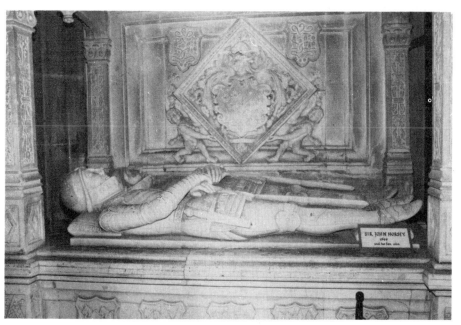

2. The Horsey tomb in Sherborne abbey.
Sir John Horsey, who died in 1546, bought the abbey and much of its property at the Dissolution, and sold the abbey church to the parishioners for £66 13s 4d. The second effigy is that of his son, also Sir John Horsey, who died in 1564.

and only a few of them can be mentioned here, but the following examples will serve to illustrate the wide differences in their background and in the sources of their wealth.

Sir John Horsey of Clifton Maybank in north Dorset was a member of an ancient county family and was very active in local affairs during the 1530s. He served on various commissions for the Crown and was sheriff of Somerset and Dorset in 1537 and again in 1544. He was steward to the lands of the monasteries of Sherborne, Athelney and Montacute, and was therefore thoroughly familiar with their nature, extent and value. He could also afford the large sums necessary to purchase some of these lands from the Crown. In March 1540 he paid £1,242 3s. 9d. for the site of Sherborne Abbey together with the demesnes, three manors and various other parcels of land. Shortly afterwards he sold the abbey church to the parishioners of Sherborne. In July 1544 he paid a further £1,451 2s. 9d. for another four manors and other lands of the Sherborne Abbey estate, and also purchased some of the lands of the Augustinian canonesses at Buckland. By the time of his death in 1546, Sir John Horsey was a major landowner in Dorset, the bulk of his estate consisting of former monastic land. Together with his son, also John (died 1564), he is buried in the former abbey church at Sherborne, the two effigies in full military armour, lying upon an old-style tomb chest.

Perhaps the best-known of local families whose future prosperity was based on the purchase of monastic land were the Horners, Thomas and his nephew John, whose good fortune is said to be the origin of the well-known nursery rhyme. Long before the dissolution the family had been tenants of Glastonbury abbey and had served the abbots in the administration of the monastic estates. During the sixteenth century they were active in local affairs and were often unpopular in consequence, as in the episode of the Taunton riot of 1536 which was mentioned in Chapter 4. Unpopularity with the rank and file was no hindrance to advancement in favour with Cromwell, however; Thomas Horner was increasingly employed on royal business in Somerset and, in spite of the long family connection with Glastonbury, he was an energetic participant in the events leading up to the execution of Abbot Whiting and his two monks. Above all, the Horners had amassed the necessary wealth to be able to take advantage of the times in which they lived and were able to find £1,831 19s. 11½d. in 1543 to buy the Glastonbury manors of Mells, Leigh-on-Mendip and Nunney – certainly a 'plum', but not dishonestly acquired as the rhyme might suggest.[20]

Others who possessed the necessary wealth and influence to purchase monastic lands were professional men, like the lawyer Richard Pate of Lincoln's Inn who was Recorder of Gloucester and acted for the Crown in surveying many of the former monastic lands in Gloucestershire. His activities brought him a large fortune, for he was able to purchase an estate at Minsterworth and also to found and

Tintern abbey church.
Soon after the Dissolution in 1536, the lead was stripped from the roofs and the site was sold to the Earl of Worcester. Because of its isolated situation, little of the stone from the church was taken for building work in the vicinity, although most of the cloister and domestic buildings were destroyed. Enough survives at Tintern to make it one of the best places in the west country to appreciate the lay-out and arrangement of a typical Cistercian house.

endow a grammar school at Cheltenham. This was placed under the care of Corpus Christi College, Oxford, which was to have a quarter of the income, 'in token of his thankful remembrance that he had been brought up heretofore in good letters.'[21]

The Bristolian, George Owen, was also well-placed to secure monastic lands through the royal favour, for he was physician to Henry VIII and acted also as physician to Edward VI and Mary. As a medical practitioner he was greatly esteemed and was left £100 by Henry VIII in his will. During the king's lifetime Owen received numerous gifts of land and he also purchased monastic lands in Bristol as well as in Oxfordshire.[22] Likewise in 1564 Queen Elizabeth's physician, Dr Richard Master, was able to purchase the site of Cirencester Abbey for £590 16s. 3d., and as a mark of her favour the queen also gave him a fine silver-gilt cup which had once belonged to her mother, Anne Boleyn, and which is now displayed in Cirencester parish church.[23]

Among merchants whose wealth enabled them to buy monastic land from the Crown, the example of William Stumpe of Malmesbury, who used many of the abbey buildings for his cloth-making business and to whose activities the survival of a part of the abbey church is due, has already been discussed in Chapter 7. Another example is the

Bristol merchant John Smythe. He amassed a great fortune in trade from the port of Bristol and used his wealth to build up a large landed estate from former monastic and chantry land. This included the house and estate at Long Ashton which had been part of Sir Thomas Arundell's estate, and which Smythe bought from the Crown in 1545 for £920, and the manor of Ashton Merrietts and the rectory of Long Ashton, formerly part of the estates of Bath Abbey which he purchased from the Crown in 1546. Like so many similar transactions at this time, Smythe paid a reasonable market price for the property he bought, for the annual value was reckoned to be £23 13s. 4d. and Smythe paid at the commonly-accepted rate of approximately twenty years' purchase, £447 6s. 0d. Later, he was to add greatly to his estate with the purchase of the lands of several dissolved chantries. John Smythe's correspondence and surviving ledger illustrate the scale of his purchases and the difficulties and bureaucratic delays which he encountered in dealing with various royal officials. In negotiating the purchase of former Church land, Smythe was greatly helped by his friendship with Dr George Owen, the royal physician. In 1548, for example, it was Dr Owen's servant who dealt with the royal officers on Smythe's behalf and represented his interests in London. He also knew how to oil the wheels of business with judicious gifts; in 1546 he sent Dr Owen a butt of sherry 'which I gave him for olde friendship', and in 1548 he instructed Owen's servant to speed one transaction, 'give you their servants somewhat to drink to make the said particulars out in a paper.'

As mayor and an active member of the ruling council of the town, Smythe was also instrumental in purchasing former Church lands on behalf of Bristol, including some of the lands of the former friaries and various former monastic properties including much land which had previously belonged to Bath Abbey. The personal estate built up by John Smythe established him as a substantial landowner, his sons were sent to Oxford and the family remained prominent, playing an important part in public life in Somerset until the twentieth century.[24] There are numerous other examples of dramatic rise to wealth, influence and gentry-status through the purchase of monastic lands. The Hippisley family were described as 'yeomen' when they leased the manor of Ston Easton from Bruton Abbey in 1525; in 1544 they purchased this and other monastic property and rapidly established themselves as one of the most wealthy and influential families in north Somerset.[25] The Bysse or Bisse family of Pensford and Stoke St Michael in north and west Somerset were clothiers, and during the early decades of the sixteenth century had made enough money to be able to take advantage of the opportunity to buy monastic land. In part their fortune rested on the export of cloth through the port of Bristol, much of it purchased for shipment by John Smythe, the wealthy Bristol merchant. Among numerous land purchases made by the family, James Bisse of Stoke St Michael bought the manor of Batcombe with its

Dunster Church.
The use of this church was shared between the parishioners, who used the nave, and the small Benedictine priory which was a cell of Bath. It was the parishioners who paid for the re-building of the tower in 1443, for which the contract survives.

fulling mills, a former Glastonbury estate in 1544. His purchases were clearly very profitable; by 1559 he had climbed so far up the social ladder that he was named as a justice of the peace and he contributed to the parish church at Batcombe in which the family is comme- morated by a fine monument.[26]

Although many of the leading men who acquired monastic lands were essentially conservative in their religious views, there were those, particularly among the local gentry families, who were enthu- siastically in favour of reform in the Church and who strongly supported the dissolution of the monasteries and friaries. Among the advocates of reform was Sir Nicholas Poyntz of Iron Acton. During the 1530s Poyntz had encouraged preachers who spread the idea of Church reform and he was noted for his advanced religious views. As steward of the abbey lands he took a prominent part in persuading the abbot of Kingswood and his monks to surrender their house in March 1538. Poyntz himself acquired the abbey site and demolished many of the buildings to use the stone on his fine new house at Newark, on the former abbey lands in the parish of Ozleworth.[27]

Even more notable exponents of reform were members of the Tracy family of north Gloucestershire. William Tracy of Toddington, who died in 1530, achieved national prominence because of the Protestant opinions expressed in his will. Tracy declared that he looked for salvation only through his faith in Christ, without need for the intercession of the Church or of prayers and masses offered on earth. In 1530 such sentiments were clearly heretical and, although by the time the will was proved Tracy's body had already been buried, he was formally declared to be a heretic and his body was dug up and burnt by the ecclesiastical authorities. William Tracy's younger son, Richard, fully shared his father's Protestant views and was able to turn these to his own advantage during the period of the suppression of the monasteries. As an executor of his father's will, as well as being a member of the Reformation Parliament, and actively agitating for an apology and recompense for the dishonour done to his father, Richard Tracy came to the notice of Thomas Cromwell and was regarded as a dependable local agent of the Crown. In 1533 Tracy was rewarded through Cromwell's influence with a lease from the Abbot of Tewkesbury of the attractive manor of Stanway, where the fine manor house and the notable monastic barn survive. He was a supporter of Hugh Latimer, the reforming Bishop of Worcester. In 1538 Tracy took part in the examination of the Holy Blood at Hailes, and it was he who took the relic to London. Bishop Latimer praised him to Cromwell

> I would wish there were many of that sort . . . He is given to hospitality . . . and he is always ready to serve the king in commissions and other ways, with most hearty fashion, according to his duty, letting for no costs nor charges at any time.

Richard Tracy was one of the royal commissioners at the surrender of both Hailes and Winchcombe, and was rewarded in October 1540 with the demesnes of Winchcombe to add to the manor of Stanway.[28] So many of those who were to rise to the top of local society and who were to become the owners of the fine country houses and elegant parklands which are such a characteristic feature of the west-country landscape, owed their advancement to the purchase of monastic lands. Such families included the Duttons, who acquired the beautiful Gloucestershire manor of Sherborne, formerly part of Winchcombe Abbey lands, and made this the centre of an estate which stretched right across the Cotswolds from Cheltenham to Oxford. Likewise, the estates of the Thynnes at Longleat, the Poyntz family at Kingswood, the Phelips at Montacute, the Rogers at Cannington, the Hoptons at Witham, the Strangways at Abbotsbury, the Pophams at Marksbury and many others were based on the acquisition of monastic lands. This social mobility meant, for example, that of the 211 leading families of Dorset at the beginning of the seventeenth century, 103, or nearly half the total number, had appeared for the first time in the ranks of the gentry between the meeting of the Reformation Parliament in 1529 and the end of the reign of Elizabeth in 1603. Many of the mansions erected by these newly risen families were built on or near the foundations of former monasteries, like those mentioned above or the houses at

Abbey Barn, Abbotsbury.
This view shows the huge interior of the Abbotsbury barn. During the Middle Ages it was even larger, and has since been reduced in length by almost one third.

The Monastic Barn, Frocester Court.
The manor of Frocester was granted to the monks of St Peter's Abbey at Gloucester early in the ninth century and remained part of the abbey possessions until the dissolution early in 1540. The huge barn (to the right of the picture) was built c1300, and is one of the finest medieval barns in England. Its size and quality reflect the wealth of the abbey and the large extent of the monastic estates.

Lacock, Wilton, Amesbury, Milton, Maiden Bradley and Forde. As a result, there are few of the spectacular monastic ruins which are such a feature of Yorkshire, and only at a few places such as Tintern in the Wye valley, Cleeve in west Somerset, in the surviving cloisters at Lacock or in the cathedrals of Gloucester and Bristol are there substantial remains of the monastic buildings. A much more wide-spread reminder of the former wealth of the monastic houses survives in the numerous barns, such as those at Abbotsbury, Tisbury, Bradford-on-Avon, Doulting, Glastonbury, Ashleworth, Frocester Court or Brockworth. Reminders of the former size and splendour of the monastic houses also survive in the large monastic precincts which remain as notable features in towns such as Cirencester, Tewkesbury, Malmesbury, Bruton, Cerne Abbas or Glastonbury. The widespread estates of the monasteries have also left their mark on place-names such as Bradford Abbas, Priorswood, Canons Marsh, Monkton Dever-ill, Monkton Combe and Monks Lane. Minchinhampton belonged to the 'Minchins' or nuns, first of Caen and later of Syon, Charterhouse on Mendip was a grange of the Carthusians at Witham, Duntisbourne Abbots belonged to St Peter's Abbey at Gloucester, and there are other similar examples.

But throughout most of the West Country the monastic houses and estates were rapidly transformed by their new owners during the sixteenth century. It was the new families who had acquired monastic lands who were to become the leaders of local society; the wealth derived from their estates enabled them to dominate the life of the region and provided the fortunes needed to build the fine mansions, manor houses and estate villages, and to lay out the parklands which remain such a common sight in the west-country landscape.

References

CHAPTER 1

1. For brief details of the west-country monastic houses and late-medieval criticisms see J.H. Bettey, *Wessex from AD 1000*, Longman, 1986, 64–75, 89–107.
2. *Somerset and Dorset Notes and Queries*, XIX, 1929, 197–201.
3. J.A.F. Thompson, *The Later Lollards*, OUP, 1965, 20– 51; K.G. Powell, 'The Beginnings of Protestantism in Gloucestershire', *Bristol and Gloucestershire Archaeological Society Transactions*, 90, 1971, 141–57.
4. A. Watkin (ed.), 'The Great Chartulary of Glastonbury', *Somerset Record Society*, 3 vols., 59, 63, 64, 1947–56.
5. G. Beachcroft & A. Sabin (eds.), 'Two Compotus Rolls of St Augustine's abbey, Bristol', *Bristol Record Society*, IX, 1938. See also Appendix IV.
6. K. Rogers (ed.), 'Lacock Abbey Charters', *Wiltshire Record Society*, 34, 1978.
7. R.H. Hilton, 'Winchcombe Abbey and the Manor of Sherborne', in H.P.R. Finberg, *Gloucestershire Studies*, Leicester University Press, 1957, 89–113; E.S. Lindley, 'Kingswood Abbey, its Land and Mills', *Bristol and Gloucestershire Archaeological Society Transactions*, LXIII, 115–41, LXIV, 36–59.
8. A. Sabin, *Bristol Record Society*, XXII, 1960, 133–40. I. Keil, 'Farming on the Estates of Glastonbury Abbey', *Dorset Archaeological and Natural History Society Proceedings*, 87, 1965, 234– 50.
9. J.W. Gough, *The Mines of Mendip*, David & Charles, 1967; M. Williams, *The Draining of the Somerset Levels*, CUP, 1970.
10. D. Knowles, *The Religious Orders in England*, CUP, III, 1971, 91–5; *Victoria County History*, Gloucestershire, II, 1907, 71.
11. E.M. Thompson, *The Somerset Carthusians*, London, 1895, 151–5, 322–3; *V.C.H.*, Somerset, III, 1911, 120.
12. J. Fowler, *Medieval Sherborne*, Dorchester, 1951, 308– 18.
13. *V.C.H.*, Wiltshire, III, 1956, 287; *Letters and Papers of Henry VIII*, IX, 160. The Bonhommes or *Boni Homines* followed the Rule of St Augustine and their life-style was similar to that of Augustinian canons.
14. G. Beachcroft & A. Sabin (eds.), *op. cit.*, 84.
15. Gloucester Public Library, *Hockaday Abstracts*, Winterborne file.
16. J.P. Traskey, *Milton Abbey*, Compton Press, 1978, 156– 7; N. Orme, *English Schools in the Middle Ages*, Methuen, 1973, 246– 7; *V.C.H.*, Somerset, II, 1911, 448; *Somerset and Dorset Notes and Queries*, III, 1892, 241–8.
17. N. Orme, *Education in the West of England 1066–1548*, University of Exeter, 1976, 4–12, 201–15.
18. N. Orme, 'A School Note-book from Barlinch Priory', *Somerset Archaeological Society Proceedings*, 128, 1984, 55–63.
19. J. Fowler, *op. cit.*, 267–8; R. Gilyard-Beer, *Cleeve Abbey*, HMSO, 1959, 16; R.W. Dunning, 'The Last Days of Cleeve Abbey', in C.M. Barron and C. Harper-Bill (eds.), *The Church in Pre-Reformation Society*, Boydell Press, 1985, 58–67; E.D.H. Williams, J. & J. Penoyre and B.C.H. Hale, 'The George Inn, Norton St Philip', *The Archaeological Journal*, 144, 1987, 317–27.
20. H. Maxwell-Lyte (ed.), 'Visitation of Religious Houses and Hospitals', *Somerset Record Society*, 39, 1924, 207–25.
21. R.W. Dunning, 'Revival at Glastonbury 1530–9', *Studies in Church History*, 14, 1977, 213–22.
22. *Letters and Papers*, Henry VIII, IV(ii), 25–6; VI, 218, 226, 304–5, 364, 374.
23. *Somerset Record Society*, 39, 1924, 207–225.

149

24. *Victoria County History*, Gloucestershire, II, 1907, 93; *L. & P. Henry VIII*, X, 382, XV, 545.
25. W.A.J. Archbold, *Somerset Religious Houses*, CUP, 1892, 55–6; T. Wright, 'Letters Relating to the Suppression of the Monasteries', *Camden Society*, XXVI, 1843, 51; *V.C.H.* Somerset, II, 1914, 141–4.
26. *Ibid.*
27. J. Fowler, *op. cit.*, 265–6; J.H. Bettey, *Wessex from AD 1000*, Longman, 1986, 105–7.
28. *V.C.H.* Gloucestershire, II, 1907, 78.
29. *V.C.H.* Somerset, II, 1914, 141, 146.
30. *L. & P. Henry VIII*, V, 322; XIII (i), 391; XIII (ii), 635.
31. G. Baskerville, *English Monks and the Suppression of the Monasteries*, Cape, 1937, 65–6; D. Wilkins (ed.), *Concilia Magnae Britanniae et Hiberniae*, 1737, III, 790–1.
32. N. Orme, *English Schools in the Middle Ages*, Methuen, 1973, 247.
33. R.W. Dunning, 'The Last Days of Cleeve Abbey', in C.M. Barron and C. Harper-Bill (eds.), *The Church in Pre-Reformation Society*, Boydell Press, 1985, 58–67.
34. J. Aubrey, *Wiltshire Collections*, (ed.) J.E. Jackson, Wiltshire Archaeological Society, 1862, 12.
35. *L. & P. Henry VIII*, IX, 228; G. Baskerville, *op. cit.*, 207.
36. The full account of this complex story is told by D. Knowles, 'The Matter of Wilton in 1528', *Bulletin of the Institute of Historical Research*, 83, 1958, 92–6.
37. J.P. Traskey, *Milton Abbey*, Compton Press, 1978, 160.
38. *L. & P. Henry VIII*, IV, 1544.
39. *L. & P. Henry VIII*, V, 1614; *V.C.H.* Somerset, II, 1911, 106.
40, *L. & P. Henry VIII*, XIII (i), 254, 391, 746, 1064; XIII (ii), 467; XIV (1), 635; *V.C.H.* Wiltshire, III, 1956, 323.
41. J. Fowler, *op. cit.*, 310–12; *L. & P. Hen. VIII*, VI, 1533; VIII, 693, 852.
42. *L. & P. Hen. VIII*, VII, 821.

CHAPTER 2

1. *L. & P. Hen. VI*, VI, 510; VII, 577; VIII, 402, 778.
2. The Commissioners' Instructions are printed before the text of the *Valor Ecclesiasticus* I; The printed edition was published in six folio volumes by J. Caley and J. Hunter, *The Valor Ecclesiasticus*, Record Commission, 1810–34. The west-country monasteries will be found in the following volumes:
Vol. I Somerset (Bath & Wells); Dorset (part of Salisbury diocese)
Vol. II Wiltshire (part of Salisbury diocese); Gloucester (part of Worcester diocese)
Unless otherwise stated, the information given throughout this chapter is derived from the *Valor Ecclesiasticus*.
3. A. Savine, 'English Monasteries on the Eve of the Dissolution', in P. Vinogradoff, (ed.), *Oxford Studies in Social and Legal History*, I, OUP, 1907; D. Knowles, *The Religious Orders in England*, III, CUP, 1971, 241–59; J. Youings, *The Dissolution of the Monasteries*, Allen & Unwin, 1971, 34–7.
4. *L. & P. Hen. VIII*, X, 1192.
5. D. Knowles, *op. cit.*, 247.
6. *L. & P. Hen. VIII*, X, 1099.
7. K.G. Powell, 'The Beginnings of Protestanism in Gloucestershire', *Bristol & Gloucestershire Archaeological Society Transactions*, XC, 1971, 141–57.
8. *Ibid.*, XII (1), 508.
9. *Ibid.*, VIII, 736.
10. The complete list can be found in *L. & P. Hen. VIII*, VIII, 149, (35–82).
11. *L. & P. Hen. VIII*, VIII, 551; IX, 383.
12. These figures are derived from A. Savine, *op. cit.*, 270–88, which remains an indispensable analysis of all the statistics in the *Valor Ecclesiasticus*.

13. Hugh Latimer, *Works*, II, (ed.), G.E. Corrie, Parker Society, Cambridge, 1845, 364.

14. R.W. Dunning, 'The Last Days of Cleeve Abbey', in C.M. Barron and C. Harper-Bill, (eds.), *The Church in Pre-Reformation Society*, Boydell Press, 1985, 58–67.

15. *L. & P. Hen. VIII*, XII (1) 4. This will be discussed in more detail in Chapter 4.

16. J.N. Langston, 'Priors of Llanthony by Gloucester', *Bristol and Gloucestershire Archaeological Society Transactions*, LXIII, 1942, 139.

17. These figures and much of the following section on monastic income is derived from A. Savine, *op. cit.*, 126f: also P.R.O. E315/397, 398, 420, 514; SC6/Henry VIII/105, 662, 7415.

18. *V.C.H. Wiltshire*, III, 1956, 313; see also P.R.O. SC6/Henry VIII/3969, 3972, E315/420, E318/18.

19. A. Savine, *op. cit.*, 131–39.

20. For details see A. Savine, *op. cit.*, 203–10; a detailed account of monastic fisheries, their management, profitability and place in monastic life can be found in C.J. Bond, 'Monastic Fisheries' in M. Aston, (ed.), *Medieval Fish, Fisheries and Fishponds in England*, BAR, 182, 1988, 69–112.

21. R.H. Hilton, 'Winchcombe Abbey and the Manor of Sherborne', in *Gloucestershire Studies*, H.P.R. Finberg, (ed.), 1957, 110–20.

22. *V.C.H. Wiltshire*, III, 1956, 237.

23. *Ibid.*, 312–3.

24. P.R.O. E315/398, f90; for an excellent account of monastic farming and estate management in the years before the dissolution see J. Youings, 'The Church', in *Agrarian History of England and Wales*, IV, J. Thirsk, ed., 1967, 306–31.

25. W.A.J. Archbold, *The Somerset Religious Houses*, CUP, 1892, 33.

26. A. Savine, *op. cit.*, 214–6; W.A.J. Archbold, *op. cit.*, 68–70.

27. R.W. Dunning, *op. cit.*, 59–61; W. Dugdale, *Monasticon Anglicanum*, 1817–30, II, 361.

28. W.A.J. Archbold, *op. cit.*, 29–33; R.W. Dunning, 'Abbey of the Princes: Athelney Abbey', in J. Sherborne & R.A. Griffiths, (eds.), *Kings and Nobles in the Later Middle Ages*, Alan Sutton, 1986, 295–303.

29. R.W. Dunning, *op. cit.*, 60–5; J. Fowler, *Medieval Sherborne*, Dorchester, 1951, 310–2.

30. R.W. Dunning, *A History of Somerset*, Phillimore, 1983, 58.

31. E.S. Lindley, 'Kingswood Abbey, Its Lands and Mills', *Bristol and Gloucestershire Archaeological Society*, LXIII, 1954, 123.

32. *V.C.H. Wiltshire*, III, 1956, 313–4; G. Oliver, *Monasticon Diocesis Exoniensis*, 1846, 338–56.

33. The accounts of St Augustine's Bristol have been printed as follows: G. Beachcroft and A. Sabin, (eds.), 'Two Compotus Rolls of St Augustine's Abbey, Bristol', *Bristol Record Society*, XXII, 1960; A. Sabin, 'Compotus Rolls of St Augustine's Abbey, Bristol, for the years 1503–4 and 1506–7', *Bristol and Gloucestershire Archaeological Society Transactions*, LXXIII, 1954, 192–207.

34. A. Sabin, *Bristol Record Society*, IX, 1938, 85.

CHAPTER 3

1. T. Fuller, *Church History of Britain*, (1655), 1837 edn., II, 214.

2. *Dictionary of National Biography*; D. Knowles, *Religious Orders in England*, III, 1967, 270–2.

3. *Ibid*.

4. J.H. Bettey, 'Sir John Tregonwell of Milton Abbey', *Dorset Natural History and Archaeological Society Proceedings*, 90, 1969, 295–302.

5. *Dict. Nat. Biog.*; W.A.J. Archbold, *Somerset Religious Houses*, CUP, 1892, 6–7.
6. D. Wilkins, *Concilia Magnae Britanniae et Hiberniae*, 4 vols., London, 1737, III, 786–91.
7. *L. & P. Hen. VIII*, IX, 1886, 42; W. Hunt (ed.), 'Two Chartularies of Bath Priory', *Somerset Record Society*, VII, 1893, lxviii–lxxi; *Somerset Archaeological Society Proceedings*, 129, 1985, 142–5.
8. *L. & P. Hen. VIII*, IX, 1886, 139.
9. *Ibid.*, 159, 167.
10. *Ibid.*, 160.
11. *Ibid.*, 160.
12. *Ibid.*, 168; W.A.J. Archbold, *op. cit.*, 38–9.
13. *Ibid.*
14. D. Knowles, *op. cit.*, 300, 481; P.R.O. SC6/Hen. VIII/3969, 3972.
15. *L. & P. Hen. VIII*, IX, 1886, 168. See also Appendix VII.
16. T. Wright, 'Letters relating to the Suppression of the Monasteries', *Camden Society*, XXVI, 1843, 65–6.
17. *L. & P. Hen. VIII*, IX, 1886, 621, 622; *Wiltshire Archaeological Magazine*, 47, 327–9.
18. *L. & P. Hen. VIII*, IX, 763, 795; W.A.J. Archbold, *op. cit.*, 53–4.
19. *L. & P. Hen, VIII*, IX, 228.
20. J. Youings, *The Dissolution of the Monasteries*, George Allen & Unwin, 1971, 153.
21. *L. & P. Hen. VIII*, IX, 1886, 280.
22. *Ibid.*, 426, 590, 685, 763, 790, 1170.
23. *Ibid*, 188.
24. *Ibid.*, 677.
25. *V.C.H.*, Glos., II, 1907, 101; *L. & P. Hen. VIII*, VIII, 79; IX, 426, 842.
26. P.R.O., SP1/89/123–35; *L. & P. Hen. VIII*, VIII, 148; K. Barker, (ed.), *Cerne Abbey Millenium Lectures*, Cerne Abbas, 1988.
27. *L. & P. Hen. VIII*, IX, 1081.
28. *Ibid.*, 1087.
29. *L. & P. Hen. VIII*, IX, 723, 1137, 1145.
30. *Ibid.*, 4, 314.
31. *Ibid.*, 934.
32. *L. & P. Hen. VIII*, VIII, 171, 747.

CHAPTER 4

1. Statutes of the Realm, III, 733, 27 Hen. VIII, c. 28. The Act is printed in J.R. Tanner, *Tudor Constitutional Documents*, CUP, 1951, 59–63, and in J. Youings, *The Dissolution of the Monasteries*, Allen & Unwin, 1971, 155–9.
2. P.R.O. E323/1(i); *L. & P. Hen. VIII*, XII(i), 143(42); XIII(ii), 457.
3. *V.C.H. Wiltshire*, III, 1956, 318–9.
4. *Dictionary of National Biography*; A.L. Rowse, *Tudor Cornwall*, Cape, 1951, 219–22.
5. R.W. Dunning, 'The Last Days of Cleeve Abbey', in C.M. Barron & C. Harper-Bill, (eds.), *The Church in Pre-Reformation Society*, Boydell Press, 1985, 58–67. Arundell's letter is printed in W.A.J. Archbold, *The Somerset Religious Houses*, CUP, 1892, 84–6.
6. The commissioners instructions are printed in J. Youings, *The Dissolution of the Monasteries*, Allen & Unwin, 1971, 160–3; see also S. Jack, 'The Last Days of the Smaller Monasteries in England', *Journal of Ecclesiastical History*, XXI, (2), 1970, 97–124.
7. W.C. Richardson, *History of the Court of Augmentations 1536–54*, Baton Rouge, 1961, 49–56.
8. P.R.O. SC12/33/37. The main findings of the commissioners are summarised in Appendix VIII.
9. *Ibid.*

10. *Ibid.*
11. D.S. Chambers, *Faculty Office Registers 1534–49*, OUP, 1966, *passim.*
12. G. Baskerville, 'The Dispossessed Religious of Gloucestershire', *Bristol and Gloucestershire Archaeological Society Transactions*, XLIX, 1927, 63–122.
    G. Baskerville, *English Monks and the Suppression of the Monasteries*, Cape, 1937, 148.
13. P.R.O. SC6/Henry VIII/7298; *Somerset Archaeological Society Proceedings*, XXXVIII, 1892, 336; LIV, 1908, 79–106.
14. *L. & P. Hen. VIII*, XIII(1), 1450. 15. *L. & P. Hen. VIII*, X, 382; XII(2), 202.
16. Quoted by W.A.J. Archbold, *op. cit.*, 56–7.
17. *L. & P. Hen. VIII*, IX, 1123.
18. *L. & P. Hen. VIII*, IX, 795; J.H. Bettey, 'Sir John Tregonwell of Milton Abbey', *Dorset Natural History and Archaeological Society Proceedings*, 90, 1968, 295–302.
19. *L. & P. Hen. VIII*, X, 800.
20. *V.C.H. Wiltshire*, III, 1956, 301.
21. P.R.O. SC6/Henry VIII/7415.
22. G.R. Elton, *Policy and Police*, CUP, 1972, 26, 112–20; J.H. Bettey, *Church and Community in Bristol during the Sixteenth Century*, Bristol Record Society, 1983, 12–15.
23. G.R. Elton, *op. cit.*, 102–5.
24. P.R.O. SP1/120; W.A.J. Archbold, *op. cit.*, 89–90.
25. W.A.J. Archbold, *op. cit.*, 87–8.

CHAPTER 5

1. W. Dugdale, *Monasticon Anglicanum*, 1817–30 edition, II, 359–60.
2. *L. & P. Henry VIII*, XIII(i) 433.
3. *Ibid.*, 505, 746.
4. J. Youings, 'The Church', in J. Thirsk, (ed.), *Agrarian History of England and Wales*, IV, 1967, 327–9; *L. & P. Henry VIII*, XIII(i), 505.
5. *L. & P. Henry VIII*, XII(ii), 744, 882.
6. A. Sabin, 'Manorial Accounts of Saint Augustine's Abbey, Bristol', *Bristol Record Society*, XXII, 1960, 16.
7. J. Youings, *op. cit.*, 328.
8. *L. & P. Henry VIII*, XIV(i), 63.
9. J. Youings, *op. cit.*, 327.
10. J.P. Traskey, *Milton Abbey*, Compton Press, 1978, 169–71.
11. K.S.H. Wyndham, *The Re-Distribution of Crown Land in Somerset 1536–72*, unpublished PhD thesis, London University, 1976, 19– 20.
12. *L. & P. Henry VIII*, XIV(i), 324.
13. *L. & P. Henry VIII*, XIII(i) 573; D. Knowles, *The Religious Orders in England*, CUP, III, 1971, 353; J. Youings, *The Dissolution of the Monasteries*, Allen & Unwin, 1971, 68–9.
14. *L. & P. Henry VIII*, XIII(i) 391; XIII(ii) 635, Appendix IV.
15. A. Watkin, 'Glastonbury 1538–9, *Downside Review*, LXVII, 1949, 437–50.
16. R. Dunning, 'Revival at Glastonbury 1530–9', in Derek Baker, (ed.), *Studies in Church History*, Blackwell, Oxford, 14, 1977, 213– 22.
17. T. Wright, 'Letters on the Suppression of Monasteries', *Camden Society*, XXVI, 1843, 236–8.
18. A. Watkin, 'Dean Cosyn and Wells Cathedral Miscellanea', *Somerset Record Society*, 56, 1941, 159–65.
19. *Ibid.*
20. W. Dugdale, *Monasticon Anglicanum*, 1817–30, II, 361.
21. *L. & P. Henry VIII*, XIII(i), 27, 42.
22. W.A.J. Archbold, *The Somerset Religious Houses*, CUP, 1892, 68–70.

23. *L. & P. Henry VIII*, XIII(i), 190(41).
24. *Ibid.*, 199, 433; Gloucester City Library, *Hockaday Abstracts*, 252, Kingswood.
25. P.R.O. Aug. Book 232/11f. 33; *V.C.H. Gloucestershire*, II, 1907, 90, the date of surrender is wrongly given in the *V.C.H.* as 10 March 1539; Gloucester City Library, *Hockaday Abstracts*, 224, Llanthony Priory.
26. T. Wright, 'Three Chapters of Letters relating to the Suppression of the Monasteries', *Camden Society*, 26, 1843, 193–6.
27. *Ibid.*, 202–3.
28. *Ibid.*, 196.
29. *Ibid.*, 198.
30. *V.C.H. Wiltshire*, III, 1956, 333–4; *L. & P. Hen. VIII*, XIII(i), 1456.
31. T. Wright, *op. cit.*, 198.
32. G.E. Weare, *A Collectanea relating to the Bristol Friars Minor*, Bristol, 1893, 67–90; *V.C.H. Gloucestershire*, II, 1907, 109–11.
33. *L. & P. Hen. VIII*, XIII(ii) 474, 482; *V.C.H. Dorset*, II, 1908, 92–4.
34. 'Wriothesley's Chronicle', *Camden Society*, N.S.XI, 1875, i, 75. P.R.O. SP1/129/120.
35. *L. & P. Hen. VIII*, XIII(i), 347; XIII(ii), 186.
36. *L. & P. Hen. VIII*, XIII(ii), 409.
37. *Ibid.*, 710, 856; *V.C.H. Gloucestershire*, II, 1907, 9809.
38. W.A.J. Archbold, *op. cit.*, 80–2, 129–31.
39. *Ibid.*; R.W. Dunning, 'The Abbey of the Princes: Athelney Abbey', in R.A. Griffiths and J. Sherborne, (eds.), *Kings and Nobles in the Later Middle Ages*, Alan Sutton, 1986, 295–303.
40. *L. & P. Hen. VIII*, XIV(i), 629.
41. *V.C.H. Wiltshire*, III, 1956, 255; *Wiltshire Archaeological Magazine*, 28, 1894–6, 288–319.
42. *L. & P. Hen. VIII*, XIII(ii), 1092.
43. *Ibid.*
44. W.A.J. Archbold, *op. cit.*, 92–5; *L. & P. Hen. VIII*, XIV(i), 324.
45. *L. & P. Hen. VIII*, XIV(i), 468.
46. *L. & P. Hen. VIII*, XIV(i), 575.
47. *L. & P. Hen. VIII*, XIV(i), 629, 664.
48. J.H. Bettey, *Wessex from A.D. 1000*, Longman, 1986, 157.
49. *L. & P. Hen. VIII*, XIV(i) 269; W.A.J. Archbold, *op. cit.*, 83–4.
50. *L. & P. Hen. VIII*, XIV(i), 145.
51. *Ibid.*; W.A.J. Archbold, *op. cit.*, 70–1.
52. E.M. Thompson, *The Somerset Carthusians*, London, 1895, 329–30.
53. *L. & P. Hen. VIII*, XIV(i), 1154; E.M. Thompson, *op. cit.*, 330–2.
54. J.H. Bettey, 'Sir John Tregonwell of Milton Abbey', *Dorset Natural History and Archaeological Society Proceedings*, 90, 1968, 295– 302.
55. *Wiltshire Archaeological Magazine*, 28, 317; 46, 1934, 421.
56. P.R.O., *Deputy Keeper's Report*, VIII, 1847, App. 2, 1– 51.
57. *L. & P. Hen. VIII*, XIV(i), 100, 324, 491.
58. *Ibid.*, 78.
59. T. Wright, 'Letters Relating to the Suppression of the Monasteries', *Camden Society*, XXVI, 1843, 236–8.
60. *Ibid.*
61. Gloucester City Library, *Hockaday Abstracts*, 208, Gloucester.
62. J. Bennett, *History of Tewkesbury*, Tewkesbury, 1830, 346–59.

CHAPTER 6

1. J. Leland, *Itinerary*, L. Toulmin Smith (ed.), 1906–8, I, 144.
2. W. Dugdale, *Monasticon Anglicanum*, 1817–30, I, 9.
3. *Letters and Papers of Henry VIII*, XIV(ii), 206.

4. *Ibid.*; Margaret Wood, 'Ashbury Manor, Berkshire', *Newbury and District Field Club Transactions*, 11: 3, 1965, 5–18.
5. P.R.O. E315/420; Dugdale, *op. cit.*, I, 10–21.
6. *Ibid.*
7. R.W. Dunning, 'Revival at Glastonbury 1530–9', in Derek Baker, (ed.), *Studies in Church History*, 14, 1977, Blackwell, Oxford, 213– 22.
8. F.A. Gasquet, *Henry VIII and the English Monasteries*, II, 1902, 327–8; *Somerset Record Society*, 55, 1940, 84–8; R.W. Dunning, *op. cit.*, 217 n25.
9. *L. & P. Hen. VIII*, XIV(i), 716; H. Ellis, (ed.), *Original Letters*, 3rd ser., III, 1846, 241–2.
10. J.R. Tanner, *Tudor Constitutional Documents*, CUP, 1951, 63–7; on the purpose and significance of this Act, see J. Youings, *Dissolution of the Monasteries*, Allen & Unwin, 1971, 81–4.
11. *L. & P. Hen. VIII*, IX, 313; XIV(i), 271. Transactions of the Newbury and District Field Club, 11, 1965, 5–18.
12. F.A. Gasquet, *op. cit.*, 337–8.
13. A. Watkin, 'Glastonbury 1538–39', *The Downside Review*, LXVIII, 1949, 437–50.
14. J. Leland, *Collectanea*, T. Hearne (ed.), Oxford, 1715, VI, 70.
15. *L. & P. Hen. VIII*, XIV(ii), 185. The complete letter is quoted by W.A.J. Archbold, *The Somerset Religious Houses*, CUP, 1892, 77–8.
16. *L. & P. Hen. VIII*, XIV(ii), 206.
17. *Ibid.*
18. *L. & P. Hen. VIII*, XIV(ii), 232.
19. *L. & P. Hen. VIII*, XIV(ii), 272, 399.
20. *Ibid.*
21. *Ibid.*
22. *Ibid.*
23. *Ibid.*, 427, 532.
24. W.A.J. Archbold, *op. cit.*, 151–2.

CHAPTER 7

1. *L. & P. Henry VIII*, XIV(i), 523.
2. *L. & P. Henry VIII*, XV, 543.
3. W. Dugdale, *Monasticon Anglicanum*, 1817–30, I, 256.
4. *L. & P. Henry VIII*, XIV(i); R.W. Dunning, 'The Abbey of the Princes', in R.A. Griffiths & J. Sherborne, (eds.), *Kings and Nobles in the Later Middle Ages*, Alan Sutton, 1986, 295–303.
5. *L. & P. Henry VIII*, VIV(i), 468; G. Oliver, *Monasticon Diocesis Exoniensis*, 1846, 338–56.
6. *L. & P. Henry VIII*, XIV(ii), 113, 660.
7. W.A.J. Archbold, *Somerset Religious Houses*, CUP, 1892, 122; *Somerset Archaeological Society Proceedings* XXXVIII, 1892, 342– 3.
8. *L. & P. Henry VIII*, XXI(ii), 775; G. Baskerville, 'The Dispossessed Religious of Gloucestershire', *Bristol and Gloucestershire Archaeological Society Transactions*, XLIV, 1927, 71; *Victoria County History, Gloucestershire*, II, 1907, 99.
9. *Victoria County History, Wiltshire*, II, 1956, 240; *L. & P. Henry VIII*, XIV(i), 597.
10. *L. & P. Henry VIII*, XIV(ii), 27, 646.
11. Gloucester City Library, *Hockaday Abstracts* (Gloucester St Nicholas); G. Baskerville, *BGAS Transactions*, XLIV, 1927, 92; Also *BGAS Transactions*, 63, 1942, 137.
12. *Somerset and Dorset Notes and Queries*, V, 1896, 268– 70, Will of Margaret Russell; *V.C.H. Dorset*, II, 1908, 90.
13. C.R. Straton, (ed.), 'Survey of the Lands of William, First Earl of Pembroke', *Roxburghe Club*, 1909, II, 487.
14. *Dictionary of National Biography; Wiltshire Notes and Queries*, IV, 1902–4, 97–107,

145–56; K.G. Powell, 'The Beginnings of Protestantism in Gloucestershire', *B.&G.A.S. Transactions*, XC, 1971, 148.

15. *V.C.H., Gloucestershire*, II, 1907, 61–5.
16. J.P. Traskey, *Milton Abbey*, Compton Press, 1978, 172; *L. & P. Hen. VIII*, XII(ii), 1008(34); *V.C.H. Wiltshire*, III, 1956, 274.
17. T. Wright, (ed.), 'Letters relating to the Suppression of the Monasteries', *Camden Society*, 26, 1843, 7–10, 58–9.
18. G. Baskerville, *B.&G.A.S. Transactions*, XLIX, 1927, 70–4.
19. J. Fowler, *Medieval Sherborne*, Longmans, Dorchester, 1951, 310–16; *Miscellanea Genealogica et Heraldica*, 2nd. Ser., II, 48; J. Hutchins, *History of Dorset*, 3rd. Edn., 1866–70, II, 248.
20. G. Baskerville, 'The Dispossessed of Gloucestershire', *B.&G.A.S. Transactions*, XLIX, 1927, 63–97.
21. J. Fowler, *op. cit.*, 316–7.
22. *L. & P. Hen. VIII*, XIV(i), 637, 1154; *V.C.H. Somerset*, II, 1911, 22.
23. G. Baskerville, 'The Dispossessed Religious', in H.W.C. Davies, (ed.), *Essays in History presented to R.L. Poole*, OUP, 1927, 454–5.
24. *V.C.H. Wiltshire*, III, 1956, 255.
25. *Ibid.*
26. See Appendix XI.
27. W.A.J. Archbold, *The Somerset Religious Houses*, CUP, 1892, 127.
28. *Ibid.*, 149.
29. G. Baskerville, *B.&G.A.S. Transactions*, XLIX, 1927, 94.
30. *Ibid.*, 149.
31. *Somerset Archaeological Society Proceedings*, XXXVIII, 1892, 340; Somerset Record Office, D/D/Ca 21, 1555–6.
32. *Historical Manuscripts Commission*, 55, (Various Collections VII), 1914, 53.
33. G. Baskerville, *op. cit..*, 84.
34. J.H. Bettey, 'Paul Bush, first Bishop of Bristol', *B.&G.A.S. Transactions*, 106, 1988–9, 169–72.
35. D. Knowles, *The Religious Orders in England*, III, 1971, 426–7; see also H. Aveling, *Ampleforth and Its Origins*, 1952, 271– 9.
36. British Library, Harleian MSS., 3881 f38b; W. Dugdale, *op. cit.*, I, 9; *Somerset Archaeological Proceedings*, XXXVIII, 1892, 338.
37. *V.C.H. Somerset*, II, 1911, 96.
38. *Somerset Archaeological Proceedings*, XXXVIII, 1892, 332.
39. P.R.O. E134/15James I/E6; I am grateful to Dr R. Dunning for drawing my attention to this reference.
40. E.M. Thompson, *The Carthusian Order in England*, 1930, 510–15.
41. J. Aubrey, *Brief Lives*, (ed.), A. Clark, OUP, 1898, I, 316.
42. T. Wright, 'Letters', *Camden Society*, 26, 1843, 258.
43. P.R.O. SC6/Henry VIII/7415.
44. W. Dugdale, *Monasticon Anglicanum*, I, 63–7; *L. & P. Hen. VIII*, XIV(ii), 232, 389, 530.
45. P.R.O. E315/494. I am grateful to Mrs Celia Bennetts for providing the reference to this survey.
46. P.R.O. SP1/157/f155.
47. C.E. Wright, 'The Dispersal of the Libraries in the Sixteenth Century', in F. Wormald and C.E. Wright, (eds.), *The English Library, before 1700*, Athlone Press, 1958, 148–75.
48. J. Aubrey, *Natural History of Wiltshire*, (ed.), K.G. Ponting, David & Charles, Newton Abbot, 1969, 78–9.
49. *L. & P. Hen. VIII*, XIV(i), 637, 1154.
50. *L. & P. Hen. VIII*, XIII(i), 42, 190(41); S.R.O. DD/PH156; P.R.O. SC6/Henry VIII/3137; *V.C.H. Somerset*, II.
51. Gloucester City Library, *Hockaday Abstracts*, 348, Leonard Stanley.
52. P.R.O. E318/2/46; *Royal Commission on Historic Monuments Dorset*, IV, 1972, 59;

C.R. Straton, (ed.), 'Survey of the Lands of William, First Earl of Pembroke', *Roxburghe Club*, 1909, II, 487.

53. P.R.O. E134/27Eliz.19; C3/184/75; C22/631/17; J.H. Bettey, 'The Dissolution and After at Cerne Abbas', in K. Barker, (ed.), *The Cerne Abbey Millenium Lectures*, Cerne Abbas, 1988, 43–53.

54. Royal Commission on Historic Monuments (England), *Churches of South-East Wiltshire*, 1987, 103–8; *V.C.H. Wiltshire*, III, 1956, 256–7; *Wiltshire Archaeological Magazine*, X, 69–82; *Wiltshire Notes and Queries*, III, 260–99.

55. P.R.O. SC6/HenryVIII/3969; 3972; *Archaeologia*, 2 ser., X, 1907, 493–520; *Wiltshire Archaeological Magazine*, XXXV, 541–81.

56. P.R.O. Aug. Office, 494/375; *Hockaday Transcripts*, 404, Winchcombe.

57. P.R.O. Aug. Office 212/102; *Hockaday Transcripts*, 228, Hailes.

58. *L. & P. Hen. VIII*, XVII, 8; British Library, Cotton Mss, Eiv, f254.

59. *Ibid.*

60. *L. & P. Hen. VIII*, XIII(i), 42.

61. P.R.O. E117/14/38; SC6/Henry VIII/7415; *L. & P. Hen. VIII*, XVII, 8.

62. P.R.O. E117/14/28, reproduced in J. Youings, *The Dissolution of the Monasteries*, Allen & Unwin, 1871, 227.

63. P.R.O. E117/14/32–40, British Library, Scudamore Papers Add. MSS, 11,041f93; J. Vanes, 'The Ledger of John Smythe 1538–50', *Bristol Record Society*, 28, 1975, 7, 16, and *passim*.

64. P.R.O. E117/14/38.

65. 'Churchwardens' Accounts of St Michael's, Bath', *Somerset Archaeological Society Proceedings*, XXVI, 1880, 113–38; J.H. Bettey, *Bristol Parish Churches during the Reformation*, Bristol Historical Association, 1979, 14–15.

66. P.R.O. E315/494. This is reproduced in Appendix XIV.

67. J.H. Bettey, *The Dissolution at Edington*, Society of Friends of Edington Priory, 1987; J.E. Jackson, 'Edington Monastery', *Wiltshire Archaeological and Natural History Magazine*, XX, 1882, 285–90.

68. W. Dugdale, *Monasticon Anglicanum*, II, 260–1; *Somerset Archaeological Society Proceedings*, XXVI, 1880, 119.

69. J.H. Bettey, *Wessex from AD 1000*, Longman, 1986, 165– 6.

70. Joseph Fowler, *Medieval Sherborne*, Dorchester, 1951, 298.

71. *W.A.M.*, 46, 1934, 433–40; R.C.H.M. *Churches of South-East Wiltshire*, H.M.S.O., 1987, 149–53. I am grateful to Dr John Chandler for information about Ivychurch.

72. J. Leland, *Itinerary*, (ed.) L. Toulmin Smith, 1906– 8, II, 24–5.

73. P.R.O. E318/1074; J. Youings, *op. cit.*, 238–43; R.H. Luce, *The History of the Abbey and Town of Malmesbury*, Malmesbury, 1979, 59–60, 69–74; *Archaeologia*, LXIV, 399–436.

74. J. Leland, *op. cit.*, 24.

75. *L. & P. Hen. VIII*, XIV, 1354(48); J. Youings, *op. cit.*, 178–9; T. Wright, *Camden Society*, 26, 1843, 198–201.

76. W.K. Jordan, *Edward VI: The Threshold of Power*, Allen & Unwin, 1970, 318–21; E. Green, 'Flemish Weavers at Glastonbury', *Somerset Archaeological Society Proceedings*, XXVI, 1880, ii, 17–22.

CHAPTER 8

1. J. Youings, 'Terms of the Disposal of the Devon Monastic Lands, 1536–58', *English Historical Review*, LXIX, 1954, 22.

2. J. Youings, 'Devon Monastic Lands', *Devon and Cornwall Record Society*, N.S. I, 1955; J.E. Kew, 'The Disposal of Crown Lands and the Devon Land Market 1536–58', *Agricultural History Review*, XVIII, 1970; K.S.H. Wyndham, 'In Pursuit of Crown Land', *Somerset Archaeological and Natural History Society Proceedings*, 123, 1979, 65– 74.

3. Richard Carew, *Survey of Cornwall*, 1769 edn., 109; T. Fuller, *Church History*, Book VI, 336.
4. *L. & P. Henry VIII*, X, 1256(5–6).
5. *D.N.B.; Wiltshire Archaeological Magazine*, XV, 189; *L. & P. Henry VIII*, XII(ii), 227; XIII(i) 575.
6. K.S.H. Wyndham, *Somerset Archaeological and Natural History Society Proceedings*, 123, 1979, 65–74.
7. *D.N.B.; V.C.H. Wiltshire*, III, 1956, 240, 294; *Wiltshire Archaeological Magazine*, 28, 1894–6, 288–319; *S.A.N.H.S. Proc.*, 123, 1979, 66; C.R. Straton, (ed.), *Roxburghe Club*, 1909, I, 2–5.
8. *V.C.H. Wiltshire*, III, 1956, 314–5; J.E. Jackson, (ed.), *Wiltshire Collections of John Aubrey*, Devizes, 1862, 91; J. Strype, *Works*, 1820–40, II, Pt. 1, 191; *Wiltshire Archaeological Magazine*, XXVIII, 315.
9. *V.C.H. Wiltshire*, III, 1956, 274; *W.A.M.*, XXXV, 1907–8, 541–81; *Archaeologia*, 2nd. Ser., X, 1907, 493f.; *L. & P. Henry VIII*, XII(i), 311(33).
10. J. Youings, 'Devon Monastic Lands', *Devon and Cornwall Record Society*, N.S. I, 1955, 13; *Archaeological Journal*, LXX, 498–9; *Dorset Archaeological and Natural History Society Proceedings*, IX, 136–46.
11. P.R.O. SC6/Henry VIII/3137f.24; *Cal. Patent Rolls*, 1555–7, 57–8; *V.C.H. Somerset*, II, 1911, 113; *V.C.H. Somerset*, iii, 1974, 214.
12. B. Watkins, *The Story of Flaxley Abbey*, Alan Sutton, 1985; Gloucester Public Library, *Hockaday Abstracts*, Flaxley.
13. *W.A.M.*, XX, 1882, 285–90; J. Kennedy, 'Laymen and Monasteries in Hampshire', *Hampshire Field Club Proceedings*, 27, 1970, 65–85.
14. J.H. Bettey, *Wessex from AD 1000*, Longman, 1986, 181– 5.
15. A.L. Rowse, *Tudor Cornwall*, Cape, 1957, 219–22; *L. & P. Henry VIII*, XVI, 379; XIX(ii), 340; XX(i), 1335.
16. *D.N.B.*; J. Bossy, *The English Catholic Community 1570–1850.* 1975, 100–3.
17. J.H. Bettey, 'Sir John Tregonwell of Milton Abbey', *Dorset Natural History and Archaeological Society Proceedings*, 90, 1968–9, 295–302.
18. *Ibid.*
19. Joseph Fowler, *Medieval Sherborne*, Dorchester, 1951, 141, 310–53.
20. K.S.H. Wyndham, *S.A.N.H.S.Proc.*, 123, 1979, 70.
21. *V.C.H. Gloucestershire*, II, 1907, 424–5.
22. *D.N.B.*; K.S.H. Wyndham, *S.A.N.H.S.Proc.*, 123, 1979, 68.
23. J. Welsford, *Cirencester*, Alan Sutton, 1987, 66.
24. J. Vanes, 'The Ledger of John Smythe 1538–50', *Bristol Record Society*, 28, 1975; J.H. Bettey, 'The Correspondence of the Smyth Family 1548–1642', *Bristol Record Society*, 25, 1982; J.H. Bettey, *The Rise of a Gentry Family, the Smyths of Ashton Court 1500–1642*, Bristol Historical Association, 1978.
25. P.R.O. SC6/Henry VIII/3137; E318/595.
26. K.S.H. Wyndham, *S.A.N.H.S.Proc.*, 123, 1979, 71; J. Vanes, *op. cit.*, 5, 93, 144, 156.
27. *L. & P. Hen. VIII*, XIII(i), 433; XII(ii), 89; Gloucester Public Library, *Hockaday Abstracts*, 252, Kingswood; K.G. Powell, 'The Beginnings of Protestantism in Gloucestershire', *Bristol & Gloucestershire Archaeological Society Proceedings*, XC, 1971, 151.
28. Catherine Davies, 'A Protestant Gentleman and the English Reformation: Richard Tracy', in *The Sudeleys, Lords of Toddington*, Manorial Society of Great Britain, 1987, 121–39; Gloucester Public Library, *Hockaday Abstracts*, 404, Winchcombe; 228, Hailes.

DOCUMENTARY EVIDENCE ON THE STATE OF THE MONASTERIES DURING THE 1530s AND CONTEMPORARY ACCOUNTS OF THE PROCESS OF SUPPRESSION

APPENDIX I

The Major Monastic Houses of the West Country

The following tables show the major monastic houses of the region and the orders to which they belonged. The figures for the net income of each house in 1535 are derived from the *Valor Ecclesiasticus*. As explained in Chapter 2, St Augustine's, Bristol and Kingswood are not included in the *Valor Ecclesiasticus* and the figures for their income are derived from other contemporary surveys of their property and wealth.

The table of net income illustrates both the great variation in wealth between the richest and the poorest houses, and also the immense fortune enjoyed by many of the monasteries of the region, especially by the ancient and well-endowed Benedictine houses. The final column lists the numbers of monks or nuns who were present at the suppression of each house. The numerous hospitals and collegiate establishments as well as a few small or subsidiary houses have been omitted from these tables. For example, Leonard Stanley, Gloucestershire, was a dependency of St Peter's, Gloucester; Cranborne, Dorset was a dependent house of Tewkesbury, and had only three monks, although like its mother house it survived until 1540.

Name	Order	Net Income in 1535	Date of Suppression	Number of Monks/Nuns at Suppression
		BRISTOL		
St Augustine's	Aug.	£670	1540	12
St James	Ben.	£57	1540	4
St Mary Magdalen	Aug. Canonesses	£21	1536	2
		*****************************		
		DORSET		
Abbotsbury	Ben.	£390	1539	10

Name	Order	Net Income in 1535	Date of Suppression	Number of Monks/Nuns at Suppression
Bindon	Cist.	£147	1539	8
Cerne	Ben.	£575	1539	17
Christchurch (formerly in Hampshire)	Aug.	£312	1539	19
Forde	Cist.	£374	1539	14
Milton	Ben.	£578	1539	13
Shaftesbury	Ben.N.	£1166	1539	57
Sherborne	Ben.	£682	1539	15
Tarrant	Cist.N.	£214	1539	14

****

GLOUCESTERSHIRE

Name	Order	Net Income in 1535	Date of Suppression	Number of Monks/Nuns at Suppression
Cirencester	Aug.	£1051	1539	18
Deerhurst	Ben.	£134	1540	5
Gloucester, St Oswald's	Aug.	£90	1536	7
Gloucester, St Peter's	Ben.	£1430	1540	36
Flaxley	Cist.	£112	1537	7
Hailes	Cist.	£3357	1539	22
Kingswood[1]	Cist.	£232	1538	13
Llanthony	Aug.	£648	1539	24
Poulton[1]	Gilbertine	£20	1539	2
Tewkesbury	Ben.	£1598	1540	30
Winchcombe	Ben.	£759	1539	18

****

MONMOUTHSHIRE (Now GWENT)

Name	Order	Net Income in 1535	Date of Suppression	Number of Monks/Nuns at Suppression
Tintern	Cist.	£192	1536	13

****

SOMERSET

Name	Order	Net Income in 1535	Date of Suppression	Number of Monks/Nuns at Suppression
Athelney	Ben.	£209	1539	9
Barlinch	Aug.	£98	1537	9
Barrow Gurney	Ben.N.	£24	1536	–
Bath	Ben.	£617	1539	20
Buckland	Aug. Canonesses	£223	1539	14
Bruton	Aug.	£439	1539	16
Cannington	Ben.N.	£39	1536	8
Cleeve	Cist.	£155	1536	17
Dunster	Ben.	£37	1539	3
Glastonbury	Ben.	£3311	1539	52
Hinton	Carth.	£248	1539	17
Keynsham	Aug.	£419	1539	11

[1] The abbey at Kingswood and the priory at Poulton were situated in detached parts of Wiltshire.

Name	Order	Net Income in 1535	Date of Suppression	Number of Monks/Nuns at Suppression
Montacute	Cluniac	£456	1539	17
Muchelney	Ben.	£447	1538	12
Stavordale	Aug.	—	1533	6
Taunton	Aug.	£286	1539	12
Witham	Carth.	£215	1539	13
Woodspring	Aug.	£87	1536	8

****

WILTSHIRE

Name	Order	Net Income in 1535	Date of Suppression	Number of Monks/Nuns at Suppression
Amesbury	Ben.N.	£495	1539	34
Bradenstoke	Aug.	£212	1539	12
Easton	Trinitarian	£42	1538	–
Edington	Bonhommes	£442	1539	13
Ivychurch	Aug.	£122	1536	12
Kington St Michael	Ben.N.	£25	1536	4
Lacock	Aug. Canonesses	£168	1538	19
Maiden Bradley	Aug.	£180	1536	8
Malmesbury	Ben.	£803	1539	22
Marlborough	Gilbertine	£30	1539	5
Monkton Farleigh	Cluniac	£153	1537	13
Stanley	Cist.	£177	1536	9
Wilton	Ben.N.	£601	1539	33

****

Ben.	=	Benedictine	Ben.N.	=	Benedictine Nuns.
Cist.	=	Cistercian	Cist.N.	=	Cistercian Nuns
Aug.	=	Augustinian	Carth.	=	Carthusians

(Source: D. Knowles and R.N. Hancock, *Medieval Religious Houses*, Longman, 1953.)

APPENDIX II

The Major Friaries and the Number of Friars at the Suppression 1538

There were far fewer friaries in the region than monasteries, and the friars were all to be found in the towns. Only in Bristol were all four major orders of friars represented. The friars were dedicated to poverty, and as is shown in Appendix IX, most of the friaries were very poor, their accommodation consisted of the bare minimum and even their churches were poorly furnished; several were in severe financial difficulty. Their suppression brought very little revenue to the Crown, and was rather designed to remove a body of preachers whose original allegiance had been to the Pope and who might have been articulate critics of the royal policy. All the west-country friaries were persuaded to surrender during the summer and autumn of 1538.

DOMINICAN

Bristol	6
Gloucester	7
Ilchester	7
Melcombe Regis	–
Salisbury	14

****

FRANCISCAN

Bridgwater	8
Bristol	6
Dorchester	7
Gloucester	5
Salisbury	10

****

CARMELITE

Bristol	4
Gloucester	3
Marlborough	5

****

AUSTIN

Bristol	8

(Source: D. Knowles and R.N. Hancock, *Medieval Religious Houses*, Longman, 1953.)

APPENDIX III

Sheep Flocks on some of the Manors belonging to the Dorset Monasteries listed in the Valor Ecclesiasticus *1535*

The Dorset entries in the *Valor Ecclesiasticus* are unique in listing the number of sheep kept by the monastic houses. Each house had many other manors where all the lands had been leased to tenants and no monastic sheep flocks were kept, but it is evident that, on the manors listed here, the large sheep flocks continued to be carefully managed and were divided into ewe, lamb, wether and hoggett or hogge, flocks. Wethers were castrated rams, kept for fattening or for folding on the arable land; hogges or hoggetts were two-year old sheep which had not yet bred. The fact that the commissioners took the trouble to list the sheep flocks belonging to the Dorset monasteries is an indication of the importance of sheep in the monastic economy, although large sheep flocks were equally important to the monasteries of Wiltshire and Gloucestershire, where the commissioners were less conscientious or interpreted their duties differently.

ABBOTSBURY

Abbotsbury	221 ewes	
	448 ewes	
	374 hoggetts	
Portesham	495 lambs	
	391 ewes	
		TOTAL: 1,929

BINDON

Burnegate & Little Bindon	368 ewes	
Woodsterte	300 ewes	
Bovington	481 wethers	
West Chaldon	389 ewes	
	655 hoggetts	
	506 wethers	
West Lulworth	500 hoggetts	
	338 ewes	
		TOTAL: 3,537

MILTON (MYDDLETON)

Myddleton	775 ewes	
	500 hoggetts	
	500 wethers	
Huish	573 ewes	
Sydling	1,060 wethers	
	587 ewes	
	460 hoggetts	
Holway	404 ewes	
Holworth	1,000 ewes	

East Ringwood	1,000 hoggetts
La Lee	470 ewes

TOTAL: 7,329

CERNE

Cerne	800 ewes
	850 hoggetts
	442 lambs
Little Bredy	500 lambs
	424 ewes
	250 hoggetts
Long Bredy	600 lambs
Winterborne	668 lambs
Nether Cerne	320 ewes
	375 lambs
Minterne	350 lambs
Mosterton	100 lambs
Milborne	350 wethers

TOTAL: 6,029

TARRANT KAINES

Tarrant	600 lambs
Keyneston	400 ewes
	500 hoggetts
Winterborne Musterton	350 ewes
Crawford Magna	160 lambs
Charleton	180 lambs
Gussage All Saints	160 lambs
Bere	600 lambs

TOTAL: 2,950

SHAFTESBURY

Barton	300 ewes
Tarrant	200 ewes 200 wethers
Donhead	250 wethers
Encombe	350 wethers
Hanley	200 hoggetts
	600 wethers
Berwick	200 wethers

TOTAL: 2,300

SHERBORNE

Corscombe	440 wethers
Wyke	190 ewes
Stawell	103 wethers
Sherborne Bertona	152 wethers

TOTAL: 885

Total number of sheep belonging to the Dorset monasteries in 1535 (excluding those on manors outside Dorset)

24,959

APPENDIX IV

Estates and Income of St Augustine's Abbey, Bristol during the Later Middle Ages

Since St Augustine's, Bristol was omitted from the *Valor Ecclesiasticus*, it is particularly useful to have detailed surveys of its properties and income at the end of the Middle Ages. This table shows the property which the monastery possessed in Bristol and the income it derived from it during 1491–2; the properties included houses, shops, inns and a water-mill. Oblations were the offerings made by visitors to the abbey, and were low in 1491–2, probably because of controversy and tension between the abbey and the townsfolk of Bristol over their respective rights, which had resulted in a lawsuit. The bulk of the abbey's income was derived from its properties in the surrounding area, and from parish churches 'appropriated' to the abbey which thus became the rector of the parish and took a considerable proportion of the tithe, appointing a vicar to attend to the spiritual welfare of the parishioners. The profits of trade included sales of malt and bread by the abbey.

	Annual Value in 1491–2		
	£	s.	d.
Property in Bristol	99	9	11½
Appropriated churches in Bristol (All Saints, St Nicholas, St Augustine the Less)	6	8	8
Oblations and fees	1	2	6½

Property in Gloucestershire

Horfield	Ham
Almondsbury	Hill
Cromhall	Stone
Arlingham	Bevington
Berkeley	Swanshunger
Blacksworth	Wanswell
Codrington	Barton Regis
South Cerney	Ashleworth

Property in Somerset

Leigh (Abbotsleigh)	Pawlett
Portbury	East Harptree
Rowberrow	Stanton Drew
Baggeridge	

Property in Dorset

Fifehead Magdalen

Property in Wales

Penarth
Peterstone

Appropriated churches

Gloucestershire

Almondsbury	Filton
Ashleworth	Horfield
Berkeley – Herons	Kingsweston
Elberton	Wapley

Somerset

Clevedon	Tickenham
Pawlett	Weare
Portbury	

Wales

Penarth	St Mellons
Peterstone	Marshfield
Rumney	

Dorset

Fifehead Magdalen

Devon

Halberton

	£	s.	d.
Annual value of manors, lands and appropriated rectories outside Bristol	595	3	10½
Profits of trade in 1491–2	65	16	2½
Total net income in 1491–2	768	1	3

(Source: G. Beachcroft and A. Sabin, eds., Two Compotus Rolls of St Augustine's Abbey, Bristol, *Bristol Record Society*, IX, 1938)

Letter from the Abbot of Athelney, Robert Hamlyn, to Thomas Cromwell,
10 April 1536

Robert Hamlyn had been a monk at the Benedictine abbey of Tavistock
in Devon and was elected abbot of Athelney in 1533. His letter to
Cromwell provides a vivid illustration of the way in which a monastic
house could get heavily into debt in spite of a net annual income of
£209. It also illustrates the financial innocence of the abbot who had
evidently hoped to clear the very large debts and financial chaos of his
house by further borrowing. The debts include payments owed to the
King, to the abbots of Glastonbury and Dunkeswell, and to local
gentlemen and merchants; there was also money due to clergy in
various abbey livings and to monastic officials and pensioners.
Another large section comprised personal debts which had been
incurred by Robert Hamlyn whilst still at Tavistock and included £40
due to the abbot of Tavistock and £20 to Hamlyn's patron, Sir William
Courtenay. Other debts to merchants and tradesmen from Taunton,
Bridgwater and Bristol suggest extravagant spending by the monastery over many years.

> Honourable and my singular good master, my duty considered, I lowly
> have me commended unto your good mastership, desiring you to be
> good master unto me and to my poor house concerning the payments of
> our debts, that I may be out of trouble and suit of the law, and I am
> contented to live as poorly as any man shall do of my degree to the intent
> that every man may be the sooner paid.
> Worshipful master, devise some means that this my petition may take
> effect and I am contented to abide your order in this behalf. I trust to
> order me and my house after such a strait fashion that I shall make
> payment of a hundred pounds every year. I have sent your mastership
> a book of debts and yearly fines that my poor house is charged with,
> which is very much. I heartily desire you to take the pains to oversee it
> and to provide some remedy, and you shall have our daily prayers as
> knoweth God who ever have you in his blessed tuition and send you
> long life.
> Written at Athelney the tenth day of April (1536) by your poor
> bedesman, Robert, Abbot of Athelney.

> If I could have a friend that would lend me iiii or v hundred pounds
> without any profit or lucre, I would gladly binde me and my house for
> the repayment of a hundred pounds yearly until the full sum be paid as
> strongly as it may be devised by the law. If I had money to make payment
> I should have much money remitted to pay the rest out of hand.

> This be owed that followeth:

	£	s.	d.
Unto the Kings Grace a hundred marks	66	13	4
Unto my Lord of Glastonbury	90	0	0
Unto the Abbot of Dunkeswell	80	0	0
Unto Master Soper of Taunton	40	0	0
Unto Master Philips of Poole	32	0	0
Unto the Vicar of More	20	0	0
Unto Master Newport of Bridgwater	27	0	0
Unto John Browne of Uffcombe	20	0	0
Unto Sir Philip Jordyne, priest	14	0	0
Unto Thomas Mord of North Curry	48	16	10
Unto Sir Richard Warre, Knight	60	0	0
Unto Sir John Curle	27	0	0
Unto one Thurstan Mede	6	13	4
Unto the church of Ilton	6	14	4
Unto Sir John Mayor, priest	6	13	4
Unto the church of Curry	9	0	0
Unto the church of Thurlaxton	5	0	0
Unto John Chapel of Glastonbury	10	0	0
Unto Master Austrayge of Bristol	8	0	0
	and odd money		
Unto Walter Young	16	0	0
Unto William Prysoe	6	0	0
Unto John Cheke	8	0	0
Unto Nicholas Browne of Taunton	42	0	0
Unto Richard Mychyll	5	13	4
Unto Robert Kene	2	0	0
Unto Joan Payne	1	3	4
Unto one Yuery	7	0	0
Unto Barnarde of Taunton	2	6	8
Unto one Moddyslye	1	2	0
Unto John Goldsmith of Taunton	2	10	0
Unto Roger Bele		17	8
Unto William Collynggs		18	0
Unto Master Smythe of Bristol	27	6	1
Unto the Prior of Taunton	10	0	0
Unto the Prior of St John's of Bridgwater	5	0	0
Unto William Harte	1	6	8
Unto John Persone	8	0	0
	and odd money		
Unto William Gredy	6	0	0
Unto Thomas Alyn	3	13	4
Unto Master Gytson	6	13	4
Unto Sergeant Thorneton his executors	7	0	0
Unto one Norman	1	13	0
Unto William Brygge	3	0	0
Unto our vicar of Wells	5	6	8
Unto one Usman		15	0
Unto Snow of Langport	3	0	0
Unto William Potter	1	0	0
Unto John Parson of Sutton	2	0	0

	£	s.	d.
Unto Master Porter of Somerton	1	0	0
Unto a furrier of Taunton	1	6	8
Unto a saddler of Taunton	2	13	0
Unto Thomas Howes		19	0

These sums following is my debts that I borrowed at my first coming to Athelney to pay my ordinary charges withall.

	£	s.	d.
Of my Lord of Tavistock	40	0	0
Of Richard Mayow of Tavistock	50	0	0
Of Sir William Courtenay	20	0	0
Of Mr Servyngton of Tavistock	13	6	8
Of John Williams of Tavistock	5	0	0

Sum Total £889 12s. 7d.

These following be the fines and pensions that our house is yearly charged withall:

	£	s.	d.
Unto my Lord Daubeny, chief steward	2	0	0
Unto my Lord Fitzwarren	2	0	0
Unto Master Secretary	2	13	4
Unto Mr Thomas Clarke	2	0	0
Unto Sir John Horsey	2	0	0
Unto Mr Phylyppes of Poole	1	6	8
Unto Mr Soper of Taunton, auditor	2	0	0
Unto Mr Cuffe, under-steward	2	0	0
Unto John Chapell of Glastonbury	2	0	0
Unto Catecote for the King's corrody	2	10	0

All those are granted by convent seal before rehearsed.

	£	s.	d.
Unto Sir John Wadham, knight	1	0	0
Unto the Sheriff	2	0	0
Unto the Escheator		16	0
Unto Mr Portman	1	6	8
Unto Mr Penny, attorney		13	4
Unto our vicar of Wells	2	13	4
Unto the vicar of Long Sutton		16	0
Unto the vicar of Lyng in money by the year	1	13	4

Unto Ambrose a singing man (who) hath by convent seal yearly £2 13s. 4d., being at liberty from the house and charged with no service

Sum Total £34 2s. 0d.

Sources: W.A.J. Archbold, *The Somerset Religious Houses*, CUP, 1892, 29–33; R.W. Dunning, The Abbey of the Princes: Athelney Abbey, Somerset, in R.A. Griffiths and J. Sherborne, eds., *Kings and Nobles in the Later Middle Ages*, Alan Sutton, 1986, 295–30.

Richard Layton to Thomas Cromwell, 7 August 1535

This letter of Richard Layton, together with his letter of 24 August 1535 which is given in Appendix VII, provides a good example of Layton's style, of his apparent contempt for the monks, his scorn of their superstitious reverence for relics, and, above all, of his determination to find faults and preferably sexual scandals which he could report to Thomas Cromwell. At Bath the Prior, Willliam Holway, was an educated man and, as shown in Chapter 3, Layton's verdict on him was quite unjust, and while there may have been sexual irregularities at both Bath and Monkton Farleigh, Layton's allegations seem wildly exaggerated. It may well have been true, however, that there were serious faults especially at the small Cluniac house of Monkton Farleigh, and we can readily believe Layton's allegations about the abuse of relics which included the *Vincula* or chains which had bound St Peter in prison and Layton seems genuinely affronted by the way in which the laity were deceived by such spurious articles. Like the heads of many other houses, the Prior of Bath was not above attempting to ensure the favour of Cromwell by gifts, and the present of hawks traded on Cromwell's well-known love of falconry. This letter, like those of Cromwell's other commissioners, reveals the almost feverish speed and energy with which the enquiry into the state of the monasteries was carried out. Whatever opinion is held on the accuracy of their verdicts, Cromwell's commissioners displayed an amazing diligence and zeal in their task, and were obviously eager to please their powerful employer and to rise in his service. The spelling in this and the following letter has been modernised.

May it may please your goodness to understand that we have visited Bath where we found the Prior a right virtuous man, and I suppose no better of his coat; a man simple and not of the greatest wit, his monks worse than any I have found yet, both in buggery and adulteries, some one of them having x women, some viii, and the rest so fewer. The house well repaired but four hundred pounds in debt. At Farleigh, cell to Lewes, the Prior had but viii whores and the rest of the monks some iiii, iii, ii as they might get them, their wills was good, the truth is the place is a very stews, and much buggery both there and at Lewes, and specially there the sub-prior as appeareth by the confession of a fair young monk, a priest, late sent from Lewes. I have matter sufficient here to bring the Prior of Lewes into great danger (if all things are true which are said). By this bringer, my servant, I send you the *Vincula* of St Peter which women of this country used to always send for in time of childbirth to put about them to have thereby short deliverance and without peril, a great relic here counted because the patron of the church is St Peter, judge you what you list but I suppose the thing to be very mockery and a great abuse that the Prior on Lammas Day should carry the same charm in a basin of silver in procession, and every monk to kiss the same after the Evangelist, with great solemnity and reverence, having therefore no manner thing to show how they first came unto it, neither having thereof no writing. You shall also receive a great comb called Mary Magdalene's comb, St Dorothy's comb, St Margaret's comb the least, they cannot tell how they came by them, neither have anything to show in writing that they be relics. Whether you will send them again or not I have referred that to your judgement and to the King's pleasure. This day we depart from Bath towards Keynsham where we shall make an end by Tuesday at night. Whether it shall be your pleasure that we shall repair unto you on Wednesday early or that we shall return towards Maiden Bradley, within ii miles whereof is a Charterhouse called Witham, and Bruton abbey vii miles from that, and Glastonbury another vii miles. What your pleasure shall be in the premises it may please you to ascertain us by this bearer, my servant. The Prior of Bath hath sent unto you for a token a leash of Irish lavers, bred in a cell of his in Ireland, no hardier hawks can be as he saith. Thus I pray God to send you as well fare as your heart desireth, from Bath, this Monday by your assured poor priest and servant.

You shall receive a book of our Lady's miracles, well able to match the Canterbury Tales, such a book of dreams as you never saw, which I found in the Library.

Richard Layton

If you tarry with the King's Grace viii days we shall despatch all the houses afore recited.

Source: *Letters and Papers, Henry VIII*, IX, 42.

APPENDIX VII

Richard Layton to Thomas Cromwell, 24 August 1535

In this letter Layton again shows his cynical contempt for the mass of so-called relics possessed by the monasteries. He also makes an interesting reference to the holy thorn of Glastonbury. The 'Gaunts' was St Mark's hospital on College Green in Bristol, the church of which survives as the Lord Mayor's Chapel. As in the previous letter, his tale of sexual irregularities and his allegations about the Prior of Maiden Bradley are, quite clearly, grossly exaggerated and seem designed for the amusement of Cromwell rather than an attempt to provide a fair picture. As before, it displays Layton's tremendous energy and eagerness to advance his career in Cromwell's service, and it is notable that this letter was written at 4 o'clock in the morning. Above all, the penultimate sentence of this letter shows the attitude which Layton and his fellow commissioners adopted towards the monks and nuns, their desperate search for scandal or irregularities, and the disappointment they felt at finding 'nothing notable'.

Please it your Mastership to understand, that yesternight late we came from Glastonbury to Bristol at St Augustines, where we begin this morning, intending this day to dispatch both this house here, being but xiiii canons, and also the Gaunts where be iiii or v. By this bringer, my servant, I send you relics, first two flowers wrapped in white and black sarcenet that on Christmas eve, at the very hour that Christ was born, will spring, bud and bear blossoms, saith the prior of Maiden Bradley. You shall also receive a bag of relics wherein you shall see strange things, as shall appear by the scripture, as God's coat, Our Lady's smock, part of God's supper, part of the stone on which Jesus was born in Bethlehem (belike there is in Bethlehem plenty of stones and some quarry there making mangers of stone). The scripture of every thing shall declare you all; and all these of Maiden Bradley, where there is a holy father Prior, and has but vi children, and but one daughter married yet of the goods of monastery, trusting shortly to marry the rest. His sons be tall men waiting upon him, and he thanks God he never meddled with married women, but all with maidens the fairest could be gotten, and always married them right well. The Pope, considering his fragility gave him licence to keep a whore, and he has good writing under seal to discharge his conscience, and Mr Underhill to be his ghostly father, and he to give him full remission, etc.

I send you also our Lady's girdle of Bruton, red silk, which is a solemn relic sent to women travailing, which shall not miscarry in childbirth. I send you also Mary Magdalen's girdle, and that is wrapped and covered with white, sent also with great reverence to women travailing, which girdle Matilda the Empress, founder of Farleigh, gave unto them, as saith the holy father of Farleigh. I have crosses of silver and gold, some which I send you not now because I have more that shall be delivered me this night by the Prior of Maiden Bradley himself. Tomorrow, early in the morning, I shall bring you the rest, when I have received all, and perchance shall find something here.

In case you depart this day, it may please you to send me word by this bringer, my servant, which way I shall repair after you. Within the Charter house have professed and done all things according as I shall disclose you at large tomorrow early. At Bruton and Glastonbury there is nothing notable; the brethren be so strait kept that they cannot offend, but fain they would if they might, as they confess, and so the fault is not in them.

From St Augustines without Bristol, this St Bartholomew's day, at iiii of the clock in the morning, by the speedy hand of your most assured poor priest.

Richard Layton

Source: T. Wright, *Letters Relating the Suppression of the Monasteries*, Camden Society, XXVI, 1843, 58–9.

*Report of the Commissioners for the Survey of the Lesser Houses in Wiltshire,
Bristol and Gloucestershire 1536*

This table gives the names of the Commissioners appointed by the
newly-formed Court of Augmentations to survey those monastic
houses in the region which were suppressed under the Act of 1536.
The details of their responsibilities are given in Chapter 4. The table
also summarises the surviving returns made by the commissioners.
The first column gives the net annual income of each house as
recorded in the *Valor Ecclesiasticus* in 1535; the second column shows
the somewhat higher valuations made by the commissioners in 1536.
Also included are the returns made by the commissioners of numbers
of 'religious', i.e. monks or nuns, their servants including those
employed on the demesne farms, the value of the most readily saleable
assets of each house, and any money owed by the monastery or due to
it. These figures are based on the full returns of the Court of
Augmentations which are in the Public Record Office SC 12/33/37.
Returns for the other monastic houses in the region which were
suppressed in 1536 do not survive.

Receivers and Auditors: Richard Paulet, John Pye, William Berners — Wiltshire
Richard Paulet, William Berners — Bristol
Richard Paulet, William Berners — Gloucestershire

Local Gentry: Henry Long — Wiltshire
Thomas White, Nicholas Thorne — Bristol
John Walshe, Edmund Tame — Gloucestershire

Name of Monastery	Valuation in V.E. 1535	Valuation in 1536	No. of Religious	No. of Servants	Value of Lead & Bells	Value of Ornaments	Value of Woods	Debts	Credits
	£ s. d.	£ s. d.			£ s. d.	£ s. d.	£ s. d.	£ s. d.	£ s. d.
Maiden Bradley	180 10 4	199 16 4	8	18	67 10 0	40 13 4	160 0 0	191 13 4	54 2 8
Monkton Farleigh	153 14 2½	195 2 8½	6	18	28 8 0	89 18 7	67 16 0	245 2 7	51 10 0
Lacock	168 9 2	194 9 2	17	42	100 10 0	360 19 0	75 14	–	–
Kington St Michael	25 9 1½	35 15 0	4	11	5 5 0	17 1 0	24 0 0	50 0 0	–
Stanley	177 0 8	204 3 6½	10	43	65 10 0	260 12 0	164 0 0	285 5 11	12 13 4
Easton Royal	42 12 0	45 14 0	2	8	6 0 0	72 3 4	17 13 4	22 2 2	–
Ivychurch	122 18 6½	132 17 10	5	17	–	183 11 0	136 4 2	–	14 10 0
St Mary Magdalen, Bristol	21 11 2	21 13 2	2	2	19 4	3 12 10	14 6 8	–	–
Flaxley	112 3 1	129 1 6½	7	18	–	69 8 6	57 0 0	17 1 4	21 8 4
St Oswald, Gloucester	90 10 2	95 2 6	7	illeg.	57 5 0	74 8 6	6 0 0	124 9 3	–

APPENDIX IX

The Surrender of the Friars

This gives three contemporary accounts of the pressure which was put upon the friars to surrender their houses and of the way in which this was accomplished. All three accounts show the poverty of the friars, the decline in contributions from the laity and the financial difficulties which they were facing. Clearly, they had little alternative but to abandon their way of life. At Gloucester the Bishop of Dover, acting as the representative of Thomas Cromwell, was obviously at pains to make it appear that the three houses of friars 'voluntarily' surrendered, even though it had been made impossible for them to continue. The friary of Carmelites or White Friars in Bristol stood near the site of the present Colston Hall. The inventory of the goods of the house reveals their extreme poverty and the paucity of their possessions which consisted of little more than a quantity of old vestments, two chalices made of copper, a few bedsteads, cupboards, a table bench and other furnishings and some pots and pans. The whole contents of the friary was worth no more than £8 2s 11d. The conduit which is referred to by the Bishop of Dover is the water supply which still flows from Brandon Hill along a channel beneath Park Street and emerges by St John's Church on the city wall.

(a) Memorandum by the mayor and three aldermen of Gloucester describing the manner in which the three friaries of Gloucester were suppressed, July 1538.

> Memorandum, this 28th day of July in the 30th year of our most dread sovereign lord king Henry the eighth, Richard, bishop of Dover and visitor under the lord privy seal for the king's grace, was in Gloucester, and there before the mayor and aldermen in the houses of friars there at two times in two days put the said friars at their liberties, whether they would continue in their houses and keep their religion and injunctions according to the same, or else give their houses into the king's hands. The injunctions he there declared among them, the which were thought by the said mayor and aldermen to be good and reasonable, and also the said friars said that they were according to their rules, yet as the world is now they were not able to keep them and live in their houses, wherefore voluntarily they gave their houses into the visitor's hands to the king's use. The visitor said to them, 'Think not, nor hereafter report not, that you were suppressed, for I have no such authority to suppress you but only to reform you, wherefore if you will be reformed according to good order you may continue for all me.' They said they were not able to continue. Wherefore the visitor took their houses and charitably delivered them and gave them letters to visit their friends and so to go to other houses, with the which they were very well content and so departed. This we the said mayor and aldermen testify by our hands subscribed.

Master William Hasard, mayor   Master William Mathew, alderman
Mr Thomas Bell the elder, alderman   Thomas Payne, alderman

(b)   Suppression of the Carmelite Friars of Bristol, July 1538.

Memorandum this 28 day of July in the 30 year of King Henry VIII,
Richard, bishop of Dover and visitor for the King's Grace being in Bristol,
brought before the mayor there iiii friars late of the White Friars there,
which confessed before the said mayor that they voluntarily did leave
their house in Bristol because they perceived that they before had divers
priors the which had sold and plundered all the jewels and substance
with the other ornaments and stuff of the house, and yet left them in debt
and no thing to live with, and considering that the charity of the people is
very small so that they cannot see how to continue and live in their
house, wherefore voluntarily they give their house into the visitor's
hands to the King's use. They also confessed that the said visitor had
given to them all their own chambers and all the books of the choir and
divers other small implements and each of them a letter and 20d in their
purses to bring them to their country, and gave them certain times to visit
their friends, and so he hath with ii honest men of the town praised all
the moveables and paid the charges and old debts and made a perfect
inventory of the stuff that is left, the custody of it with the house in the
hands of John Mercke.

> Thomas Clifton sub-prior
> Thomas Wraxall
> Simon Wagon *als* Vagan
> John Hooper

(c)   Richard, Bishop of Dover's description of the Bristol Carmelite
      Friary, July 1538.

The White Friars in Bristol, the which all that was in it is little more than
paid the debts. It is a goodly house in building, meet for a great man, no
rents but their gardens. There is a chapel and an aisle of the church, and
divers gutters, spouts and conduits of lead, the rest all tile and slate. A
goodly laver and conduit coming to it. This house was in debt above £16,
of the which paid £8, the rest discharged by pledges.

Sources: a)   T. Wright, *Letters*, Camden Society, 26, 1843, 202–3;
           b)   G.E. Weare, *Collectanea*, Bristol, 1893, 75;
           c)   G.E. Weare, *Collectanea*, Bristol, 1893, 74.

APPENDIX X

Letter to Thomas Cromwell from Thomas Arundell, 18 December 1538

This letter is particularly interesting since it gives a rare insight into the attitude of the monks and nuns to the suppression of their houses. There are few indications of whether the religious welcomed the opportunity of release from their cloisters or resented the total upheaval of their lives, but it is clear that for the nuns who had few opportunities of alternative employment, the suppression came as a total disaster. Many nuns would, inevitably, suffer much hardship and the wealthy convent of Shaftesbury was prepared to pay the large sum of 100 marks (£66 13s 4d) to the King and £100 to Thomas Cromwell if they were allowed to continue in their communal life, even in some different form. Their offer was ignored by Cromwell. It is interesting to see that the abbot of Cerne also wished for his house to continue, although his offer was likewise ignored. The letter also incidentally reveals the sort of pressure which had been put upon the abbess and nuns of Shaftesbury by Dr John Tregonwell, and the attempts which had been made to secure their 'voluntary' surrender. The writer of this letter, Thomas Arundell, was to be rewarded for his services by acquiring the site and lands of Shaftesbury, while John Tregonwell was to obtain Milton.

18 December 1538

My singular good Lord, after my lowly and most hearty recommendations, this shall be to advertise the same, that forasmuch as your good Lordship, at my departure, did by occasion ask of me whether the abbess and convent of the monastery of Shaftesbury would surrender their house unto the King's hands, whereunto I answered as I then thought, that considering the King's Highness was so liberal to all such that so would surrender, they would rather be contented to follow the more than otherwise. Nevertheless, since the coming hither of Master Dr Tregonwell, the King's Highness commissioner in that behalf, I have perceived them to be of other sort; for notwithstanding the long and earnest practising of the said Mr Doctor for their surrender, they have in right lamentable wise answered, that having the favour of the King's Majesty, they will not by any means willingly thereunto agree. Whereupon they have most heartily desired me to write unto your good Lordship, to move their petition that it might please the same to move the King's Majesty that they may remain here, by some other name and apparel, his Highness poor and true Bedeswomen, for the which they would gladly give unto his said Majesty five hundred marks, and unto your Lordship for your pains one hundred pounds. And (they) have also required me to desire your good Lordship to accept this their most humble petition in good part, and that they mean in no wise to offend the King's said Majesty on his behalf. And now, my good Lord, even so I have desired your Lordship for them, so must I and do heartily pray the same to have me excused of this my bold enterprise. But your gentle goodness always towards me hath been the cause thereof, which enforceth me thus to entrouble you. And since my coming home, the abbot of Cerne hath desired me to make the same offer, which I would be bounden to see performed also, if it may so stand with your good pleasure. As our Lord knoweth, who send your good Lordship good and long life.

From Shaftesbury, the 18th day of December.

Your Lordship's with my service,
Thomas Arundell.

Source: H. Ellis, *Original Letters*, 1846, III, 229–31.

The Surrender of the Nunnery at Shaftesbury, 23 March 1539

This example of a pension list gives a complete roll of the nuns at Shaftesbury, and illustrates the way in which the pensions were awarded by the royal commissioners. In spite of the much greater difficulties they would face in the world outside their convents, the nuns were awarded smaller pensions than most monks. The same pattern is followed, however, of awarding very high pensions, often accompanied by other perquisites, to the heads of the religious houses, and graduated pensions to the religious, depending on age, seniority and the wealth of their houses. This list of the Shaftesbury nuns also reveals their connection with many of the landowning and gentry families of the region, with names such as Zouche, Mayo, Horsey, Gerard, Lovell, Champneys, Ashley, Rogers, Ashe and Bisse representing many of the wealthiest families of the neighbouring district, some of whom were to profit greatly from the suppression of the monasteries. Dorothy Clausey who was awarded a pension of £4 13s 4d was Cardinal Wolsey's daughter.

Pensions assigned to the nuns by John Tregonwell, William Petre and John Smythe, royal commissioners.

* Elizabeth Zouche, abbess		£133 6s. 8d.		
Katherine Hall, prioress		£20 0s. 0d.		
Elizabeth Monmouth, sub-prioress		£7 0s. 0d.		
Elizabeth Bryther	£6 13s. 4d.	* Margaret Hymerford	£6 13s. 4d.
		Elsie Jakes,	
* Joanna Amys	£6 13s. 4d.	sicke & lame	£6 13s. 4d.
Philippa Cattisby	£6 0s. 0d.	Margaret Cocks	£6 0s. 0d.
* Elizabeth Godwyn	£6 0s. 0d.	* Ursula Payne	£6 0s. 0d.
* Amys Ball	£6 0s. 0d.	* Jane Farendon,	
		sicke & lame	£6 0s. 0d.
Avice Brente	£6 0s. 0d.	* Alice Champneys	£6 0s. 0d.
* Joanna Kelly	£6 0s. 0d.	Alice Payne,	
		sicke & lame	£6 0s. 0d.
Joanna Longford	£6 0s. 0d.	Edith Kemer	£6 0s. 0d.
Brigett Fauntleroy	£5 6s. 8d.	Katherine Gelise	
		or Giles	£5 6s. 8d.
Alice Baker	£5 6s. 8d.	Elizabeth Care	£5 6s. 8d.
* Joanna Benbury	£5 6s. 8d.	Jane Perceval	£5 6s. 8d.
* Margaret Mewe		* Anne Audeley	£5 6s. 8d.
or Mayo	£5 6s. 8d.		
Alice Pecocke	£5 6s. 8d.	* Elizabeth Core	£5 6s. 8d.
* Mary Cressett	£5 6s. 8d.	Juliana Burdeaux	£5 6s. 8d.
° * Joanna Towse	£5 6s. 8d.	* Anne Phillpot	£5 0s. 0d.
* Margaret Butsett	£5 0s. 0d.	* Elizabeth Ashley	£5 0s. 0d.

* Christiana Weston	£4 13s. 4d.	* Edith Magdalen	£4 13s. 4d.
* Elizabeth Horsey	£4 13s. 4d.	* Margaret Nuton	£4 13s. 4d.
* Alice Gerard	£4 13s. 4d.	* Ursula Johnson	£4 13s. 4d.
* Elizabeth Larder	£4 13s. 4d.	* Alice Rogers	£4 13s. 4d.
* Dorothy Clausey	£4 13s. 4d.	* Anne Bodenham	£4 13s. 4d.
* Elizabeth Denham	£4 13s. 4d.	* Thomasine Hussey	£4 0s. 0d.
* Alice Bonde	£4 0s. 0d.	* Elizabeth Wortheton or Wroughton	£4 0s. 0d.
Margaret Keyleway	£4 0s. 0d.	Margaret Ashe	£4 0s. 0d.
* Jane West	£4 0s. 0d.	* Katherine Hayward	£4 0s. 0d.
* Margaret Lovell	£4 0s. 0d.	* Elizabeth Babington	£3 6s. 8d.
* Margaret Frye	£3 6s. 8d.	° Alice Bisse	£3 6s. 8d.

Total sum of all yearly pensions : £431.

* = still drawing pension in Mary's reign
° = formerly a nun at Cannington, Somerset.

Source: W. Dugdale, *Monasticon Anglicanum*, 1817–30 edn., II, 474–6.

APPENDIX XII

The Collapse of Monastic Resistance: the West-Country Surrenders of January to March 1539

Many of the greatest and most ancient of the west-country monasteries which had successfully resisted all previous attempts by successive royal commissioners to persuade them to surrender, finally collapsed very rapidly, one after the other, during the early months of 1539. Many of these surrenders were received by Dr John Tregonwell, who made a remarkable sweep through the west country, starting in Wiltshire and proceeding through Somerset, Devon and Cornwall, and then to Dorset and once more into Wiltshire and Somerset. Notwithstanding all the difficulties of travel and communications, riding on horseback through the worst of the winter weather, in just over ten weeks Tregonwell received the surrender of twenty-one monasteries. It is another good illustration of the fact that those men who served Thomas Cromwell in this business and who were later to be handsomely rewarded, were obliged to work exceedingly hard for their master. At each house, Tregonwell or one of the other commissioners generally took two or three days to receive the formal surrender, allocate the pensions of the religious, arrange for particular treasures to be safeguarded or sent to London, give orders for the oversight of the buildings and the care of the demesne lands and ensure the closure of the monastery and the dispersal of its inmates. As a result of this dramatic collapse of monasticism through the region, by the spring of 1539 only a few monasteries such as Tewkesbury, Christchurch and Glastonbury remained, isolated and vulnerable, and their end was to come during the winter of 1539–40.

1539	Monastery	Order	Number of Monks/Nuns
16 January	Poulton	Gilbertine	Prior + 2 monks
18 January	Bradenstoke	Aug.	Prior + 13 canons
21 January	Lacock	Aug. canonesses	Abbess + 15 canonesses
23 January	Keynsham	Aug.	Abbot + 10 canons
27 January	Bath	Ben.	Abbot + 20 monks
1 February	Kingswood	Cist.	Abbot + 13 monks
8 February	Athelney	Ben.	Abbot + 6 monks
10 February	Buckland	Aug. canonesses	Abbess + 14 canonesses
12 February	Taunton	Aug.	Prior + 11 canons
8 March	Forde	Cist.	Abbot + 13 monks
10 March	Llanthony	Aug.	Prior + 24 canons
11 March	Milton	Ben.	Abbot + 12 monks
12 March	Abbotsbury	Ben.	Abbot + 9 monks

182

1539	Monastery	Order	Number of Monks/Nuns
13 March	Tarrant	Cist. Nuns	Abbess + 19 nuns
14 March	Bindon	Cist.	Abbot + 7 monks
15 March	Cerne	Ben.	Abbot + 16 monks
15 March	Witham	Carth.	Prior + 12 monks
18 March	Sherborne	Ben.	Abbot + 16 monks
20 March	Montacute	Cluniac	Abbot + 13 monks
23 March	Shaftesbury	Ben. Nuns	Abbess + 57 nuns
25 March	Wilton	Ben. Nuns	Abbess + 33 nuns
31 March	Edington	Bonhommes	Rector + 12 monks
31 March	Hinton	Carth	Prior + 16 monks
1 April	Bruton	Aug.	Abbot + 14 canons

APPENDIX XIII

The Last Days at Glastonbury, from the Letters of Cromwell's Commissioners

The following series of letters from Cromwell's commissioners gives a dramatic contemporary account of the end of the greatest of all the west-country monasteries, and leaves no doubt of the harsh way in which the elderly, sick abbot, Richard Whiting, and his two monks, Roger Wilfred *alias* James and John Arthur *alias* Thorne, were dealt with by the royal commissioners. The letters also reveal the admiration of the commissioners for the excellence of the buildings, treasures, grounds and estates of this wealthiest of monasteries. It was this wealth which was in large part responsible for the downfall of the abbeys, and the letter from Richard Pollard shows in the most blatant form the eager ambition of the local gentry to share in any distribution of the monastic spoils.

(a)   Richard Pollard, Thomas Moyle and Richard Layton to Thomas Cromwell, September 1539.

> Please it your lordship to be advertised, that we came to Glastonbury on Friday last past, about ten of the clock in the forenoon; and for that the abbot was then at Sharpham, a place of his, a mile and somewhat more from the abbey, we, without any delay, went unto the same place; and there, after communication declaring unto him the effect of our coming, examined him upon certain articles. And for that his answer was not then to our purpose, we advised him to call to his remembrance that which he had as then forgotten, and so declare the truth, and then came with him the same day to the abbey; and there of new proceeded that night to search his study for letters and books; and found in his study secretly laid, as well a written book of arguments against the divorce of the King's majesty and the lady dowager, which we take to be a great matter, as also divers pardons, copies of bulls, and the counterfeit life of Thomas Becket in print; but we could not find any letter that was material, and so we proceeded again to his examination concerning the articles we received from your lordship, in the answers whereof, as we take it, shall appear his cankered and traitorous heart and mind against the King's majesty and his succession; as by the same answers, signed with his hand, and sent to your lordship by this bearer, more plainly shall appear. And so, with as fair words as we could, we have conveyed him hence into the Tower, being but a very weak man and a sickly. And as yet we have neither discharged servant nor monk; but now the abbot being done, we will, with as much celerity as we may, proceed to the dispatching of them. We have in money £300 and above, but the uncertainty of plate and other stuff there as yet we know not, for we have not had opportunity for the same, but shortly we intend, God willing, to proceed to the same; whereof we shall ascertain your lordship so shortly as we may. This is also to advertise your lordship, that we have found a fair chalice of gold, and divers other parcels of plate, which the abbot had hid

184

secretly from all such commissioners as have been there in times past; and as yet he knoweth not that we have found the same; whereby we think, that he thought to make his hand, by his untruth to his King's majesty. It may please your lordship to advertise us of the King's pleasure by this bearer, to whom we shall deliver the custody and keeping of the house, with such stuff as we intend to leave there to the King's use. We assure your lordship it is the goodliest house of that sort that ever we have seen. We would that your lordship did know it as we do; then we doubt not but your lordship would judge it a house meet for the King's majesty, and for no man else; which is to our great comfort; and we trust verily that there shall never come any double hood within that house again. Also this is to advertise your lordship that there is never a one doctor within that house, but there be three bachelors of divinity, which be but meanly learned as we can perceive. And thus our Lord preserve your good lordship.

(b)   The Commissioners to Cromwell, 28 September 1539.

Pleaseth it your lordship to be advertised, that since our letters last directed unto you from Glastonbury, we have daily found and tried out both money and plate hid and mured up in walls, vaults, and other secret places, as well as by the abbot and others of the convent, and also conveyed to divers places in the country. And in case we should here tarry this fortnight, we do suppose daily to increase in plate and other goods by false knaves conveyed. And among other petty briberies, we have found the two treasurers of the church, monks, with the two clerks of the vestry, temporal men, in so arrant and manifest robbery, that we have committed the same to the jail. At our first entry into the treasure-house, and vestry also, we neither found jewels, plate, nor ornaments sufficient to serve a poor parish church, whereof we could not a little marvel; and thereupon immediately made so diligent enquiry and search, that with vigilant labour we much improved the same, and have recovered again into our hands both money, plate, and ornaments of the church. How much plate we know not, for we had no leisure yet to weigh the same; but we think it of great value, and we increase it more every day, and shall do, as we suppose, for our time here being. We assure your lordship that the abbot and the monks aforesaid had embezzled and stolen as much plate and ornaments as would have sufficed to have begun a new abbey; what they meant thereby, we leave it to your judgement. Whether the King's pleasure shall be to execute his law upon the said four persons, and to minister them justice, according to their deserts, or to extend his mercy towards them, and what his majesty's pleasure is, it may please your lordship to advertise us thereof. The house is great, goodly, and so princely as we have not seen the like; with 4 parks adjoining, the furthermost of them but 4 miles distant from the house; a great mere, which is 5 miles compass, being a mile and a half distant from the house, well replenished with great pike, bream, perch, and roach; 4 fair manor places, belonging to the late abbot, the furthermost but 3 miles distant, being goodly mansions; and also one in Dorsetshire, 30 miles distant from the late monastery. We have despatched the servants, with their half-year's wages, giving humble thanks to the King's majesty for the same; the monks also, with the King's benevolence and reward, and have assigned them pensions. We find them very glad to depart, most humbly thanking the King's majesty of his great goodness most graciously shown unto them at this time, as well for his grace's regard as for their pensions. Cattle we intend to sell for ready money; and to let out the pastures and demesnes now from Michelmas forth quarterly; until the King's pleasure be further known, to the intent (that) his grace shall lose no rent, for the abbot has much pasture ground in his hand. Other news we know none, but that almightly God have you in his tuition.

(c)   Lord Russell to Cromwell, 16 November 1539.

. . . My lord, this shall be to ascertain (you), that on Thursday the 14th day of this present month the abbot of Glastonbury was arraigned, and the next day put to execution, with two other of his monks, for the robbing of Glastonbury church, on Tor Hill, next unto the town of Glastonbury, the said abbot's body being divided into four parts, and (the) head stricken off; whereof one quarter standeth at Wells, another at Bath, and at Ilchester and Bridgwater the rest, and his head upon the abbey gate at Glastonbury. And here I do send your lordship enclosed the names of the inquest that passed on Whiting the said abbot, which I assure you, my lord, is as worshipful a jury as was charged here these many years. And there was never seen in these parts so great appearance as were here at this present time, and never better willing to serve the king. My lord, I assure you there were many bills put up against the abbot by his tenants and others, for wrongs and injuries that he had done them. And I commit Your good Lordship to the Keeping of the blessed Trinity From Wells, the 16th day of November.

Your own to command,
John Russell.

(d)   Richard Pollard to Cromwell, 16 November 1539.

Pleaseth it your lordship to be advertised, that since my last letter sent unto your lordship bearing date the 15th day of November, the same 15th day the late abbot of Glastonbury went from Wells to Glastonbury, and there was drawn through the town upon a hurdle to the hill called Tor, where he was put to execution; at which time he asked God mercy and the king for his great offence towards his highness, and also desired my servants then being there present to see the execution done, that they would be means to my lord president and to me that we should desire the king's highness of his merciful goodness and in the ways of charity, to forgive him his great offences by him committed and done against his grace, and thereupon took his death very patiently, and his head and body bestowed in like manner as I certified your lordship in my last letter. And likewise the other 2 monks desired like forgiveness, and took their death very patiently, whose souls God pardon. And whereas I at my last being with your lordship at London moved your lordship for my brother Paulett, desiring your lordship to be a means that he might have the surveyorship of Glastonbury, which I doubt not but he will use and exercise the said office to the king's most profit and advantage, and your lordship's goodness herein to him to be shown he shall recompense to his little power, I assure your lordship he hath been very diligent and divers others by his means, to serve the king at this time, according to his duty and right. So was Nicholas Fitz-James, John Sydenham and Thomas Horner, your servants. Also this is to advertise your lordship that the late abbot of Glastonbury, afore his execution, was examined upon divers articles and interrogatories to him ministered by me, but he could accuse no man but himself of any offence against the king's highness, nor he would confess no more gold nor silver nor any other thing more than he did afore your lordship in the Tower. My Lord Russell taketh his journey this present day from Wells towards London. I suppose it will be near Christmas before I shall have surveyed the lands at Glastonbury, and taken the audit there. Other news I know none, as knoweth God, who ever preserve your lordship. From Wells, the 16th day of November.

Your assured to command,
Richard Pollard.

Sources: a) *L. & P. Hen. VIII*, XIV(ii), 232.
          b) *L. & P. Hen. VIII*, XIV(ii), 272.
          c) *L. & P. Hen. VIII*, XIV(ii), 530.
          d) *L. & P. Hen. VIII*, XIV(ii), 531.

APPENDIX XIV

The Buildings and Possessions of Tewkesbury Abbey at the Suppression

These extracts from a survey of Tewkesbury Abbey made immediately after the Suppression, illustrate the extent of the buildings, the splendour of the furnishings and the vast wealth of a typical Benedictine monastery. They also reveal the grandeur of the separate establishment kept by the abbot. The last abbot, John Wakeham, received the large pension of £266 13s. 4d. per annum; in 1541 he was consecrated bishop of the newly-founded diocese of Gloucester. Thirty-six monks received pensions, and wages were paid to 144 servants. The commissioners were at pains to list the silver, jewels, treasures, vestments, bells and lead since these were the most readily saleable items. A fodder or fother of lead weighed 19½ hundredweights. Although the commissioners regarded the great abbey as 'superfluous', part of it had for long been used for parochial worship so that it was not totally demolished like the cloisters and most of the other buildings of the abbey, but it was purchased by the parishioners of Tewkesbury for £453 and remains as a powerful reminder of the splendour of monastic architecture and of how much has been destroyed.

Tewkesbury late Monastery
Surrendered to the use of the King's Majesty and of his heir and successors for ever . . . 9 January 31 Henry VIII(1540).

The clear yearly value of all the possessions belonging to the said monastery   £1,195 15s. 6½d.

Pensions assigned to the Abbot   £266 13s. 4d. per annum
Pensions assigned to 38 monks, in total   £284 13s. 4d. per annum

Records and Evidences belonging to the said late monastery remain in the Treasury there under the custody of John Whittingdon, Knight. The keys whereof be delivered to Richard Poulet, receiver.

Houses and Buildings
Assigned to remain undefaced
The lodging called the New Walke leading from the gate to the late Abbot's lodging, with buttery, pantry, cellar, kitchen, larder and pastry there adjoining.
The late Abbot's lodging
The hostery
The great Gate entering into the Court with the lodging over the same
The Abbot's stable, bakehouse, brewhouse, slaughterhouse
The Almery barn
The Dairyhouse
The great barn
The maltinghouse with the garner in the same

The ox house in the barton
The barton gate and the lodging over the same

Deemed to be superfluous
The Church with chapels, cloister, chapter house, misericord, the ii
dormitories
The Infirmary with chapels and lodgings within the same
The convent kitchen
The library
The old Hostery
The chamberer's lodging
The new hall
The old parlour adjoining to the Abbot's lodging
The cellarer's lodging
The poultry house
The garner
The almery

Lead remaining
The quire aisles and chapels
The cloister, chapter house, frater   } 180 fodders
St Michael's chapel
Hall, fermery and gatehouse

Bells In the steeple there viii

Jewels to the use of the King's Majesty
ii Mitres garnished with silver gilt, ragged pearls and counterfeit
stones

Plate to the same use
Silver gilt   329 ounces
Silver parcel gilt   605 ounces   } 1,431 ounces
Silver white   497 ounces

Ornaments reserved to the same use
One cope of silver tissue with one chasuble and one tunicle of the
same
One cope of gold tissue with one chasuble and tunicle of the same

Source: P.R.O. E315/494.

APPENDIX XV

The Surrender of Christchurch, 28 November 1539

The following letter was written from Christchurch on 2 December 1539 by the five royal commissioners who received the surrender. The abbey church which they describe survives because it was granted to the parishioners in 1540. The commissioners also describe the prior's lodging with its hall, buttery, pantry, kitchens and lodgings, the cloister, chapter house and all the domestic buildings of the abbey. The lead on the church and other buildings they estimated at 38 fodders (or 741 cwts.), there were seven bells, 26 ounces of gold plate, 1,907½ ounces of silver plate, and other ornaments worth £177 0s. 10d. The gold and silver was reserved for the King. Raynolde or Reginald Pole who is referred to and whose mother's tomb was defaced by the commissioners was a prominent churchman and an outspoken critic of the religious policies of his cousin, Henry VIII. He had incurred the King's wrath through his support for Catholicism and had fled abroad to escape persecution. He was to return as a cardinal and was made archbishop of Canterbury during the restoration of Catholicism during the reign of Queen Mary. The prior, John Draper, was granted a pension of £133 6s. 8d. *per annum* together with the mansion house at Somerford Grange for his lifetime. At the time of the suppression the net annual income of the house was £519 3s. 6½d. The community consisted of a prior, sub-prior and seventeen canons, all of whom received pensions.

We found the prior a very honest conformable person, and the house well furnished with jewels and plate whereof some be mete for the king's majestie in use, as a little chalice of gold, a goodly large cross double gilt, with the foot garnished and with stone and pearl; two goodly basons double gilt. And there be also other things of silver right honest and of good value as well for the church use as for the table reserved and kept for the king's use. In the church we find a chapel and monument curiously made of Caen stone prepared by the late mother of Raynold Pole for her burial which we have caused to be defaced and all the arms and badges clearly to be delete. The surveying of the demesnes of this house which be large and barren and some part thereof xx miles from the monastery which we also survey and measure hath caused us to make longer abode at this place than we intended.

Source: *Victoria County History, Hampshire*, II, 1903, 159.

Select Bibliography

(A comprehensive list of sources is contained in the Notes to each Chapter)

ARCHBOLD, W.A.J.   *The Somerset Religious Houses*, CUP, 1892.

ASTON, M. (ed.)   *The Medieval Landscape of Somerset*, Somerset County Council, 1988.

BARKER, K. (ed.)   *The Cerne Abbey Millenium Lectures*, Cerne Abbas, 1988.

BASKERVILLE, G.   'The Dispossessed Religious of Gloucestershire', *Bristol & Gloucestershire Archaeological Society Transactions*, XLIX, 1927, 63–122; *English Monks and the Suppression of the Monasteries*, Cape, 1937.

BEACHCROFT, G. & SABIN, A. (eds.)   Two Compotus Rolls of St Augustine's Abbey, Bristol, *Bristol Record Society*, IX, 1938.

BETTEY, J.H.   'Sir John Tregonwell of Milton Abbey', *Dorset Natural History & Archaeological Society Proceedings*, 90, 1968–9, 295–303; *Wessex from AD1000*, Longman, 1986.

BOND, J.   'Monastic Fisheries', in M. Aston (ed.), *Medieval Fish, Fisheries and Fishponds in England*, BAR British Series, 182, 1988, 69–122.

DUNNING, R.W.   'Revival at Glastonbury', *Studies in Church History* 14, 1977, 213–22; 'The Last Days of Cleeve Abbey', in C.M. Barron & C. Harper-Bill, (eds.), *The Church in Pre-Reformation Society*, Boydell Press, 1985, 58–67; 'The Abbey of the Princes: Athelney Abbey', in R.A. Griffiths & J. Sherborne, (eds.), *Kings and Nobles in the Later Middle Ages*, Alan Sutton, 1986, 295–303.

FOWLER, J.   *Medieval Sherborne*, Longmans, Dorchester, 1951.

KNOWLES, D.   *The Religious Orders in England*, III, CUP 2nd. Edn. 1971.

KNOWLES, D. & HADCOCK, R.N.   *Religious Houses in England and Wales*, Longman, 1953.

SABIN, A. (ed.)   'Some Manorial Accounts of St Augustine's Abbey, Bristol', *Bristol Record Society*, 22, 1960.

THOMPSON, E.M.   *A History of the Somerset Carthusians*, London, 1895.

TRASKEY, J.P.

Milton Abbey: A Dorset Monastery in the Middle Ages, Compton Press, Tisbury, 1978.

VICTORIA COUNTY HISTORY

Dorset	II, 1908
Gloucestershire	II, 1907
Hampshire	II, 1903
Somerset	II, 1914
Wiltshire	II, 1956

WYNDHAM, K.S.H.

'In Pursuit of Crown Land: The Initial Recipients of Somerset Property in the Mid-Tudor Period', *Somerset Archaeological Society Proceedings*, 123, 1979, 65–74; 'Crown Land and Royal Patronage in Mid-Sixteenth Century England', *Journal of British Studies*, 19, 1980, 18–34.

YOUINGS, J.

'Landlords in England: The Church', in J. Thirsk, (ed.), *The Agrarian History of England & Wales*, IV, 1500–1640, CUP, 1967; *The Dissolution of the Monasteries*, Allen & Unwin, 1971.

Index